PRAISE FOR

COMPLETE TRAINING

'Rol
of v   He excels in questioning
attit   This book is due for re   epted thinking that has allowed much
of L   exception
and   reac   the industry.'
Jon   ngzone.co.uk

'Bri   of theoretical understanding and rich
ope   perience in this practical book that supports and
cha   s to make training serve organizational performance as well
as i   ual development needs.'
**Phil .een, Writer and Consultant at Onlignment and Former Chair
of the e-Learning Network**

'Based on many years of experience in adult learning, working with
a variety of clients, including big multinationals with dozens of thousands
of people to develop, Robin summarizes here his uncompromising views
about what's wrong with corporate training and development and how
it can be put right. It provides vital advice for anyone interested in
developing an organization's most valuable resource – its people.'
**Svetlana Omeltchenko, Vice President, Global Marketing Insights,
Coty Inc, Paris**

Complete Training

Complete Training

From recruitment to retirement

Robin Hoyle

KoganPage

LONDON PHILADELPHIA NEW DELHI

First published in Great Britain and the United States in 2013 by Kogan Page Limited

120 Pentonville Road	1518 Walnut Street, Suite 1100	4737/23 Ansari Road
London N1 9JN	Philadelphia PA 19102	Daryaganj
United Kingdom	USA	New Delhi 110002
www.koganpage.com		India

© Robin Hoyle 2013

The right of Robin Hoyle to be identified as the author of this work has been asserted by him in accordance with the Copyright, Designs and Patents Act 1988.

ISBN   978 0 7494 6899 6
E-ISBN   978 0 7494 6900 9

British Library Cataloguing-in-Publication Data

A CIP record for this book is available from the British Library.

Library of Congress Cataloging-in-Publication Data

Hoyle, Robin.
   Complete training : from recruitment to retirement / Robin Hoyle. – 1st Edition.
      pages cm
   Includes bibliographical references and index.
   ISBN 978-0-7494-6899-6 – ISBN 978-0-7494-6900-9 (ebk.)   1. Organizational learning.
2. Employees–Training of.   I. Title.
   HD58.82.H6965 2013
   658.3'124–dc23
                                                                                2012051524

Typeset by Graphicraft Limited, Hong Kong
Printed and bound in India by Replika Press Pvt Ltd

For Jan

CONTENTS

ACKNOWLEDGEMENTS

It would be wrong not to acknowledge the assistance of many people in bringing this book to fruition. Many of the ideas expressed here first found their initial life via articles on TrainingZone.co.uk, and Michael Strawbridge and Jon Kennard deserve thanks for encouraging my contributions. Their readers and subscribers also deserve some credit for their comments and for endorsing my approach. Alison Church and Jim Riley and many others at Venture Marketing will also recognise some of the concepts as ones which were initially floated in the pages of *Learning Magazine*. I'd also like to thank former work colleagues and clients at ebc and at Infinity Learning for their support and encouragement and for asking interesting questions over the years. These interactions all helped hone the Complete Training approach. Thanks to the many people who have shared a platform with me or come up to me at the end of sessions and conferences and whose kind words encouraged me to believe that I might have something to say and – most importantly – something worth hearing. Thanks to Martina O'Sullivan and Fiona Dempsey at Kogan Page for backing the idea and for their subsequent practical advice and support. To Ilsa, Rory, Hamish, Calum and Robbie – you have inspired some of what appears here more than you can know. Finally, my eternal gratitude goes to Jan Holden who read every word of every draft of every chapter and was always on hand with comments and feedback and inspiration. This wouldn't have happened without you.

RH

Introduction: a manifesto

Why a manifesto? Am I standing for office, running in an election? Not exactly, but I want to start this book with a public declaration of principles and intentions – which is what a manifesto is supposed to be all about. I also want to lay out a philosophy of how workplace learning could, should and in some cases, does happen.

The manifesto is also part of the evaluation of this book – your evaluation as a reader and mine as writer. It lays out the goal of the book and starting with the end in mind is part of the approach which *Complete Training* advocates so it seems appropriate I should start as I want everyone else to carry on.

The Complete Training Manifesto

1 People of all ages are efficient learning machines

2 The aim of workplace training is to enable people to do things differently and do different things

3 People are varied and one size and one approach will not fit everyone

4 Evidence-based techniques are more likely to work

5 Language matters

6 What gets measured gets done

7 The best training requires a coherent, joined-up approach

Principle 1: People of all ages are efficient learning machines

The received wisdom, handed down by years of cliché, is that 'you can't teach an old dog new tricks'. If this is to be believed we lose learning capability as we age and progress through our careers and jobs. While it may be true that we will never be the learning dynamo we were when we were pre-five years of age (I am assuming no precocious four-year-old is reading this) it certainly isn't the case that we can't continue to learn and do new things – at whatever age.

Work by Professor Andrew Meltzoff of the Washington Institute for Learning and Brain Sciences describes the incredible learning capability of very small children. Even though this is at a point in their lives before language, at a time when the average parent may not have a clue how much brain activity is going on, children are learning and putting together pictures of the world. Think about it, the baby who can barely focus their own eyes becomes the only person in the house who knows how to programme the digital TV to record your favourite programme in just five years! And this capability as a learning machine – making new connections in our incredibly powerful and active brains – is not somehow lost after childhood. Yes, the habits we display as adults are formed at this time. Many psychologists believe that the blueprint for the adult is made right there. As the Jesuits had it in medieval Europe: 'Give me a child until he is seven and I will give you the man!'

But research by Meltzoff and others would seem to show that not only do we learn at that age, but that we learn how to learn by the time we are toddlers:

> ...the capacities that allow us to learn about the world and ourselves have their origins in infancy... The scientist peering into the crib, looking for answers to some of the deepest questions about how minds and the world and language work, sees the scientist peering out of the crib, who, it turns out, is doing much the same thing.[1]

Certainly pre-school education, care and development is a political hot potato in most of the developed world. While we may not all agree on how important getting the right start in life is for today's babies – we can all agree it is important. Building the toolkit of learning skills early on is a matter well beyond families or compulsory education. It has become a matter for the progress of our economy, if not our whole civilization.

In fact, our capability as learners would appear to be one of the differentiators – if not the key differentiator – between us and the rest of the animal kingdom. The first humans with larger brains than the other primates with which they shared the savannahs and gorges of Africa provide a blueprint for how modern humans still think, process information and learn. We are all aware of the flight or fight syndrome – the response to danger which was first hard-wired into our beings when we faced daily danger from predators and competitor humans. You also may be aware that our initial reaction to information and being able to subconsciously filter out things we consider irrelevant is based on an ability first developed when we walked the savannah and had a split second to respond to movement – instantly working out whether the animal we glimpsed was food or whether we were.

To quote the Director of the British Museum, Neil MacGregor, talking about the Olduvai Stone Chopping Tool, found in modern Tanzania and now the oldest object in the British Museum's collection at 1.8 million years old:

> What sets us apart from them [other primates] at this moment in our
> evolution is that, unlike them, we make tools before we need them.
> And once we have used them we keep them to use again. It's the
> beginning of the tool box.[2]

Inherent in this primitive capability is the need to learn and to anticipate when we have discovered or learned something and may need that information, and the tools inherent in its application, in the future.

So our survival as a species derives from some fundamental competences which hark back millions of years. Our ability to survive as modern individuals and our ability to succeed as adults are based on abilities most of us are born with. How did early humans learn? How do pre-school children learn?

The truth is they learn all the time and from lots of different stimuli and opportunities. To appropriately harness our learning capabilities into adulthood and throughout our life in work requires a range of learning opportunities. What's more we need to learn how to take these opportunities when they arise.

And that's where the 'old dog, new tricks' defence comes in. The truth is not that we can't learn but that we choose not to expose ourselves to learning opportunities when we are older. We embrace the fixed, the comfortable and the routine rather than the uncertain, the disruptive and the challenging. There may be all kinds of reasons for this reluctance. Simply, it may be down to the individual. But when I hear people reject learning, citing age, inability or lack of time, I have come to expect that there is something else which underpins their reticence. Some of it may be societal – the idea that education is for the young. Some may be about a previous bad experience either in school or afterwards. Often it will be a lack of motivation – there will be a lack of clarity about what's in it for them. Even when the potential rewards have been spelled out, there may be a lack of trust or belief that learning something new will deliver the benefits described.

Often the issue is the culture of the organization and how it reflects the external culture. If you are anxious about being seen to be incapable or lacking in knowledge, exposing yourself to a situation, where the whole reason for being there is that you lack knowledge or capability, could be horribly stressful. Without doubt, many within organizations find admitting to a development need a significant barrier. In fact in some organizations, not to be constantly projecting an image of hyper-capability is to run the risk of being side-lined or worse. Without a little humility – an open recognition that we don't know everything or how to do everything – can we really learn and develop as well as we might?

Engaging the capabilities of people as learners is one of the main challenges facing those involved in Learning and Development (L&D) and one which only a wholesale review of how we do what we do will bring into focus.

Principle 2: The aim of workplace training is to enable people to do things differently and do different things

Change is central to learning, training and development. When organizations require their people to change the way they do things or to undertake completely new tasks, some form of learning and training intervention is required. Occasionally this change and the associated training and learning interventions are planned for. Often they are not and members of staff simply muddle through. Over time, yesterday's quick fix becomes today's habit.

Behavioural change eventually happens – whether it is the optimum change and the right set of behaviours may be questionable, but the role of L&D teams is to ensure that the change required is supported and accelerated by the behaviour adopted. But behavioural change – when new activities become habitual – takes time. It's not one day in a classroom or one hour using an online module which powers that change.

Change is scary. Wherever change happens, it will be people who make it happen or become the biggest barrier. Wherever change happens, learning and development has made it happen – whether formal courses and programmes or informal adoption of new behaviours. To deliver change through people is a real skill and requires concerted work and detailed planning. It also requires a feedback loop, because people are not machines and what we think might deliver knowledge, skills, motivation and the intrinsic desire to embrace change and the new possibilities it offers, doesn't always work first time. Learning designers understand this.

To deliver change requires a clear understanding of what change looks like – a vision of the future and means of evaluation which go beyond a simple tick box or happy sheet. The feedback loop needs to transparently make the programme more effective and more efficient. Delivering change through development requires joined-up thinking and integrated activities to enable your people to make the change you and they would like to see.

Principle 3: People are varied and one size and one approach will not fit everyone

If everyone was a homogenous every-employee, then designing training would be easy. One course would enable everyone to be trained to the required standard.

Although we know instinctively that such an approach is doomed to deliver disappointment, work-related training is most often managed as though this self-evident fact isn't the case. In order to effectively deal with the myriad of different experiences, motivations, capabilities and expectations, we need a range of different interventions. As many of them as is feasible should be capable of being tailored to an individual's needs – accessing different workshops, selecting alternative routes through online modules or working on discrete work-based tasks with a supportive mentor or coach. The more a learner is in control of their own learning journey, the more committed they are to the outcomes.

If we are serious about improving performance we should harness the wide mix of options available. Inevitably this requires a certain in-built redundancy. Some programmes – with time taken for design, implementation and delivery – will be used by relatively few learners. The question is, 'how important is it that everyone has this skill or that knowledge?' If it's not important, then putting all your eggs into the basket of a single course may be an affordable luxury. If it is important, then delivering the required skills and knowledge as efficiently and effectively as possible becomes a no-brainer. The cost of a range of appropriate courses and training activities is much less than the cost of incompetence.

A course may not be the only solution. Resources and tools are everywhere. The growth of communication technologies enables a library of unimaginable scale to be on everyone's desk. But having access to information – assuming you can find what you need – is not the same as learning. Resources are not the same as courses.

For learning to take place we need to remember, to sort things in our brain's personal directory. You may call your training all sorts of things – interventions, workshops, courses or modules. But the learning process requires more than a seemingly inexhaustible torrent of data and opinion. However you describe your training, a course which enables information to be processed and reflected upon, plans to be formulated, and skills and activities to be tried out, is so much more than a collection of resources.

However, not everything needs training. Being a skilled information seeker – knowing when and how to look things up and how to critically analyse the information discovered – is a vital 21st-century skill. It means that we don't have to learn everything about our jobs or the challenges which we face. The process of looking things up – the **find, use and forget** model – is fine if potentially wasteful, but not for all circumstances. Sometimes your people will need to learn things. Roles are becoming more complex. Judgement and rapid, reliable responses to previously un-encountered situations will become more valued. In those circumstances, the time required to look things up as and when required is not an option – especially in a web-focused world which presents many options when what is required is a single answer – now! There are many circumstances where information resources may be unavailable or – worse – unreliable.

Every organization needs its employees to learn. At the core of everyone's work will be a set of capabilities or competences for which courses and structured, joined-up development programmes are the only answers.

Principle 4: Evidence-based techniques are more likely to work

There's a lot of wishful thinking – or sloppy thinking – in the world of training and learning. But enough research has been done over the last 120 years for us to understand a lot about how people learn. The learning options may evolve and proliferate, but the brain is largely the same thing which enabled the dominance of the species of homo-sapiens several millennia ago.

Understanding the research which has been done empowers L&D professionals to make effective choices. Through exercising these choices judiciously, the L&D team can genuinely contribute to the strategy of the organization.

There is a problem here though. Whereas we may think that the research on how people learn is well known, actually what is understood is neither the whole story nor indeed the real story. There's a famous quote attributed to Einstein: 'You should make things as simple as possible, but no simpler.' Now some researchers and academics have taken this to heart and explain their findings and their breakthroughs – whether in the field of neuroscience, social science, psychology or business – in ways which everyone can understand and take on board. Many do not. This is where the interpreters of the latest new thinking pounce. When the training industry is so fragmented – there are literally millions of businesses who provide training as part of their market offer – the chance to hook their products and services up to the latest research, even where the fit is tenuous, is too great to resist. If there's a bandwagon rolling by, you can bet a training company will jump on it.

These simplifications of evidence and research – coming from a vested perspective – are often unreliable. Add to this the power of the internet and the half-baked and the half-truths become accepted as fact across the whole industry in a click of a mouse.

How to overcome this problem? I think we all need to become our own researchers. First, we need to do our own desk research and question anything which is presented as scientific. Whether that is the definitely dodgy, like neuro-linguistic programming or the decidedly doubtful, like some of the personality profiling tools, we owe it to ourselves and our clients to investigate and read widely, rather than taking as gospel whatever some self-appointed master practitioner tells us.

We also need to research what works in our organization with our people and our culture. Evaluation of training programmes and calculating the impact of courses on performance has ranged from non-existent to patchy. We need to incorporate into the training mix opportunities to pause, reflect and gather the evidence about how well our activities have delivered against their objectives. That always assumes there are some objectives we can measure.

Undertaking research, evaluation, measuring outcomes and testing our ideas, contributes to the evidence base and our knowledge of what works within our own organizations. If we can then compare and contrast those findings with some of the universal truths about learning and how we change behaviour, then we have a blueprint for future success. That success will be based on our ability to critically analyse new trends, fads and psychological breakthroughs so that we can select approaches which deliver real benefit. This approach relies on support from across the organization not merely from those in the HR team. The role of Complete Trainers is to become trusted advisers to their clients and the organizations with which they work.

Principle 5: Language matters

As a flip side to the issues of using external evidence properly and codifying our experience of what works, comes the challenge of what we call things. Training within organizations often and rightly becomes part of the communications process. Despite this, training teams are often pretty lax about the terminology they use. I was once on a conference call with a major telecommunications company. There were over 70 people on the call – a significant challenge in itself. About 30 minutes in, I realized that although we were discussing agile development within their network team, it was pretty clear that there were at least 70 different definitions of agile amongst those on the conference. It was a 'flavour of the month' word and became meaningless as everything which could conceivably be called agile, was – along with a few activities which could lay no credible claim to the terminology.

This is but one example of fashion dictating the jargon we use. Remember when empowerment was the big buzzword? It seems to have disappeared without trace. Now autonomy seems to have replaced it – same stuff, different label. Along with autonomy comes the idea of everything being social.

Now I have to admit to this being a particular bugbear of mine. I'll expand on why in later chapters, but the essential problem is that social learning means something other than the current fashion for describing everything from Twitter, Facebook, blogs and wikis as part of the social learning revolution. Trouble is, as many first-year psychology students will know, Social Learning is what Albert Bandura called his theory of child development following his experiments with BoBo dolls in the 1960s.[3] In short, Bandura recognized that young people learn through observation of others and that they build a picture of what is OK to do and not OK to do based on what they see. Is that similar to the use of social media in learning? Not really, because the central process – observation – is missing. Being told what someone did is not the same as watching them do it. There is no excuse for this misappropriation of the terminology. This is not some esoteric theorist of whom no one could be expected to have heard. Bandura is probably the world's most often cited living psychologist.

Why does it matter? Because I think a relatively under-researched set of tools and opportunities which the read–write capability of Web 2.0 provides seem to be borrowing the credibility of the terminology of a great mind in modern cognitive research. Simply put, one is rigorously researched while the claims for the other are somewhat unproven. If we are trying to be taken seriously, and we should be, then sloppy use of today's jargon undermines our credibility. Borrowing fashionable terminology and making it mean whatever we want it to mean is worse and jeopardizes our efforts to change corporate behaviour and improve organizational effectiveness. Complete Training relies on the support of the whole enterprise. We should be interpreting the latest terminology and language for the rest of the business, not scattering our conversation and our PowerPoint slides with half-understood jargon just so we seem in touch and up to date.

Principle 6: What gets measured gets done

Think about what you measure in your organization. Think about how individuals are rewarded, paid bonuses or even just left in place to fight another day. Is development amongst those things measured?

I mean really measured. Not just an HR person sending around an e-mail bemoaning the fact that team members have been pulled away from training courses at the last minute. Not just the fact that so many people-days of training have been delivered.

If we're serious about training people – that is, supporting them in changing their behaviour to increase effectiveness and efficiency or to embrace and adopt new ways of working – then training can't be left to the L&D team alone. Everyone is involved.

We know that learning doesn't only happen on courses. We can all identify someone who taught us a lot – not through flip charts and formal presentations – but through their willingness to share their experience, to provide advice, give feedback or just act as a great role model.

Too many organizations seem to operate on the principle that training is just the preserve of the L&D team. It isn't. But if every-one's doing it, why do we need an L&D team at all? Because it's not easy and not everyone is. Courses and training programmes might not be the only game in town but they are the ones which attract the biggest crowds. Focusing on the formal and ensuring that it is as good as it can be encourages the informal and ad hoc to happen; sets expectations that it will happen; and creates an insatiable desire for learning across the organization.

Unquestionably there is at best a grudging support for training initiatives, especially from those whose support we need most – the line managers. In fact, on occasions they express outright hostility.

One example which comes to mind is a major UK company which had many compliance-related programmes online. Managers were given a target of ensuring a certain proportion of their team members passed these mandatory courses within a fixed time period. Top marks for initiative must go to the team leader who copied all the test questions, annotated them and circulated the resulting document to his team so they could pass the test first time and not 'waste valuable time' actually doing the learning!

That example highlights one of the problems of engaging manager support for people development activities. With the advent of Learning Management Systems and e-HR software, which demon-strate who has done what, when and how well, the L&D team are cast in the role of the corporate development police rather than a business partner.

So how do we get line managers involved? It seems the first task is to give them a clear job! Sounds straightforward doesn't it, but I often talk to trainers bemoaning their lack of support and, when questioned, it becomes clear that the only job the managers have been asked to do is to release their team members to attend courses or complete online programmes. There are a number of different jobs we can give them which not only engage them with the process, but actively help us to achieve our and the organization's objectives.

But before we can ask them to do these jobs we need to make sure that our objectives coincide with theirs. Simply put, if they can't see the benefit of being involved then they won't be. Again this is all a bit motherhood and apple pie, but ask yourself, what role did line managers – who will be expected to invest their team's time – play in determining what was needed, how it was to be delivered and how much time and energy could/should be invested in its completion? For training, ie enabling people to undertake their present job more effectively and efficiently, this seems to me to be a minimum first step.

Thereafter, involving these managers in supervising work-based tasks, monitoring performance, providing feedback to the learners and supporting people as they try to change behaviour, becomes much more straightforward.

That doesn't always work with development activities. Here, I am defining development as learning experiences designed to equip our people to do something in the future – ie not their current job but a new activity they may wish to take on or a new role within the organization. Managers facing short-term performance pressures – deadlines, quality, cost control etc – are much less likely to commit precious resources to addressing needs some way off, if they are constantly fighting fires which are springing up today. Here a two-stage process may help.

The first stage is to build support for development into the manager's targets and reward them accordingly. This avoids the impact of systems theory – the process of measuring one thing leading to a lack of focus on other, equally valuable activities which are not measured with quite the same rigour. A manager targeted – and paid a bonus – on achieving results this quarter is clearly more likely to concentrate his or her efforts on achieving those targets than longer-term objectives which are not going to influence their end-of-year performance-related pay. I have come across some organizations which actively reward managers who receive positive staff feedback for their role in supporting training and development. Those managers have key result areas and performance indicators which may include the proportion of team members undergoing training programmes and achieving competences. For the most part, I have encountered such initiatives while attending sessions as part of the innovations strand at training conferences. If it's considered innovative it speaks volumes for how common this might be. I suspect that hens' teeth appear slightly more often.

The second stage is to create some 'pull' to go alongside the 'push'. Put simply, this means rewarding learners who learn and making it clear that one of their responsibilities in driving their own development is to make demands of their line manager. In the professions, the idea of Continuing Professional Development, and CPD points which need to be earned over the course of a year, drives individuals to demand time for training and updating. Being refused access to training causes a major issue in the team and tends not to happen. Of course, CPD points can be earned for things other than attending courses. Sometimes simply subscribing to a journal counts towards the total. The eternal problem with measuring what's going on is that sometimes we don't always measure the right things. It is very easy to accord importance to the things which can be easily measured rather than measure things which are important. These input measures are too easily focused on the wrong things. However, expecting people to undertake n amount of training within a given time period is at least a start to ensuring that training doesn't get relegated to one of the things to be done when everything else has been taken care of.

It won't be all your managers who routinely pull their team members off booked courses at the last minute. It won't be that everyone thinks coaching is a waste of time (although if no one else is doing it, it will be much harder for individual managers to swim against the tide of corporate culture). This is where the L&D team still need to have something of the role of enforcer about them.

Enforcement is impossible without data. Often e-HR systems, Learning Management Systems or simple training records only tell you which learners have or haven't attended course X, downloaded the pre-attendance material for course Y, or undertaken the work-based activities following on from course Z. But if the organization has a problem with managers supporting learners, then that data is insufficient. Effective tracking and monitoring of training should identify what individuals are doing *and* what teams are doing. If the available data indicates that Fred Smith's team are not getting involved in training and development, then we need to speak to Fred Smith or the head of Fred's department rather than focus on the individual team members who, more than likely, have little or no say in whether or not they can take up the training on offer.

It's a lot easier to have this conversation with senior managers if it is a regularly scheduled meeting with each department head where usage and attendance statistics, results and future training requirements are discussed. This doesn't have to be every week – probably as infrequently as once a quarter is sufficient – but this has a real impact on culture. If these meetings can be arranged, where figures or indicators are discussed alongside plans for the future, this will soon cascade its way through the organization. At least the amount of time you spend chasing course participants should reduce dramatically.

According to Gary Wyse[4] – who has counted this stuff – knowledge workers spend on average around 4.8 per cent of their working time actually being trained – ie attending courses or using training resources such as e-learning. Now assuming that they spend some of the remaining 95.2 per cent of their time learning on the job and undertaking activities during normal day-to-day schedules which help them develop new skills, it is clear that the impact of these activities needs to be optimized through linking the on-the-job, informal learning closely to the formal training programmes. That means enrolling individuals and their managers into a much broader approach to workplace learning and development and ensuring coherence between what happens in the training room and what happens in the workplace.

Coming back to the main issue, if they are not tasked with getting involved in this way – and either recognized for positive efforts, or chastised for failing to get involved – then training activities will rank much lower down their priority lists than the tasks which are measured – and rewarded.

Principle 7: The best training requires a coherent, joined-up approach

When e-learning first became a real option for training and development, it was heralded as the answer to everything. One of my then clients closed its management and customer service training department because everything could be covered via programmes on the organization's intranet. Of course this was at best an ambitious commitment to technology but in reality it was hopelessly misguided. After trying to convince them to reverse their decision, this organization – along with many, many others – finally wiped the technological blindness from their eyes and agreed that e-learning couldn't do everything and would need supplementing with other types of training.

Blended learning was born. Those wedded to the classroom and slightly scared of anything to do with computers immediately hailed it as the death of e-learning and the final vindication for their rubbishing of the medium up to that point. Some e-learning companies immediately re-branded themselves as blended learning companies – despite the fact that they had no experience of training outside computer programs. In fact, they had no experience of learning and development before someone decided that e-learning would be 'the killer app' (as it was described in *Wired* magazine in 1999). It took some time for trainers and development professionals to fully get on board with the whole blended thing, but as e-learning became more business as usual, even the technophobe trainers put down their squeezy stress balls and embraced the new medium as one of the tools available.

Over recent years the blend has been expanded. In some genuinely good examples, development programmes might include a four-stage sequence of activities: pre-workshop activities such as doing some initial reading and setting some goals (preferably in association with the boss); course attendance – ideally over more than one day with work-based activities and self-directed learning in between; follow-up by the line manager or coaching provided by someone with the skills to undertake the coaching activities; and finally a work-based implementation programme which is monitored to enable competence to be recognized. In and amongst this, there will be conversations with line managers, coaches, mentors, peers and others which will identify the next set of development goals and off we go again to continue our learning journey.

Let's be honest – it doesn't happen like that too often, and yet if we look at our own learning experiences – those times in our career when we really learned something new, mastered new skills or had a personal breakthrough in our capabilities – that's what happened. These disparate and different activities were coherent – one led neatly to the next. The activities which we used were staged so that achieving one level led naturally towards increased capability. What's more, those joined-up, coherent learning activities, supported by someone outside who is concerned with our development, mirror our experiences as the most phenomenal learning machine when we were young children.

The joined-up, the coherent and the supported approach to learning and development is not only good practice: it feels natural to us as learners. It is an all-encompassing view of what it takes to develop our knowledge, our skills and for us to change our behaviour. We might call it Complete Training.

Employee life cycles

...one man in his time plays many parts,
his acts being seven ages...

WILLIAM SHAKESPEARE, *AS YOU LIKE IT*

We define our life in work through stages. Are we the new boy or girl just starting out or are we an old hand, seasoned, experienced, seen it all, done some of it? Have we got 20 years' experience or just one year's experience which is now 19 years out of date?

Where we are in relation to these various stages influences how we do things, not least of which is how we approach learning new things and developing our skills. From a work perspective there are five stages which really make a difference for training teams and for those who are undertaking learning and development activities. At each of these stages there are different expectations, challenges and opportunities. Regardless of where the learner is in their career, the L&D team still has the same job to do – enable people to do things differently and to do different things. However, we may find the tactics and techniques we need to use subtly change to take into account different challenges. Some of these are an inevitable part of the career stage – people who have been around for a while have learned things and therefore we need to acknowledge and build our approach based on their existing knowledge and capability. In some cases, the capabilities which have been proudly achieved are no longer relevant. Moving from a position of seeming competence to a position in which the newly required capabilities do not draw on those hard earned skills presents a unique set of circumstances.

Other challenges may be linked to the attitudes which may be prevalent in those who have worked in the organization some time or have reached a certain status. This is a combination of personal outlook – receptiveness to change, willingness to learn, reluctance to embrace new thinking – and organizational culture. While it may not be universally the case, it should be acknowledged that a certain blindness to new ways of doing things can come hand in hand with longevity in employment and particularly longevity in role. The stages which are most significant from a training perspective are:

- new recruit;
- new manager;
- leader;
- specialist;
- retiree.

Let's look at them in turn.

The new recruit

Remember what it felt like when you started a new job? We can characterize a new starter's expectations of induction (albeit these may be unspoken) by looking at the areas of 'discomfort' a new starter may have to deal with in their first few days and weeks:

- Organizational disorientation – that feeling of being a new starter that most of us find uncomfortable. Being an outsider without a clear understanding of where things are, how things get done and what is expected. This can create a sense of unfocused anxiety about work and about building relationships with colleagues.

- Being useless – or at least less than useful. This is a symptom of disorientation and makes people feel uncomfortable at a time when they want to re-pay the organization after being given the job, having experienced the euphoric feelings, or at least relief of being the chosen one and having had their sense of self-worth boosted.

- Specific anxiety – about practical issues such as getting paid, not making a bad first impression, getting on with people etc. In practical terms this amounts to an anxiety that they will 'pass' the probationary period.

- Risk aversion – not wanting to make mistakes or be perceived negatively by their co-workers and supervisors.

- Fears of dependency – being to some extent 'out of their depth', new starters want to move beyond the feeling of being a passenger – overly dependent on more experienced colleagues – as quickly as possible.

- Wanting to make a mark – positively. A desire to be seen as capable and competent and able to fit in with the team and the organization's ethos.

These areas of discomfort amount to a positive desire to learn – a hunger for information and education as a route to addressing these potentially unsettling feelings as a new starter. From an organizational perspective, it is helpful when learners are excited about the learning journey they are on (as opposed to displaying the more cynical frame of mind occasionally exemplified by more entrenched members of staff).

Although we can determine with certainty that they will have some gaps in their understanding and knowledge of the organization, its culture, procedures and policies, we shouldn't make the mistake that these newbies know nothing. This is even more the case in a world of online information where those applying to work within an organization will do their homework pre-interview and may know more about some of the things the organization boasts about on its web pages than those who have been there for years.

The new manager

I'm referring specifically here to those who have been promoted into their first role as a supervisor of others. Whether they're called line manager, team leader, supervisor, NCO, ward sister or foreman is unimportant. For the most part these individuals have made the transition from being part of the team to being a leader of the team.

No one is more aware than the new manager that managing and leading people is about much more than putting on the captain's armband. The trouble is that management is rather like sex – everyone thinks they're good at it despite the limited evidence which underpins such confidence.

The chances are that most new managers will have been promoted to a role where they are responsible for the output of others without any specific training and support to undertake that side of the job. Many of those elevated will have been an able and capable team member – perhaps the best. When I worked with an extremely large engineering enterprise, the supervisors were almost always selected on the basis of being 'good with the tools' and 'having some years on their back'. It was a form of 'Buggin's Turn', a state of affairs where if you work in the same place for long enough, eventually it will be your turn to be manager.

The problem was that this organization was the Signals and Telecoms department of British Rail, who used to run all the railways in the United Kingdom. The issue of poor preparation for supervisors was highlighted by the Hidden report into the Clapham rail crash, an incident in which 33 lives were lost. Thereafter, when anyone was promoted to a supervisory role, they were supposed to have been through a preparatory training course. It just so happens I was involved in its delivery. It was a very tragic reason to be commissioned to design and run such a forward-thinking training innovation, but – for an incredibly traditional organization – it certainly represented a major breakthrough. This bold experiment ended when, shortly thereafter, British Rail was broken up and sold off and the work of signalling maintenance was contracted out. Some years later, in 2003, the Potters Bar rail crash claimed seven lives. The Health and Safety Executive investigation laid the blame squarely on poor maintenance of signals. Draw your own conclusions.

The other challenge with promoting from within is that the new manager faced with complexity for which she or he is under-prepared can always find enough to keep them busy in actually doing the job.

The leading, directing, monitoring and motivating is left to one side in favour of hands-on operational work – especially when fires need fighting.

When interacting with their team, the under-prepared manager sometimes seeks to act as some kind of representative of the team they now lead – taking their concerns and grievances to management. If you can remember the TV quiz show *The Wheel of Fortune* you'll remember that at the end of the advert break the host would skip down the stairs to the whoops and hollers of a studio audience who by this time were in a frenzy of toddler-like over-excitement. As the applause died down, our host would inform us that during the break he had 'put another 1,000 on the wheel' – in other words the competitors now had twice as much chance of achieving the top prize. But – pause for sombre face – '**they** had put another bankrupt on the wheel' – in other words twice the opportunity to lose everything.

Who were the 'they' that he referred to? Apparently, a shady and misanthropic cabal, hell-bent on creating misery amongst those hard-working contestants as they tried to spin a massive roulette wheel. Many first-time managers, uneasy in their new role as an authority figure, having previously been 'one of us', seek sanctuary in this kind of 'them and us' representation of the organization's activities and policies. A new target has been set which is stretching and will require significant extra effort? 'They' set it. A change in travel expenses, office layout, car park places or just about any apparently minor thing which will be unpopular while giving the impression that the top brass don't care about the poor bloody infantry? It was 'them' again. Unfortunately, new managers need to be prepared for the situation explained to me by my boss when I was in a similar situation. 'You don't get a salary[1] **and** a round of applause,' he said. He was right. Attempts to court popularity from those who reported to me were never successful. The best I could hope for was respect and trust. Incontrovertibly, though, I was no longer 'Us'. I had become 'Them'.

As well as learning that trying to be Mr Popular was doomed to failure, I also learned a genuinely shocking fact. Management is an activity, not a status. Who knew? Having only seen management from the other side of the delegation dance, a *paso doble* in which I was certainly not leading, I had no real understanding of the combination of wit, charm and low cunning routinely employed by successful managers. I had little awareness of results and perform-ance being monitored and relationships with the rest of the team being observed. I was blithely ignorant of the role in building a team, with a sense of purpose and a focus on the mission and vision of the organization. I had only the barest inkling of the requirement to com-municate and motivate and inspire.

So what was the activity of management? I soon learned that it was to enable people to do – willingly and well – those things which needed to be done.

Let's unpack that statement. 'Enable' suggests a kind of flexibility, equipping the team's members with the skills, resources, including time, and direction to do things and then getting out of their way, giving them the space to do a good job. 'Willingly' talks about motiv-ation – from why this is necessary to the wider enterprise to the benefits for the individual. 'Well' means a common understanding of what good looks like – the standards required in terms of quality, quantity, cost or time. These are the key measures used across all organizations. 'Things which need to be done' necessarily involves communication, ensuring everyone knows the immediate priorities, the direction of travel and the longer-term goals.

This was a revelation to me and – I suspect – to many newly pro-moted managers. It was only when I was called to account at the weekly management meeting – a truly terrifying experience for the new manager who is barely on top of their brief – that I realized I was actually supposed to do something beyond swanning around looking important. After all, I'd bought a new suit!

I was trained and supported not by the L&D team but by an incredibly understanding, patient and committed manager. I was lucky. Many I know were not. In the absence of such a role model – who not only walks the talk but takes time out of their day to talk it as well – many managers simply muddle through, replicating how their boss treats them or how the previous team leader used to do things or, in some cases, trying to be exactly the opposite of their predecessor.

This interface between the organization and the individual teams of workers is hard. It is especially hard if you have moved from the managed to the manager. Getting the support right for these individuals is crucial. Preparing them for the role (preferably before they are considered for promotion) and then supporting them once they are in the role presents a unique set of challenges for the L&D team.

The leader

The leader differs from the manager in two particulars. Firstly, they are now more established in the position, management of people has become habitual with both good and bad habits developed. Secondly, they are less operational and more strategic – responsible for setting organizational direction. Typically they will not only manage a team, but manage managers, setting immediate priorities and also focusing attention on future requirements.

I'm not talking about 'Leadership development' here in the rebranding sense. About 20 or so years ago what had been management training suddenly got a make-over. Out went the focus on **management** and in came the focus on **leadership**. I'm prepared to accept that there is a very real difference in these two skill sets, but unfortunately for most of the audiences for these courses what was needed was management training, not leadership development. In any case, management training was what the course delivered. In the new leadership orthodoxy, however, we weren't allowed to call it that. I was developing and delivering those courses at the time and I, like a whole series of others in the field, went through our course material using find and replace. Out went management, being replaced by leadership. If we're all honest, the remainder of the course content – motivation, communication, delegation, coaching and monitoring performance – stayed exactly the same. Only the words changed. While language develops, the new terminology adopted has to mean something to really matter. Linguistic fashion is a disease which regularly affects the L&D field. It is a game you may have to play, but never forget that that's what it is – a game.

But there are programmes which are and should be called leadership development which are targeted at developing leaders. They are, and should be, provided for and with those senior managers of other managers who set the strategy of the organization and lead the whole enterprise as opposed to a small part of it.

In many organizations, the development of leaders at this senior stage of their careers barely features on the L&D team's radar. Where leadership development for senior managers does take place it is undertaken by external providers – either through conference attendance or courses from business schools and one-to-one sessions with executive coaches. But avoiding a disconnect between the learning and development strategy across the organization and the business strategy being developed by those leaders requires a closeness which, invariably, is threatened when the internal training team have fewer chances to interact with those leaders in the day-to-day execution of that training strategy. It is imperative that the leadership team have a hands-on appreciation of what L&D is doing within their organizations.

But how is that going to happen if the leaders know everything? What on earth are we going to teach them and what skills will they need to develop?

Well, actually there's more scope for leadership engagement with learning and training than you might think. Three specific areas of engagement spring to mind. It is pretty clear that you would want to harness the skills of these leaders within course delivery. There is rarely a substitute for having a member of the senior leadership team actually having an input into a workshop, or blogging or engaging in a webinar. The trick is to ensure that they are working within a learning framework, otherwise there is a tendency for your carefully designed training programme to be hijacked and reduced to no more than glorified communications. Nothing wrong with internal comms – a necessary thing and ideally led from the top, but this is not the same as designing and delivering a training intervention.

The other two areas relate to their own development. When leaders commission their own internal training team to deliver their own development or components of the programmes required to make sure that they are at the forefront of organizational leadership, they provide a massive endorsement which is seen and heard by everyone else in the enterprise. Any talk about a learning organization in which the very top people do not apparently do much learning can only be so much hot air.

There are numerous issues associated with top leaders being senior to the people delivering the course and the extra stresses and strains that that puts upon the trainers involved. But judicious use of external inputs within a programme which is devised and primarily implemented in-house adds greatly to the status of the internal L&D function and also provides for a programme focused on organizational needs, strategy and direction, using the insights of those actually working within the business. Of course, this means that the L&D team who are involved will need to be absolutely on top of their game, in tune with where the organization is going, the challenges it must address and the opportunities it must take. I think most training professionals would want to think of themselves in those terms, otherwise why are they doing the job?

In a constantly changing world those who make the strategy and set the course of the organization need real clarity about how the world is, where the competition is coming from and how smart organizations are responding to evolving trends and disruptive newcomers. Is this learning? I believe so, in the widest sense but also in the sense of benchmarking with others and assessing organizational performance relative to other, similar businesses. In a fast moving world, standing still is going backwards. The oft quoted maxim attributed to W. Edwards Deming applies here: 'Learning is not compulsory – neither is survival.'[2] New environments, new challenges, new opportunities – all require new leadership strategies, styles and behaviours. As we know, the job of Learning and Development teams is to support those required to adopt new behaviours. Doing things differently and doing different things is our job at all levels of the business.

I trained a group in Buenos Aires a couple of years ago. The senior leader, who was supposed to be joining the course as a participant alongside his team members, decided this was the perfect opportunity to stage a number of one-to-one meetings with those from different countries he hadn't seen for a while. The guys from Mexico were invited to pull up a chair and give him a progress report. That problem in Chile was discussed during one of those interactive sessions. It's not as if any learning was going on – no one was giving a presentation! Finally, his colleagues from Argentina were asked not just to have a conversation, but leave the session to make a presentation about a forthcoming project. Those of you who are new to training, don't worry. This was an extreme case.

It is clear that senior personnel often need to address not just the skills gaps around dealing with a constantly changing environment, but also the older skills gaps which they may have. Very often they are what we may describe as 'legacy learners'. Assuming they were ever in a junior position, when they held that role much of what now passes for business as usual didn't exist. They have effectively missed much of the learning which many of us take for granted. Whether this was how to use a particular piece of technology or how to comply with the Sarbanes–Oxley Legislation[3] these gaps should be filled. But God forbid that senior staff would join in a classroom as a punter! In many cases, God forbid that most trainers would want them there. The senior leader can be a hugely disruptive presence, even when they don't mean to be. In many organizations the level of deference given to the top team is such that the other course participants won't say anything unless he or she has given them express permission. The chance of saying the wrong thing keeps many of the other trainees completely silent throughout. When and if a discussion is attempted, this is invariably interpreted as an opportunity for the leader to give us all the benefit of his (and it usually is male) experience and opinions.

On odd occasions – for example a course associated with a new centrally mandated project, procedure, policy or approach which applies to all – the leader may need to be present. On some other training activities about using the tools of the trade such as a bespoke software or just the organization's information systems it may also be appropriate for the CEO to be alongside the customer service assistant, not only learning with the remainder of the team but being seen to do so.

Unfortunately it rarely happens. Senior staff members often admit – with a degree of pride – that they can't work the e-mail or understand simple procedures which are commonplace to their more junior staff. This kind of senior team response to skills development does need to be challenged and addressed if training and development is to achieve its potential across organizations.

Addressing the needs of senior staff to play the new game or change the game completely is an L&D challenge. It's one which many have been reluctant to accept. A more collaborative and collegiate approach might be required. Smart senior leaders are hungry for this input. The real role models are keen to bring expertise from within the organization – the specialists with unique mastery of their discipline – alongside that from outside. Often this external stimulus comes from academics from centres of learning. They will have researched the field, published articles, and presented papers at esoteric conferences. But the wheels of academia sometimes turn a little slowly. Learning about how other organizations addressed issues a couple of years ago may not be appropriate in the face of the opportunities of the here and now. As well as academics, L&D teams should build a network of other senior staff from comparable, but non-competitive organizations who can act as a kind of mutual brains trust to provide a stimulating, blue sky environment. This may not sound like the average L&D intervention but these kinds of networking opportunities are rarely effective unless trainers are driving events.

The specialist

In many organizations, there are long-serving members of staff who are very capable at what they do and have little or no desire to advance up the greasy pole into positions of management.

In some cases they have built a small world around themselves in which they operate with the impunity only ever given to those whose output we don't quite understand but whose expertise is rarely questioned. We don't know quite what they do, but we do know it's important.

In other cases they are just too damned good at what they do to be sacrificed to the corner offices of management. They may be the hot sales person, the experienced production engineer, the great teacher or efficient nurse or empathic counsellor. The organization would be much the poorer without their quiet assuredness, the safe pair of hands they provide and the trusted services they deliver. In both these cases let's call them the specialists.

Given that these people know what to do, it would seem that there is little if anything that L&D need to concern themselves with. Certainly, in the face of capability gaps elsewhere, it would seem sensible to address those priorities before turning our attention to the people who have everything under control. But this would be a short-term attitude. In truth, training and development is a vehicle for generating loyalty and commitment to the organization. Now, it is self-evident that lots of other things also do this, from good pay and other terms and conditions to satisfying work, autonomy and sharing a set of values with the organization. But one of the values which individuals in work would apparently want to share with their employer is the one which talks about achieving potential and continually learning.

The Chartered Institute of Personnel and Development (CIPD) in its Recruitment, Retention and Turnover Survey of 2009, said:

> In an increasingly knowledge-based economy, human capital is fast becoming the most valuable business asset. Labour turnover is one measure of human capital reporting, among others, that can provide a powerful business case in influencing senior management decisions and agenda.

The labour turnover feedback showed that 37 per cent of those leaving an organization voluntarily (not for reasons of dismissal or redundancy) cited a lack of development or career opportunities as the key reason behind their decision to go elsewhere.[4] While we could accept that not all those who would figure in our specialist category would be seeking career advancement and enhanced capabilities, some would. Even if progression up the pay scales was not the major driver behind our specialist's work, the recognition which is inherent in someone receiving an investment in their development and training should not be overlooked. Not many workers ever rejoice in being ignored.

To some extent, therefore, it could be said that involvement in training is a good thing in and of itself. Not quite. I was working with a group from a hospital a couple of years ago. One specialist – a highly respected clinician – told me the story of her annual attendance at the fire safety training workshop. Having been in the same hospital and the same role for around 15 years, there was not a great deal to be gained from repeating the fire safety messages year after year. However, someone had set a measure some time previously that every member of staff should attend an annual refresher about the fire triangle and not overloading electric plug sockets, a great example of giving importance to that which can be easily measured rather than measuring those things which are important.

Duly she turned up year after year – and took a novel with her! She described it as one of her favourite days in the calendar. Four hours left uninterrupted by pagers and telephones, undisturbed except for the steady and unobtrusive burble of the presenter as she got on with her recreational reading. It might have been her favourite day in work and presumably one of the least stressful, but did it really lead her to think more highly of the training department?

Compliance training is rife with problems for the L&D team and for our specialists. Very often it is barely training at all, merely a communications exercise which gains a few ticks in boxes and covers someone's back if things go pear-shaped. This belief that the existence of a course and an attendance register is sufficient protection in the eyes of the law is a chimera, however. There have been numerous instances where a legal authority has investigated some regulatory foul-up only to find that the training records kept were largely meaningless because the training which they recorded was equally meaningless. Ticking boxes is neither an appropriate defence in the event of a transgression nor a useful investment of training resources.

In fact, programmes such as the hospital fire safety training programme (and others I have come across) actually harm the image of the whole of the human resources function in the eyes of those who should be clamouring for our services.

So, giving some thought to the needs of our specialists for training and development is a really important process. The considerations fall into two distinct areas. The first is the need for engagement with the wider enterprise – understanding strategy and being able to position their work in relation to the organization's direction. In the case of our super salesperson that might just be about understanding new product launches or the development of new services. For our true specialist – the individual who has a specific but quite esoteric responsibility – he or she may be in a small department with relatively low numbers of people compared to their potential impact on day-to-day work, or in some cases be the only person looking after a particular discipline. These people will require clarity about the way ahead and space and time to reflect on what this means for their area of specialism. One of my clients is a major brewer and bottler of soft drinks. Their activities span the globe. In many of the countries in which they operate, water scarcity is a very significant issue and one which impacts their work every day. It is, after all, impossible to make beer or soft drinks without using water. From a total workforce of around 75,000 people, the number of individuals in this organization who would consider themselves specialists in the use of water across the supply chain is probably fewer than 20, worldwide. All of them have various specialisms within their distinct field: those who look at water tables and the preservation of the watershed, those involved in public policy, those looking at the water use in crop growing, as well as those who investigate reducing water in their breweries and bottling plants. Despite their relatively low numbers, their impact is potentially huge. If the organizational strategy is to expand in Australia (for example) what are the water challenges in a country which has suffered a period of continual drought between 2003 and 2012? Advance warning and then a focus on the implications – mapping the potential scenarios and making recommendations is both important and urgent. The route to understanding company strategy is – or should be – the work of the training department.

Similarly, the work of understanding the specifics of water use and the strategies for its reduction is – or should be – the work of the training department also. This must be done in concert with the specialists. This is the second area of L&D interaction with our specialists. As well as ensuring they are up to date, a good L&D department utilizes their skills to support other functions in making the right management decisions and in adopting the appropriate behaviours.

Unfortunately, it is not always the case that those who are exceptionally learned and passionate about something specialist, are that good at communicating it to others. What's more, what is communicated may be difficult to understand by the uninitiated. The idea of knowledge management in organizations is usually a conversation between those who already know. Continually describing their own opinions or points of view to the equally knowledgeable, who may or may not share these positions, hardly counts as knowledge management. What's actually needed is a process of engaging with people and jointly working out how something can be achieved – let's call it not knowledge management but **wisdom management**.

At the heart of wisdom management is recognition of what knowledge is required, by whom in what circumstance. It is also a process by which our main aim is to inspire – to create a desire to learn more and to catalogue our collected wisdom in such a way that the intrigued may find that which they need at each level of their interest in the subject. This requires our specialists – whether top sales people, skilled and experienced nurses or technocrats in their realms of special study – to work with their L&D colleagues to spread what they know, their capabilities and their recommendations for those who are less experienced, less special and less committed than themselves. Levelling up is another way to change behaviour.

The retiree

Our last group are relatively easy to identify. Those who are approaching the time when their career within the organization is over require support too. About three years ago, I undertook a survey plotting attitudes towards training which utilized technology in some way. Counter-intuitively, those in the survey aged 45 to 55 were far more positive than other age groups about learning online and having opportunities to plot their own development using online tools.

The use of a mix of learning resources – often referred to as blended learning, linking online resources to other courses and development – was also widely favoured by the older employees. There was one fairly large fly in that particular ointment, though. Of those in the over 45 age bracket, unlike those who were younger, not one had regular access to a coach. In an organization which laid great store on senior staff and line managers coaching their team members there was a paradigm which suggested such one-to-one support was available only for those recently out of college or those on the way up through the ranks. Those who had plateaued in their career were considered beyond the reach of any training other than the minimum of check-box compliance courses, with little or no work-based follow-up. It is perhaps fair to say that the enthusiasm for self-directed development was so great because one of the drivers for this apparently out-of-character hunger was that *nothing else was available*.

Most of these older survey respondents were in the 45 to 50 age group. For many of those a future working life of 25 years may not be that far-fetched. Despite this reality, the focus of L&D activity was firmly on younger, new entrants who were likely to stay in role for only two to three years before moving on.

Certainly when I have had the opportunity to deliver courses to a mixed age range group, the enthusiasm and insights of the slightly greyer-haired participants is always welcome. In fact, with their experience and stories they can be a really useful addition to the programme. Ignoring the 'old dogs, new tricks' stereotypes introduces the trainer to a group who can respond positively to a changing work environment and learn new skills as they do so.

Harnessing their potential as learners may require different techniques to those used when we only focus on the bright young things who haven't seen it all before and haven't got more experience than the trainer. But it's a really stimulating challenge and one that trainers should be happy to embrace.

With over a third of a million workers over pensionable age in the UK workforce, it's one we'd better get to grips with pretty quickly.[5]

Those approaching retirement also have a major change coming up. Part of the L&D team's responsibility – to help people do things differently and do different things – also extends to this change, the step between paid work and no work. I also think that this is an issue when organizations are going through redundancies as well. If the support offered to those required to leave the organization does not match up to that offered to those joining the business, current and potential employees will form a view about the way in which the organization values its most important asset.

As well as preparing our older colleagues for their time after work, it is also important to develop an **organization with a memory**. One of my very early jobs was working for an organization which had gone through significant mechanization. About 90 per cent of the operation had been converted to new, computer-controlled machines with an attendant reduction in headcount. But some activities were simply too small or too infrequent for the computerization process to be worthwhile. Without the business case being made, a relatively low number of the old machines were still operating, undertaking important work albeit on a reduced capacity. Until they went wrong. When a problem arose with one such machine – originally installed almost a century before – it became apparent that the early retirement approach to headcount reduction had one major, unseen consequence. Not a single person left in the business had any idea how to fix these machines. No records had been kept, no capability retained. As a very junior employee, I was detailed to go knocking on doors asking if one of them wouldn't mind coming back in to help us. It was not a pleasant conversation. That company's magnificent 19th-century premises are now a business park and mixed residential development. Can't think why. Can you?

The L&D team need a proactive approach to harvesting the intelligence of those approaching retirement. It's not enough to create the über-operating manual either. There's a well-known phrase in technology circles: 'When all else fails, read the manual'. In most organizations, the manuals have a similar status. Even if you can find them you risk an asthma attack opening their dust-embalmed pages.

Gathering the real stories from those who have been around a while, learning their lessons and bringing these potentially dry histories to life is a skill and a process which requires time and resources. It is, though, an essential step to understand the history of which decisions were made and why and the accumulated knowledge of why the organization does things the way it does. For these older men and women to tell their stories and share their experiences requires them to adopt new behaviours, to use new skills, to do things differently and do different things. Guess whose job that is?

Throughout the chapters which follow, I will illustrate the different approaches I advocate in relation to these different career stages, pointing out how the application of each technique and strategy may need to subtly change to meet the needs of these different groups.

Complete Training tools: the starting point

> *I suppose it is tempting, if the only tool you have is a hammer, to treat everything as if it were a nail.*
> **ABRAHAM MASLOW, *THE PSYCHOLOGY OF SCIENCE: A RECONNAISSANCE*, 1966**

From a Complete Training perspective the trainer's toolkit comprises the full spectrum of different interventions, resources and courses which are melded together to create training programmes. The decision about which tool should be used for which job in the training panoply can be tricky. We tend to think of training and development as one word (perhaps 'training-and-development') as though there was no difference in these two very distinct activities. Now we have the idea of 'learning' as a distinct activity within the training process, albeit a term which is often used interchangeably with training or development. Yet these processes *are* different and when we start to devise a training programme we should understand how they are different and choose from the tools available with care.

Training is the process by which we equip learners with the skills and underpinning knowledge required to undertake their existing role. Development is the process by which learners are equipped similarly for some future role such as a promotion or a move into a different function within or beyond the organization. Learning is what the people using our courses and resources do.

Most training or development programmes start with a series of required outcomes. These are usually described in the form of learning objectives or learning outcomes. I'm not entirely certain if there is an intended differentiation between objectives and outcomes, but it would appear that years of interchangeable usage have led to these terms being practically the same thing.

Here's a definition from the University of New Mexico, USA:

> A learning objective is an outcome statement that captures specifically what knowledge, skills, attitudes learners should be able to exhibit following instruction.

And another from Birmingham City University, UK:

> Learning outcomes are the specific intentions of a programme or module, written in specific terms. They describe what a student should know, understand, or be able to do at the end of that programme or module.

Clear on the difference between outcomes and objectives? No, me neither.

I think one of the issues which led to the adoption of outcomes as the noun rather than objectives was because of the perceived over-use of objectives across the organization. Specific, Measurable, Achievable, Relevant and Time-based (utilize your own version of SMART here); there was an enormous enthusiasm for MBO or Management By Objectives around the end of the 20th century. Over time, L&D teams wanted to distance what they were doing from the MBO process which – in some organizations – had got a bad reputation. Mostly, this was because the wrong things were being managed or significance was only accorded to things which were easily quantifiable and easily measurable.

The other reason that I suspect the word outcome was adopted was because the measurement of learning and achievement of learning outcomes/objectives was so tricky, especially outside education. In formal education at least someone's assignment or examination could be marked and, hopefully, an objective score given. The challenge of the corporate trainer has always been the 'measurable' bit of the objective.

Whether the linguistic orthodoxy of your organization is objective or outcome, the element of measurement is not only an essential part of defining the purpose, and supporting the development, of a training programme, it is vital if the correct components are to be included in the eventual learning design. Effectively, if you can't say what is going to happen at the end, you can't build the things which lead up to it.

To put it another way: *Ignoranti quem portum petat nullus suus ventus est.* Or: 'If one does not know to which port one is sailing, no wind is favourable' (Seneca The Younger 4BC – AD65).

Unless you are in the habit of just randomly making up objectives and courses which you think might be useful and/or interesting to people within your organization – a more common activity than one might think – it helps to have undertaken some kind of Training Needs Analysis.

Training needs analysis or TNA

You may not be surprised that Training Needs Analysis (also called Learning Needs Analysis or even Training and Learning Needs Analysis, but we'll content ourselves with TNA for simplicity) describes two related but different things. L&D has a habit of imprecision about terminology which is really quite scary given what it is we're supposed to be about.

The first kind of TNA is an organizational one – as the Chartered Institute for Personnel and Development describe it in one of their fact sheets, it is:

> based on the systematic gathering of data about existing employees' capabilities and organizational demands for skills, alongside an analysis of the implications of new and changed roles for changes in capability.[1]

The other TNA is an individual one. It looks at one individual, their current role and the skills needed to be successful and possible future roles along with the skills needed to ensure their fitness to progress in their career. Having defined the skills (perhaps through the organizational process described above) each individual should have been helped to identify a series of skills and capability gaps which result in a training plan often called a Personal Development Plan (PDP).

Beginning to get the idea about TLAs (Three Letter Acronyms)? Believe me, if you don't have a facility with acronyms and mnemonics, then L&D may not have been the most appropriate career choice.

At the heart of starting the process of designing training interventions – whether we call them training, development or learning is unimportant at this stage – we must have some kind of specification or requirement against which we can design the programme. This is where the organization TNA comes in. The organizational component of the TNA requires the definition of the skills required across the organization for the different jobs which people do – a competence framework perhaps or at least something similar. Unfortunately, it is done with such varying quality that in many organizations they'd be best advised not to bother. In fact, poorly conceived and implemented TNAs damage the reputation of the L&D team and fuel the often unkind commentary about our relevance from other business functions.

The competence framework – or perhaps the application of it – is one area where things go wrong. The process of assessing individuals – and TNA requires some kind of individual assessment – is one of the responsibilities delegated to line managers as part of the annual appraisal process. The trouble is most managers – though not all – consider this process an unnecessary chore. In fact, in a survey I did of around 700 managers a couple of years ago, more than one third quite specifically said that this is a role which should be carried out by HR.

One of the reasons for their reluctance is that the competencies – the organizational standards defined for each job in the enterprise – are defined in 'trainer speak'. With good reason. Defining unambiguously what individuals need to do in each job requires a great deal of detail. The trouble is that most statements of capability don't define what 'good' looks like in a way which the team leader or coach can support. If the shift manager can't make head nor tail of what is written then the whole process comes to a halt and the individual's training – if it is discussed at all – is relegated to a performance appraisal after-thought.

Think about a skill most of us are familiar with – driving a car. A competency statement could be: 'Can smoothly shift into the correct gear for the speed of the car and the road conditions.' You might want to put a few caveats around that – how do you know what is the correct gear? Is it just that the driver doesn't stall the car or do you want something more, such as the sound of the engine or the read-out from the rev counter? So, as well as the statement you might have a number of measures.

The problem is that that's just changing gear. Once you break the task of driving a car into such small competence statements, you need hundreds of them just to drive to Tesco. These become unwieldy when we try to break down all the tasks someone would undertake to such a degree of granularity.

So why not make them simpler and more wide ranging? Problem number two. We want the training needs identified to be as actionable as possible and to be applied fairly and objectively. The less precise we become, the more likely these are to be interpreted subjectively. If we link TNA into the performance appraisal process, we get a reluctance to define someone as 'incompetent' when issues of performance-related pay are added to the mix. Using our driving example again: 'can drive safely with regard to prevailing road conditions' sounds OK, but what does that mean? If you've ever had a white knuckle experience as a passenger you know that what driving safely means to one person is a different matter to others.

Competencies can be unwieldy and most line managers don't take the time or effort to understand them and apply them correctly. It's entirely the line manager's fault!

Not really. I think as L&D professionals we have to take some of the blame. We define roles at such a granular level of detail that the people supervising those who actually do the job find them difficult to understand and interpret. Then, because we have different pay grades, we add to the complexity by differentiating the exact same competencies across the hierarchy.

To overcome this problem, we might seek to revise or create our competencies by consulting widely with the line managers. Getting them on board at the start is a great idea. Again, my experience of doing exactly that has been somewhat flawed. In a previous life, I was involved in making business and management TV programmes. I interviewed many hundreds of people who were good at something. I found that many peak performers are actually not very good at articulating what it is they do. In the absence of an analysis of what makes them effective – or at least the language to express it – they fall back on homilies and clichés which don't give someone new to a role much to go on. I was recently working with a team who had used the interview method to define a series of competencies. One of the ones they came up with was 'Demonstrates a can-do attitude'! What, in the name of everything sacred to a training professional, does that mean? How do I train that? How do I measure it? Most importantly, how do I know it when I see it and will it look the same in both Penge and Paris?

There's the secret – the ability to observe someone doing something and recognize the essential activities, skills and behaviours which define what 'good' looks like. I was team training with a colleague some years ago. At the end of the course, the group were asked to define what they were going to do differently on their return to the workplace. My colleague who was leading the session said: 'I want you to describe it as if you were watching a video of yourself doing it.' I thought it was a stroke of genius. If you can't see it happening – and therefore video it – assume it isn't. The best competencies use this 'video technique'. They describe what someone actually does.

Over many years I have worked with an international sales training organization. They have conducted 35,000 observations of effective sales people and boiled down the skills that differentiated the good ones from the less good ones into just four stages. It was wholly based on observation. It removed any issue about the ability or otherwise of the effective sales person to describe what they did. Because of the sheer volume of observations it was robust and – most importantly – simple to understand and interpret.

The challenges for the rest of us seeking to define the secrets of effective performance include: Who do we observe? – it's pretty clear which sales people are the most effective – what about someone handling something less black and white? Once we know who we're observing, who does the observations? How skilled are they at analysing what they are looking at? If the observation process is to be considered robust and relevant to a whole range of different contexts it will be time consuming. Is this time investment the right thing to do? By the time we have observed enough good people in different contexts, different countries and different environments, might it be the case that what we have observed is what good performance was rather than what it will be in the future?

We don't want to fall at the first hurdle. So we should learn to be smart in how we do the observations as well as looking at what is currently happening and invest our resources in cataloguing the future needs of the organization. Observing skills and behaviours which the organization doesn't yet use is going to be pretty tricky. The simple fact is that what each organization needs is changing and changing pretty rapidly.

A simple example: 53 per cent of senior executives see social media use and its impact on their business increasing in the next 12 months and yet 76 per cent of organizations have no social media policy for employees[2]. Sad to say, that the only social media-related training or communications I've seen in many organizations has been 'don't use it or else – and by the way, we've blocked access to Facebook and Twitter!' In this respect, and I think many others, the L&D team are lagging behind the organizational reality.

In their 2001 book, *Funky Business*, Swedish economists Kjell Nordström and Jonas Ridderstråle asserted that '80 per cent of the technology we will use in 10 years' time hasn't even been invented yet'. Now, I'll be honest, I haven't gone back and checked. But on the face of it that assertion seems OK in principle even though we might argue about whether it was 74.7 per cent or 82.1 per cent. The thrust of their argument – that technology is evolving at a rate we could only have imagined in the early years of the 20th century – is indisputable. What was science fiction in the not too distant past is now just work.

We desperately need L&D people to be futurologists. There is only limited benefit in the L&D team spending all their time looking at what the organization does now. Some of that energy should be focused on what it might need to do in the next three to five years. A number of organizations spend a great deal of time doing exactly this in respect of their products, their services and their customers. But as every annual report tells us, people are our most important asset so what are we doing about ensuring that we have defined the skills needed *in the future*?

For TNA to adequately enable L&D teams to specify what it is that needs to be developed and delivered requires:

1 Simple process-based competencies which are drawn from observation, accurate enough to be clear, but expressed well enough to be usable by those for whom L&D is not their main job. It may not be possible to undertake observations of 35,000 sales calls like the sales training company I mentioned. But it is possible to watch people doing their job and specifically to shadow, interview and analyse what it is that those who are considered high-level performers actually do all day. The competencies thus developed should follow my colleague's video test. Describe what it is that is observed and that is different from what others do and boil that down to a process. To quote W. Edwards Deming again: 'If you can't describe what you are doing as a process, you don't know what you're doing.'

2 Training (and associated competencies) for those who will identify training needs – ie the line managers.

I once asked a group I was speaking to how many of their organizations withheld performance pay from those managers who didn't play a full role in identifying training requirements for their teams and supporting team member development. One hand was raised from an audience of about 70. What gets measured gets done – the whole organization needs to sign up to this or it is best not to bother.

For fear of contradicting myself about setting measures which in themselves prove nothing, but at least are easy to count, I do think some kind of target works. What is the amount of training which would seem to be a bare minimum for the people in your organization? One course per year, two? How about a number of days? One organization I work with simply expects everyone in the business to have a Personal Development Plan which is recorded on their central HR system. The PDP is only marked as complete when the team leader or line manager signs it off.

The system has been set up to alert HR teams when an individual still has no PDP logged on the system 30 days after the deadline and then again at 60 days if the gentle reminder has been ignored. It places the HR team in the policing role again and I feel uncomfortable about that monitoring and enforcing role, but I'm enough of a realist to suggest that it's not only carrots which get results, sometimes it's the odd stick as well. Is everyone who doesn't complete the PDPs with each of their team members pulled up and reprimanded? Not frequently enough, unfortunately. In some cases it is addressed by the senior leaders, in others lip service is paid at best. What actually happens is that those managers who were borderline at appraisal time – that is under-performing in some areas – suddenly find that there is a new-found enthusiasm for analysing figures like the number of incomplete PDPs and the number of times team members have been removed from courses at the last minute. This is not an uncommon message given to managers: It's OK to flout the rules if you're really, really good at everything else. Blind eyes will be turned, indulgence will be granted. Just don't slip up or these instances of rule bending may come back and bite you! We all love a maverick until they stop performing.

3 A continuous process of looking at the future requirements for the organization – reviewing what other organizations are doing in other sectors and charting trends in your particular area of activity. Every employee should be engaged in at least one programme per year which is looking at the future and the kinds of things which the organization will need to be doing over a three- to five-year time horizon.

Shared learning outcomes: getting better at the things which matter

Fundamentally, the L&D team need to be able to answer a question for every member of staff who is to be involved in a training intervention: Why is this person enrolled on the training programme? 'Because they have to be' rarely works. Each individual needs a personal training or development plan which identifies their needs and the routes to satisfying them. The rationale for them putting in the required effort needs to be clearly articulated in a manner which appeals directly to them. There should be pain removed and opportunity realized, both the carrot of being able to do more, gain promotion or other reward or simply be more effective; along with the stick of dire consequences if they don't. Of course, if we need the learner to be supported by their line manager (and we do) then we need to include carrots and sticks for the manager too.

If the TNA merely responds to a competence framework (ie plugs competence gaps) then its success as a carrot or a stick will depend wholly on whether the competence framework is owned by the team member and the team leader. As we've already seen, the chances are that the existing competence framework, expressed in training terminology and based on a detailed outline of each activity required by someone in the role, isn't perceived as the primary tool in managing capability by the line manager and their team members. They will more than likely have come up with something more related to the outputs of their team than the competence framework. Whether we like it or not, competence frameworks are viewed by those outside HR as being of marginal relevance to the real work of getting things done. Better to ensure that the review which identifies the need for new skills is based on a real business need and expressed in terms of being able to do things which are integral to the current role, essential for the planned or anticipated changes in this area of work or the individual's desired future role. In reality, line managers already know who their best performers are and they already know who needs more help to get up to speed. They will have an informal league table of performance based on more subjective measures and reinforced by the existing business measurements which they and their team are expected to deliver against.

For example, I was working recently with groups of salespeople in the motor trade. To gain the necessary buy-in to the programme I needed to express the programme's outcomes in terms of unit sales, profitability per unit and increased cross selling of finance and insurance products. These are things which this group are measured on and gain rewards for.

Sales teams are relatively easy because of the close association between results and reward. Outside sales it's more difficult but not impossible. The issue is looking for clear performance measures. If you have customer service teams, do you gather information from customer satisfaction surveys and set targets for that feedback? If you're looking at marketing teams, do you evaluate response rates to each campaign? If you're dealing with factory workers, do you gather information about production machine usage, productivity, efficiency, waste levels, etc? For administrators do you set targets for the costs and time required to process invoices, customer records, or respond to information requests? The chances are you do and the importance of metrics which the organization already uses cannot be underestimated. The job of L&D teams is to help the organization do the things it does better. If you can't link your programme to the measures of success already in place in the organization, you need to think again.

Having identified our learning objectives, our line managers – with the assistance of our training programmes – can assess each individual in their teams and identify the gaps which need to be filled. This process is simpler if the objective measures of capability are closely related to those performance measures which are assessed by the organization to determine success or failure.

Matching these gaps to a programme can be tricky as the programmes we will create need to be designed to meet the complete demand for skills and capabilities which may be found in an individual. In other words, a programme designed at the global, corporate level may include all the knowledge and skills required. It is based on a fictional every-employee who rarely if ever exists – essentially, an employee who knows nothing. Thus, the general course differs from the individual's needs as they will have some of this knowledge already. It seems pretty self-evident to me that training people to do things which they already know how to do will result in some resistance from learners and a lack of desire from their line managers to undertake the assessment process or release people from day-to-day tasks to take part in our carefully crafted training programmes.

Any programme designed to meet the competence framework, therefore, requires a series of discrete components. Think of it rather like building something with Lego. The major feature of Lego or similar construction toys is that any piece can be put together with any other piece. So it should be with competence framework-derived courses. The individual learning activities which comprise our toolkit should be capable of being used in isolation or combined with others to meet each individual's specific requirements. When stitched together into a programme, we may describe this collection of resources and courses, activities and work-based tasks as a blended learning solution. The combination of self-directed learning, with or without the assistance of technology, courses and classroom activities, on-the-job learning and guidance provided by an expert or coach should be merged together to deliver one, coherent programme. Each component should lead sensibly to the next activity designed to develop the individual's competence. What helps this seamless progression between learning activities is having a sequence of learning – a kind of hierarchy of objectives.

Practically, a measurable objective contains an active verb which describes what the participants should do during the programme (which extends to workplace implementation activities in the case of behavioural objectives). Because of the inclusion of this description the activities required as part of the objective's achievement are included in the learning objective.

Knowledge, skills and behaviours

Learning objectives are available in three flavours – knowledge, skills and behaviours, supplemented by awareness-raising as shown in Figure 2.1.

Before embarking on supporting knowledge acquisition, the trainer needs to ensure a basic level of awareness. This might be the scope of

FIGURE 2.1   The triangle of learning outcomes

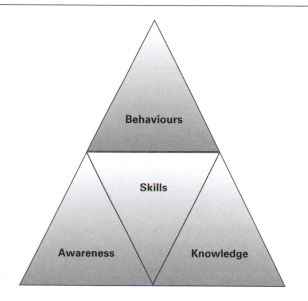

the learning to be undertaken, the context (why and why now?) and at least a broad appreciation of the benefits to be achieved from completing this learning journey.

Learning objectives describing the knowledge to be gained are the ones which most often miss out the process of measuring achievement. That's because we're trying to describe something going on in someone's head. We need to come up with some active verbs to describe the knowledge acquired. These active verbs will be observable. How we observe the activity will be a clue to the way we design the activities throughout the training programme. For example, a learning objective which expects participants to describe a process or success criteria will need an activity in which participants do some describing! This may be a report on an analysis of a case example, a question and answer session or a presentation of research.

While it may not be universally the case, often the development of skills and behaviours is built on a solid foundation of knowledge. For this reason, it is common for knowledge objectives to be required early in the training process. As a result many training workshops start with what is effectively a lecture. As a general rule, 'telling' is not a great vehicle for delivering knowledge to a group. A quick search on the web will bring you to 'The Learning Pyramid'. Here you will be told that learners only retain about five per cent of what they have heard in a lecture within a couple of weeks. Now this seems instinctively about right – it passes the common sense test. As with many of the 'scientific' studies of learning this is the only test it will ever pass. The learning pyramid is variously attributed. Most talk about Dale's 'Cone of Learning', an illustrative model first put forward by Edgar Dale in 1957 in *Audio Visual Methods in Teaching*. The problem is that Dale made it clear that this was a wholly illustrative model and he declined to put any numbers alongside the 10 components which made up his 'Cone of Experience'. In fact he pointed out it would be a dangerous mistake to regard the bands in the cone as rigid and inflexible divisions moving from direct experience to the most abstract method, verbal symbols, or being told about something.

There is a distressing tendency of the L&D profession to latch on to half-read and barely understood concepts, misrepresenting the original author's intentions, and the research which underpins them, as they do so.

Studies have been conducted into how more knowledge can be retained for longer. Despite the variable interpretation which is put upon this research, I think we can accept that a lecture is neither the only option available to us, nor the ideal way of ensuring the messages we wish our learners to take away with them will stick. Any active involvement by participants in discovering facts or exploring theories, through discussion, research or presenting back their understanding, significantly increases knowledge retention. As does writing an assignment or an essay, but this more academic approach is not appropriate for all programmes.

Interestingly, presentations/lectures which include real stories – particularly those including the more gruesome horror stories of how things can go wrong – do have greater impact. Telling stories as a route to engaging the audience and then asking participants to reflect on the experience described and extract the key theoretical points is a very valid route for experienced practitioners to share their knowledge.

The most effective way of determining what types of activity to incorporate into the programme in order to achieve the knowledge required is through taking time to craft robust knowledge objectives. The more specific the objective the more effective the pointers to the learning design. That specificity derives from the use of active verbs. 'Understand...' is not helpful because it lacks any mechanism for measurement. 'Demonstrate an understanding of...' at least requires some means of demonstration and words such as 'List', 'Describe', 'Identify' are much more helpful to the programme designer who can then build opportunities for learners to build a list, describe features and factors and recognize examples of good and not so good practice.

Where knowledge objectives naturally precede the development of skills or adoption of behaviours, it may make sense entirely to do away with the workshop as a route to knowledge acquisition. Much of the knowledge we wish to impart to our trainees can be delivered to them through other, more effective means. This pre-loading of knowledge-based learning also assists individuals to tailor the programme to meet their specific training requirements. Rather than spend time in a workshop with everyone going through the essential knowledge pre-requisites, some kind of self-directed learning based on resources which learners can be directed to in advance of any group-based learning can help 'level the playing field'. If we can create a situation in which everyone has the required initial knowledge then we can reduce repetition or redundancy during the group-based sessions for those participants who already have progressed along the knowledge acquisition path. Once everyone in the training room can be said to be on some kind of equivalent level of knowledge, the organization has assured that it is maximizing the value of the expensive process of bringing people together in a group-based, social experience.

Self-directed learning or pre-workshop activities

This pre-workshop activity is sometimes called 'pre-read' or 'pre-work'. I don't think that either of these terms is helpful. 'Pre-read' seems un-necessarily to limit the kind of initial activities which could and should be included. We've already seen that, for many organizations, the pre-workshop activity is an online module. Now it may well be the case that for some examples of the medium, these could easily be called pre-read without it being a misnomer, but one would hope that for the most part something more than merely reading is required to utilize a preparatory online programme.

Similarly, the knowledge required in advance of the workshop or group component may not be easily distributed via a book, paper or link. It may be that the learner needs to do some research work to present their own perspective on the subject under discussion. A fast-moving consumer goods company – the sort of people who manufacture and market the products and brands you find on your supermarket shelves – recently organized a programme for brand managers across its portfolio of household names. Each brand manager was supplied with a $100 video camera in advance of the one-week workshop. They were expected to go out and interview consumers in their country – identifying what was behind the brand choices that they made and the considerations which influenced their shopping decisions. The brand managers were asked to film these interviews and post them up to a 'YouTube-style' channel a couple of weeks in advance of the workshop. These interviews and the data and insights generated formed a significant element of the raw material for the programme itself. New theories about consumer and shopper behaviour were reviewed through the prism of the consumer interviews and analysis was conducted about the global relevance of these theories. Were the new ideas equally relevant in Boston and Bogota? Were shoppers in Lagos behaving in a similar or divergent way when compared with those in London?

Supplying video cameras? Setting up a dedicated YouTube-style channel? Seems expensive doesn't it? It isn't a decision taken lightly, but with accommodation, travel, catering, trainer fees and venue costs taken into account this programme cost around half a million dollars a year – around $12,500 per person per programme. When total training costs are calculated, intensifying the value of experience through this kind of innovation becomes a relatively easy decision to make and sell to the budget holders.

The answers arrived at during the workshop were a composite of the global trends observed by the course tutors and the insights gained from the streets of the cities in which the participants work. Describing this kind of activity as a pre-read would be to do it a major disservice.

Similarly, calling it 'pre-work' suggests that the work hadn't yet started, that no learning takes place (if that is the work of the workshop) before the trainer opens their mouth and shows the first PowerPoint slide. So pre-work doesn't accurately describe what it is that training participants should do in advance of coming together with their peers. What's more it seems to me to underestimate the importance of this stage of the learning activity. In fact, I would suggest it makes it seem optional. In truth, the major challenge for trainers who wish participants to undertake some activities in advance of a workshop is whether or not those participants have done anything at all. Describing the activity as 'pre-work' may feasibly contribute to the relatively low completion rates we sometimes see.

Of course the main reason there are low completion rates of activities which we define as a pre-requisite for workshop attendance is cultural. Traditionally in most organizations training has equated to attending a workshop or training course for a day or so. It has not extended to describe anything which happens or should happen beyond the training room door. In establishing the tools we must use to deliver a Complete Training experience, we have to challenge that cultural belief and establish the validity and vitality of other activities. In fact, these learning activities may be sufficient for the achievement of individual capability **without requiring attendance at a workshop at all**. For the moment, however, let's recognize the reality that the workshop – while it may not be the only tool in our kit – is a pretty important weapon in the training team's armoury.

Having defined why the programme is important, you need to activate the learner's current knowledge and bring everyone to the same place so that they can contribute equally to the debates, discussions and exercises in the classroom. Obviously, by using an e-learning programme for the pre-workshop activity, you can ensure that the material can be tracked and completion monitored. Having recorded who's done what online, you can ensure those who haven't completed the material don't progress to the next stage.

This move may seem somewhat draconian. Certainly, organizations are reluctant to take this step. For external training providers, it becomes even more difficult to exclude people from workshops onto which they have been booked. Furthermore, the benefits of involvement that we have outlined through our thorough, comprehensive and usable TNA, become a little meaningless when we introduce an element of compulsion. Compelling people to do something, when we should be assisting them in selecting the elements they need, seems contrary to the idea of selling the programme's importance and the value of its individual components.

I advocate thinking a little more laterally about pre-workshop activities. First of all, think about the medium used. With content management systems available, posting information on to an online resource, and being able to set up some form of monitoring of who is accessing what, is relatively simple. OK, not tracking as understood by those using proprietary Learning Management Systems (LMS) and not necessarily fully functioning e-learning – but does that matter? Surely, if we've done our homework on proving the relevance of the course, helping people to access information which is 'fit for purpose' may be enough.

These resources, therefore, may be a traditional online course, but it may also be a YouTube-style video or a podcast to be downloaded onto a mobile device and listened to on the move. It may also be a document that can be read on screen or printed out if that is the individual's preference. Don't think that this rules out any kind of personalization or click through to additional information which you may have usually associated with an online programme. By encouraging users to read on screen (iPads and similar make this much more practical and portable) and by embedding links into the document, you can enable your learners to click on a simple link and explore any of the other materials you may want to make available – from hints and tips delivered using mini e-learning modules, to websites, videos, podcasts or further documents.

The mini e-learning idea is an interesting one. By mini, I mean three, four or five minutes maximum – just two or three screens.

Wherever you're introducing a new concept or some unfamiliar vocabulary, perhaps include a little help icon which, when clicked, launches a short module. These can be as simple as you like – maybe created using an authoring tool and capable of being re-used in many different settings. Think of each of these resources – whatever the medium – as a store cupboard of communications, training and information. By creating them as simply as possible, you will be able to tailor them to the requirements from your TNA without needing to take ages to either create the programme (so it's out of date before it goes live) or spend a massive budget.

Specially prepared reading – such as short articles or fact sheets – should equip participants with the vocabulary relevant to the course including a definition of some of the key terminology which will feature in the programme. However, a glossary would be a pretty dry read and unlikely to be consulted. Using the necessary vocabulary within a fact sheet or article (with explanations where required) – is more likely to be completed.

There is a relationship between the length of the proposed workshop and the proposed pre-workshop activities to prepare participants to properly engage and take part in the classroom part of the activity. For a one-day course, I would suggest there is a strong likelihood of completion of the pre-workshop activity if it requires no more than 30–45 minutes. A 1,500 word article or fact sheet (between three and four A4 pages) will take an average reader around 20 minutes to read and digest. If you are concerned that some individuals might not have completed it in advance, you can always have some copies around in the coffee area prior to the commencement of the group-based session.

If you think about the amount of material covered in 1,500 words and translate that into a presentation, this may represent as many as 10 PowerPoint slides. How long would that take you to go through in a workshop session – 20 minutes, half an hour, an hour? Initial presentation material (ie the stuff you usually do to ensure everyone is on the same page at the start of a workshop) can almost always be covered through self-directed learning in advance of any workshop session and sometimes covered by simply giving someone a document to read. Once the learners are together, it helps to re-visit the materials you have distributed – perhaps just to check that the level of understanding you expected to be demonstrated after access to the pre-workshop activity has been achieved. The 'checking-they've-got-it' activity is almost always shorter and is also a more fun, dynamic and energetic start to the day than being an audience to a lecture or Power-Point presentation. Active involvement in the learning and engagement with the topic is of significant benefit in itself, but the benefit doubles if it allows you to dispense with upfront presentations and spend more time on new and exciting material, rather than information which may be new to some but not to others.

Initial self-directed learning – whether reading a document or responding to a research brief or completing one or more modules of e-learning – may include some questions which the participants should have answered. The discussion, therefore, can relate to the outcomes of these questions. An alternative for fact-heavy information or a refresher from a previous course might be a light-hearted quiz (undertaken in groups so that it also acts as a kind of ice-breaker which gets the group members talking to each other). You can always emphasize the fun part by having small prizes, such as chocolate bars, stress balls or fruit.

Life cycle tips

How do you start the training process, utilising TNA and initial, knowledge-based learning resources? The hints and tips that follow are designed to provide ideas for how to begin the process for each of our five employee stages outlined in Chapter 1.

The new recruit

For new starters within your organization, you can utilize their enthusiasm for the new job and their new role in advance of them actually starting their employment. Much of the induction process concerns itself with assisting new starters in getting to grips with the organization – its values, business models and services, as well as how the organization is structured to deliver its products and services to its clients.

Once your new recruit has signed up to join the organization, the welcome e-mail could include the log-on details of a specially constructed induction e-learning portal. If you work for a large organization you may well have much of the required material already available via your careers pages – the kind of information designed to attract new graduates or similar. Typically this will include the history of the organization, main products and services to enable people to grasp the organization's vision and mission. This information works well when tied together via stories from real people – employees, customers and service users.

This section could include some kind of assessment tool, designed to ensure your new hires complete the required pre-start learning and give confidence to line managers and others involved in the formal post-joining induction process that these new recruits have consulted and completed – to a defined standard – the initial training materials. One idea might be to include the assessment at the start of the e-learning with the remaining materials organized as a mechanism to help individuals fill the gaps that the initial assessment has identified. This sets the tone of the Complete Training philosophy – the learner is in control of identifying their needs and making the required effort and arrangements to plug any gaps identified.

This initial on-boarding also helps reduce some of those areas of discomfort we know new starters experience. If you can justify creating a simple induction for each location where new starters will be based, you can include everything from pay dates to which bakers serve the best lunchtime sandwiches, where you can safely park a bicycle and an agenda for their first few days in the business.

Try to keep it simple. Identify the 10 things every employee in your organization should know within the first week of joining and cover those things in this online tool. Remember also that many of your new employees might have been applying to a number of organizations for jobs. You are still in marketing mode. Spending a significant amount of time during this online pre-start induction explaining the disciplinary system and how you can get sacked might be counter-productive.

CASE STUDY

Cabin crew in all the major airlines require a rigorous initial training regime covering health and safety and customer service before being allowed to actually board an aeroplane in their shiny new uniforms. International carrier Virgin Atlantic won the best *Return on Investment award* at the 2006 *e-Learning Age Awards* by creating an online training programme which covered the majority of the theory behind the stringent health and safety rules required by the Civil Aviation Authority and other national regulators. The return on their investment in creating a five-hour e-learning programme was achieved very simply.

Even if the company disregarded the number of training days which were no longer required when a new member of cabin crew was recruited – and these reduced significantly – a few recruits simply selected themselves out of the process of undertaking the training. New starters were not allowed to progress to the face-to-face elements of the training until they had successfully completed the pre-starter induction materials.

When the new members of cabin crew turned up for the remainder of the hands-on training – using a dummy aircraft rig, known fondly in the training team as Diana – they found that all of those who had completed the initial online programme successfully completed the course and commenced flying shortly afterwards. The ability to complete the initial e-learning on time and to the required standard, proved to be a matchless indicator of future success and suitability to the role. The savings on administration, workshops, training materials and personal equipment which would otherwise have been provided to those who would have been unable to complete the training paid for the e-learning in less than nine months.

The new manager

In this model, those identified as potential supervisors or team leaders should undertake an introductory front-line manager training programme before being considered for promotion into the role.

Unfortunately, for many organizations, this seems to be considered an egregious interference in the autonomy of a function, area office or department by the training team. As a result, even where something similar is in place, it is more honoured in the breach than in its observance.

These approaches do work, however. I've already outlined the British Rail experience, but there have been other, more long-term approaches in some obvious but occasionally overlooked situations. Police sergeants have specific legal responsibilities which are greater than those of the constables they supervise. As a result, no police constable is promoted who has not achieved the required sergeant's qualifications. The same holds good in the military and in some civil service roles. Teachers wishing to make the step up to management – especially for a deputy headship or head teacher role – are not considered without the requisite training in leading a school.

In many professional disciplines we expect a level of training and an assessment of capability and suitability prior to advancement. If our people are our greatest asset (see every company annual report ever published) why would we risk their management to someone who has no training, no qualifications and no track record in providing those management services to their team and to the organization? As Tom Peters says in *In Search of Leadership Heroes*: 'Leadership should be seen as an honour – you have an astonishing responsibility to those in your care.'

Some of the initial theories and values associated with management in the organization can be covered in advance of anyone being released for training courses or workshops. I also don't think it is unreasonable to expect the investment being made in the individual by their employer to be matched by the employee. They could/should undertake some of this learning outside the normal nine to five. The follow-up workshops – unavailable for those who have not completed the pre-requisite materials – provide an opportunity for groups to come together to do those things which can't be dealt with without a face-to-face experience. This is when groups will discuss how to recognize and address under-performance, practice quality conversations designed to help people develop and deliver of their best, and – perhaps most importantly – explore strategies for how to manage their manager!

The specialist

The initial challenge with both defining competence and delivering pre-workshop activities to a specialist is: who determines what it is they need to be able to do and who would then create the resources required to bring them up to speed? Working in the specialist's area of expertise is probably too tricky for the humble L&D generalist.

But specialists are part of the organization too and the competence framework should define generic knowledge and skills required for everyone, regardless of role, determined by their level of seniority. This is particularly true of specialists whose area of expertise is increasingly important to the organization and therefore there is the potential for them to be charged with working in, or leading, a larger team in order to deliver the results required.

These generic competences are often the difference between making the impact required and specialists being under-used. All members of L&D teams who work with employees from outside the HR function will have a story to tell of the individual who feels they are a lone voice, battling organizational indifference when things could be so much better/different/efficient/etc if only the rest of the enterprise paid more attention to what they were saying. Usually, the isolated specialist feels that the organization is at fault. In my experience, however, it is that the specialist has never properly mastered the communication of their ideas to the wider business nor understood enough about how the other functions work, for their ideas to be comfortably integrated alongside business as usual.

I would strongly advocate that a section of every competence framework should concern itself with communications skills – influencing, managing meetings, report writing, presenting and the like. Similarly, a section should be devoted to the widest appreciation and understanding of the organization, what it does and why. Unless you are working in a particularly unusual industry, this will change – albeit subtly, perhaps – as the organization matures and develops and service users, customers and society at large changes. Standing still and making no change isn't particularly fashionable in 21st-century management thinking. Learning about what the organization does is not a one-off activity only undertaken during induction. This is knowledge which should be regularly updated.

If your specialist is required to lead on a specific area of the business, then the chances are they will have been recruited on the basis of their knowledge of that specialist area. But knowing as much as they do about their little corner of the business is only as much use as their ability to communicate what should be different and why to those who need to implement any required change. One of the keys to being able to communicate in this situation is being able to frame their arguments in ways which focus on the day-to-day concerns of those in the remainder of the organization. The primary skill set for the specialist is not only about knowing more and more in their own area of specialism, though keeping themselves up to date in their field may be one of the responsibilities we would set for them. It is vital, if they are to educate, influence and develop the remainder of the organization, that they know a good deal about what the other functions do. If your competence framework doesn't specify this broad understanding of the enterprise coupled with effective communication skills, you have the wrong competence framework.

The leader

Who assesses the leader's competence and capability? In many organizations, this activity includes a 360-degree appraisal tool in which those who work with and for the leader are asked their views about their capabilities. Those completing the questionnaire may be from inside or outside the organization depending on the role of the individual being assessed. The 360-degree tool deployed, whether a simple questionnaire or an online form to be completed, should be based on the leadership competences which your organization has adopted. The challenge here is to ensure that those completing the tool actually understand what it is they are looking at. You will only find out how reliable and understandable your 360-degree feedback tool is once you have piloted it and tested it thoroughly. In the same way that a competence framework is only helpful if the people required to interpret it can do so with a high level of objectivity and rigour, then a 360-degree tool will only help if the assessment statements mean the same thing to everyone who reads them.

Those who make a living from creating and administering such assessment surveys will argue – quite rightly – that the organizational culture needs to be supportive of the use of such assessment tools. The top leadership needs to actively support them and those being appraised need to be open to the comments received and seen to respond to the feedback. Otherwise, like much else in learning and development, the exercise is reduced to a box-ticking activity.

Whatever the culture, however open and trusting, there are two specific requirements for this to work. The first is that completion of the questionnaires should be anonymous. As a supplier, I have been included in the list of people asked to complete a 360-degree feedback questionnaire reviewing the performance of a budget holder with whom I was working. I would have loved to say that I was scrupulously honest in my comments despite the fact that this individual was re-sponsible for a significant chunk of my income. I'd love to say that, but probably couldn't. The issue here was not just the lack of ano-nymity; it was also my second specific requirement. In this instance, the feedback tool wasn't simply being used for determining training requirements, it was also being used to assess suitability for promo-tion and annual bonus. If you are serious about finding out what training is needed by people at all levels in the organization, then you should de-couple the process of assessing performance for purposes of annual bonus from the process of determining training needs. This is especially important with leaders, where admitting certain areas of weakness may require a good deal of courage. To further disincentiv-ize such candour seems destined for failure.

The retiree

When a member of staff has been in the organization for a length of time, they are an invaluable resource to support L&D activities because of their wealth of stories and their ability to set context for current initiatives. It may not be appropriate to have them involved in delivering the training, but tapping into the organizational memory of which they are custodians is a potential rich source of material for learning designers. If you need to create a fictional yet realistic scen-ario, ask an old hand. If you need to ensure that your presentation of a new approach or process doesn't ignore lessons learned from a previous era, consult those who were actively involved during that era. In non-work settings some of the most effective history exhibits I've ever seen have involved oral history – older people captured on tape reminiscing about their experiences during periods in recent history. While consulting with your more experienced colleagues, think about capturing what they say for use in podcasts or similar to support the provision of digital learning content.

The provision of training to a more experienced member of staff, especially as it relates to undertaking a job they've done for absolutely ages, can often be tricky. Either the learner adopts an attitude of 'seen it all before' or the trainer assumes they will. Worst of all is where the training team make no provision for this group because the expectation is that they have nothing to learn and won't be around to implement the new approaches for long in any case.

This is where resources come into play. As I have said, resources – like the podcasts we hope they will have contributed to – are not the same as courses. However, using job aids, articles and repositories of information can ensure this group stay up to date in an appropriate way and are able to take control of their own learning – identifying the further information or experiences which will help them make sense of any changes to the role they are expected to play.

When I produced a strategy for an organization which had a number of long-serving staff members, I suggested using online resources. Apart from technical barriers about staff being able to access the material I recommended on the computer terminals available to them, the other barrier was that a proportion of these more experienced members of staff never logged on to a computer at all. Although key tasks were computerized – such as booking holidays on the HR system – staff would trade duties with more tech-savvy colleagues. In some cases, this meant taking on jobs which were probably significantly less pleasant than sitting at a desk for half an hour in order to avoid the embarrassment of not being able to work out how to use the system, not being able to operate a mouse or keyboard or simply being scared that they'd break something. I enquired about the kind of training that had been provided for staff members when the new systems were introduced and I was told that it was all computer centre-based with tutor support and some e-learning. In other words, to access training on equipment which made you anxious required you to conquer your fears in a public setting like some kind of aversion therapy. The training was advisory (rather than compulsory – this was an organization which ran a large number of compulsory courses each year) and surprise, surprise the hardest to reach technophobes remained out of reach.

A Complete Trainer would have recognized the issues with computer literacy (and, in some cases, literacy full stop) and put in place a mandatory element of the training with one-to-one support at the place of work. I recognize that this is a potentially pretty heavy resourcing issue for an organization like this one with over 25,000 staff. The only practical way of addressing it is to convert those with some technical literacy into coaches and mentors of those with less. Ideally, this will enable a just-in-time learning process rather than creating scheduled sessions which do nothing more than raise participants' anxiety levels. If some of these tech mentors can be the older hands so that there is a peer-to-peer training opportunity between more experienced staff, then so much the better. This has the potential to reduce the levels of embarrassment about their incapability when everyone else seemingly finds this stuff so easy and addresses issues of seniority and status – a bigger issue than you might expect in many organizations. If these mentors can also advocate the use of some of those resources such as step-by-step guides and job aids, then you have some reassurance that there is a consistency of approach.

Complete Training tools: workshops

The workshop is an oft maligned component of the training mix. The issues include people waiting for ages to be able to book on to an appropriate event, the difficulty of ensuring everyone in attendance is at a similar level, the endless presentations which neither inform nor inspire and – worst of all – that everyone with a laptop thinks they can be a trainer, regardless of all evidence to the contrary. Yes, the workshop has something of a PR problem.

It's not my intention here to defend some of the things which happen in training rooms the world over in the name of the workshop. For the most part, the critics of the classroom event are right. In practice, the course, workshop or class sometimes barely deserves to be referred to as training. They are often hideously one-directional events in which PowerPoint slide after PowerPoint slide is read out to a bored group who are buoyed only by the fact that they've got out of the office for the day and will be fed by the company.

Workshops should not be the same as a day-long lecture, even when the organizer has had some consideration for the audience member by arranging a revolving rota of presenters to take charge of the remote mouse. This is not to say that all presentations should be removed from the workshop experience in favour of endless games designed to get us all in touch with our inner juggler. Far from it. Some of the highly interactive workshops are equally irritating and, being so wonderfully content free, almost impossible to justify in times of austerity. To be worth doing at all, the workshop must assist in achieving a defined learning objective for the participant which is an outcome which the organization is prepared to invest in. Too often, classroom event objectives are simply not tied into what the organization needs, nor indeed do they match the requirements of the individuals who attend.

There are face-to-face training events which are somewhat better than this, and the mix of discussions, activities and presentations provides an interesting and often stimulating day for participants. Calculating the return on the training investment in organizing such a classroom event is possible. Often these impressive calculations are undermined by the sneaking suspicion that the significant resources in room hire, trainer fees, resources and materials, food, drink and – the biggest expense – paying the participants, could have been put to better use. This is true, however apparently successful the programme may seem.

The real costs of the training room

The simple fact is that these group sessions represent by some distance the most expensive training intervention in the organizational learning toolkit. The CIPD Learning and Talent Development Survey of 2011[1] identified a median annual training spend of £350 per employee, purchasing around five training days. A similar survey by Bersin Associates[2] found that in the USA, per capita training spend was $800 representing a scant 15.3 hours of formal learning per employee. There are two interesting ideas here. In the Chartered Institute of Personnel and Development's report, training is still recorded in training *days* and in the USA, where training is apparently much more expensive, it is calculated in *hours*. The US survey goes on to confirm that a greater proportion of formal training is now being undertaken by methods other than the traditional classroom event, especially one that takes all day to attend. This difference might be a function of geography. Pulling your workforce together across a continent and many time zones must make each training workshop somewhat trickier to organize. Maybe in the UK, the relative ease of bringing people together from across the country means it has been less pressing to question the relevance of all the group training events which are organized.

Whatever explains it, the average full-time employee is at work for around 200 days per year. Spending less than 0.5 per cent of their time engaged in formal training is really not very much. If the main tool we use for this – the group workshop – is not being used effectively we had better be concerned. Each day of training which fails to deliver represents a very significant proportion of the opportunity for formal training available for each individual. We'd better get it right.

The amount of money spent on training is always difficult to assess. Different organizations and different surveys seem to include different things in the calculation. For some organizations budget reports simply cover external costs – venue hire, materials development, trainer fees. For those organizations with in-house training teams, these costs may be included too. Individual programmes may be charged out to different functions and this may include residential costs, though the cost of travel to attend is rarely calculated because it comes out of a different budget heading. What about catering? Usually this is included in the costs, but handout printing may not be. However you calculate and report your training budget, a lot of money is spent on organizing workshops. Despite this very significant cost, there is one area of expenditure that is rarely included – the salaries and wages of those who are in attendance.

CASE STUDY

I was once asked to help a major supermarket chain to design some training about new customer care policies and behaviours. As a retailer, customer care was pretty high on the organization's agenda – so high, in fact, that every one of the 120,000 employees of the company was expected to complete this training programme. I had a budget to work to and a specification which outlined that the intervention should have a duration of only one hour. I protested and outlined the amount of information I had to cover. Couldn't we make it an hour and a half so we could build lots of nice exercises in, I pleaded? That was the point at which I discovered that every person undertaking any training – from induction to management development – was paid for from the training department's budget for the time they were involved in the training session, whether it was an online module or a classroom event. The reason for this was that the organization didn't want store managers to be deterred from releasing people for training. At the corporate level, it was so important that everyone undertook their duties in a way which reflected the company's standards that the individual store manager's budget did not have to bear any of the cost of having their team members trained. When I did the sums, every 15 minutes of training time for every employee, at roughly average wage costs, added more than an extra £200,000 to the cost of each programme. It made me realize that if I was going to take people away from their front-line jobs for a period of time, I had to make sure that I generated extra benefit for the organization which at least met the cost in wages of the people being trained.

Developing skills

Given that it's such a costly business to have everyone in the same place, why do you bring people together? To give them more information? Is that really the best use of everyone's time and the considerable resources their attendance represents? For the Complete Trainer, the purpose of the workshop is to do things which can only be done when there is a group of people with a common aim, gathered in one location. And this may seem really obvious, but the skills which are the subject of the workshop need to be skills those attending actually need and will be able to practise in the near future. The common aim, therefore, is determined by a real requirement for those participating to develop capabilities which they will need *immediately* on their return to the workplace.

Notice the focus on skills. Things which can only be done in a group setting are rarely activities designed to impart more or new knowledge. The role of the workshop is to involve people in doing things, and being able to act on and with the information and knowledge they have.

FIGURE 3.1   The competence ladder

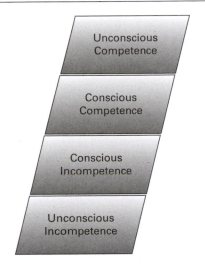

To make sense of this, it helps to understand the competence ladder. This was a model developed by Noel Burch of Gordon Training International in the 1970s. The ladder (see Figure 3.1) starts with:

Unconscious incompetence. Put simply this is when a person doesn't know what he or she doesn't know. Information-seeking skills are of no assistance if a learner has no framework into which to fit the information they discover. If we introduce new skills to someone without them recognizing that they need those skills or why, then the skill development process is at best a mechanical, stage by stage, rote learning. Think about a child in a car. Perhaps they have been given a plastic steering wheel which sticks to the window. They will 'steer' by maniacally wiggling the plastic steering wheel from side to side, pausing only to beep the horn. They do not yet know how the wheel in their hands would affect the wheels on the car and have no need to do so. Once that child observes his or her parent driving and is able to visualize one day driving themselves, they make progress. They understand that they do not know precisely how the steering wheel works or how the engine sound relates to the act of changing gears, but they do know there is a relationship. They have moved to the next stage...

Conscious Incompetence. This stage is characterized by the learner understanding where their knowledge and skills gaps are. They now know what they don't know or don't know how to do and are, therefore, capable of asking questions. They have a framework into which they can fit the answers they receive and what they discover from their observations.

Conscious Competence. This stage is where we would hope to get someone by the end of a training workshop. At this stage, the learner knows what they should do and has the basic awareness of how to do it. However, each time they attempt to complete the task using the steps they have learned they need to think very carefully. This is analogous to when you first sat behind the wheel of a car – and unfortunately this stage of conscious competence lasted until well after you passed your driving test. While you were technically competent, road craft and driving skills were less than habitual and would only come from experience using trial and – one hopes – not too catastrophic error.

Unconscious Competence. The habit stage or mastery of a skill. This is when things are so straightforward we undertake quite complex tasks without even thinking about it. We are able to complete actions we once found quite tricky or which left us both mentally and physically drained with relative ease. It's why we can drive a car to a familiar destination without being able to remember anything of the journey. Interestingly, achieving unconscious mastery is also why some highly skilled practitioners do not make good trainers. Along with Unconscious Competence can come a lack of analytical ability – ie being able to say why something works. This translates into an inability to explain what it is you do and how you do it, to someone else. If you've ever taught a teenager to drive a long time after you yourself obtained a driving licence, you may be familiar with the experience of having to rethink automatically performed tasks into useful steps and stages.

Most skills development benefits from being broken into steps and stages. For the purpose of our workshop we can easily differentiate knowledge from skills by accepting that a skill is something which gets better with practice. Or at least should do. The issue here is that the practice is good quality with feedback to support each individual in identifying areas for improvement and a way of closing gaps between actual performance and the required level. In order to develop individual capability to the conscious competence stage requires individuals to act as well as to listen and observe.

The use of competence as a marker of achievement is another of those areas of linguistic fashion in training and development circles. For many, competence or competency is different from, and currently inferior to, capability. In some respects the difference between the two terms is moot. In some references to human capital there is the recognition that capability speaks to the idea of potential or an aptitude which may be developed. In that way, capability is a description of conscious competence – not yet mastery but a collection of knowledge and skills which will lead to mastery at some future point. There is also an idea here of latent adaptability or the capacity to be more flexible in the face of changing circumstances. To some extent, competence has been saddled with baggage which suggests formulaic or unbending ability to perform a certain task within a defined set of conditions. It does not have that cachet of flexibility associated with it. Bluntly, competence and competencies are not sexy any more.

I think this is a misunderstanding of the ideas which underpin competence and another example – if any further were needed – of the need of those expressing new ideas to reject the language of the preceding period. This ever moving lexicon means that the L&D professional is always standing on shifting sands. For my purposes a working definition of competence is 'the confidence to undertake a task repeatedly to a given standard'. I make no judgement in this definition about what constitutes a given standard. I know that in most organizations quality, quantity, cost or time are the only measures anyone is really interested in.

What I do expect though, is that confidence to perform – a self-belief that the skills one possesses are fit for purpose in the circumstances one now faces. The requirement for new terminology – which, in common with many training evolutions in recent times will be used interchangeably with its old and no longer zeitgeist-y predecessor

– seems to me to be unproven. To say that capability is somehow better than competence is to misunderstand what competence really means.

Efficiency and effectiveness

If we are to develop the confidence to undertake a task within a workshop, it seems self-evident that the individuals within our workshop will need to do a bit of undertaking of those tasks in order to know whether they are good, average or poor at their execution. To improve, they will need feedback on not just what they have done but how they have done it to enable efficiency and effectiveness to be achieved.

Once again, efficiency and effectiveness are different things. Simply, effectiveness is doing the right things and efficiency is doing things right. I was training in a venue I had never been to before and found that I was short of a vital ingredient for one of the training activities I was running. I approached the reception desk and asked for some paperclips. 'How many do you need?' was the reply. I was expecting a box to be handed over with however many were inside, but as the question had been asked, I requested about a hundred. I was then given two A5 envelopes containing exactly 50 paperclips each. Someone had obviously been tasked with counting them out into batches of 50 to avoid profligacy. I would argue that while it is possible to be efficient in undertaking that task, it is never possible to be effective.

In order to develop effectiveness, the learner needs to know when and in what circumstances this would be the right thing to do. In other words, knowledge cannot be dissociated from the development of skills, but as we have already outlined in Chapter 2, this information need not only be given during the workshop. Some of it could be provided in advance and this may be the most significant factor in ensuring that a workshop represents good value.

To develop efficiency, the learner needs to develop the skills through practice, feedback and re-application of the skills. The more this can be done in a safe environment – that is, where there are no penalties for failure – then learners can be encouraged to stretch themselves, take risks and develop their capabilities sequentially. This is known in formal education as scaffolding and is a learning process common to all of us from childhood. We learn skills through incrementally increasing the degree of difficulty and combining one routine with the next. By breaking tasks down into a series of component routines, the feedback becomes more specific and actionable. Putting these different routines together into a final activity ensures that all-important growth in confidence.

In short, our workshop needs to build these incremental skills, creating a scaffold which rises through different levels and which is based on a firm foundation of why, what and how well each task needs to be undertaken. Furthermore, like building something from the ground up, when the scaffold is removed, the remaining edifice needs to be self-supporting and capable of performing its function. In the case of a building, this means it stays up! In the case of skills and the application of knowledge, this means that things are not only done, but done well. Without knowing what 'good' looks like, the attainment of the confidence inherent in any achievement of competence is shaky in the extreme. Without a good proportion of our workshop being devoted to the skills we need people to be able to practise on the job, the ideal of performance improvement through training will be unrealized.

The role of the trainer – or facilitator as they are often called these days, though the difference is not always obvious – is to do the following five things:

Planning and preparation. This seems obvious, but unless each session is really well planned in order to meet the required objectives and resources are available to ensure that each activity runs well, the fall-back position is usually to throw a few text-heavy PowerPoint slides together and talk at people. The time spent on identifying the needs of the group to be brought together and devising a lively, stimulating and action-packed day to achieve those goals is always time well spent. It is certainly the least expensive component of the whole training event.

Eliciting. This part of the role involves ensuring participants contribute their ideas and thoughts, describe their beliefs and express their values during the session. It is also an opportunity afforded to the trainer to check participant understanding. Having the confidence to ask questions and admit not knowing is a significant step within the learning process. How else are we to help new understanding and help our learners move from a position of unconscious incompetence to a position of conscious competence? As the saying has it (variously attributed but most often accorded to Carl Rogers): 'I can teach a person nothing, I can only create an environment in which they can learn.'

Focusing and summarizing. The good trainer regularly ensures everyone understands not just what to do, but why they are doing it. Now, this may be more necessary than ever. If you have recently watched a documentary on television, you may have noticed the regular updates, usually delivered in a shouty voice-over for the hard of thinking. The simple fact is that broadcasters and programme makers have worked out that we rarely give our undivided attention to the TV any more. We are likely to be rapid task-switching between domestic jobs, making a cup of tea or using the plethora of communications devices available – from social media to text messaging and occasionally, unfashionably making telephone calls. Just like a TV documentary, summing up where you've got to and signposting where you're heading is an essential component of any training programme.

Providing feedback. The most important skill for a trainer. If the participant who is doing something is not given appropriate feedback they will not improve. By appropriate, I mean specific and with enough detail to result in a change of practice and matched to the situation so they are not destroyed and unwilling to take the next risk. Remember our competence definition – to have the confidence to undertake a task repeatedly to a required standard. Confidence is built on praise as much as anything.

I have already alluded to the fact that we are efficient learning machines from birth. Think about a toddler taking their first steps. Very small children always seem to have heads that are slightly too large for their bodies – evidence should it be needed of the massive computer they are carrying around in there. As a result of this bodily imbalance, when a small child pulls themselves up on whatever furniture is available and then lets go, the weight of the head propels them forwards. If their legs are strong enough to do so, they automatically take a step forward to prevent themselves falling, and then another and another and another, until gravity wins and they land on the carpet, hopefully without significant injury. They have taken their first steps. As a parent or carer, what do you do? Usually, you'll pick them up, shower them with affection and rush for the phone and camera to let everyone know that your beloved baby can walk. What you don't do is shout 'why can't you walk yet?' and drop-kick them out of the sitting room window! Unfortunately in some sessions I've observed this is what feedback is like. Instead of the praise required as part of our child-like learning skills, the 'constructive criticism' reduces our participants to gibbering wrecks who have certainly learned one thing – they're not going to try that again.

Delivering input. It is necessary to do some presenting and, where required, delivering input is much more effective as a (short) discussion and a debate, illustrated by stories. In fact, stories are another way of tapping into a primeval learning skill. In our pre-literate past, where communication was exclusively verbal, it was the stories that carried the values, beliefs and behaviours which ensured survival and group cohesion. They still are. Though not many of us need to be worried about becoming prey, we do value security and belonging. The stories told in organizations are one of the ways that group identity is reinforced and can be a powerful learning medium. If you need to provide input, ask yourself:

1 How can I present this/demonstrate a model/concept/theory as simply and quickly as possible enabling the whole group to get on with the practical application part.

2 Can this presentation slide be an activity? If I have a slide, for example, describing the customer requirements, can the

participants tell me what they understand these needs to be first? This is a route to building energy in the room.

3 Can I rephrase what I am *telling* the group so that I am *asking* the group?

4 Can I illustrate and illuminate the theory with a story from my own experience?

Presenting

Of course, somewhere in the story-telling/presenting mix is the motivational speaker. I'm not referring here to the self-important expressing the self-evident. The cliché-mongers and pedlars of homilies for the hopeful are not the models I would want anyone to emulate. But there are speakers of real quality who can simply draw a word picture for you which builds both interest and desire. By the end of their input you are ready to climb mountains if not move them.

I was lucky enough to meet just such a speaker when I was only 18 years old and a first-year student who had chosen philosophy – mostly because it fitted the timetable with my other subjects. Gathered with others in a self-conscious gaggle in a small lecture theatre, I was somewhat sceptical of the man who shambled in. He was an archetypical academic of the time – leather elbow patches on a baggy corduroy jacket which had more than a hint of yesterday's lunch about it. His grey hair was long and straggly and very thin on top. He had what charitably could be described as a lived-in face. Had he been sitting on a street corner with a dog tied to a piece of string, he wouldn't have looked too far out of place. In one hand he carried a battered leather briefcase, which looked to be about the same age as him. He placed it on the table in front of him and cleared his throat. The assembled students slowly redirected their attention to the man who stood in front of them.

'My name is Stuart Linney. I am a professor of philosophy and, as you can probably tell from my accent, I am a South African. As a result of my nationality, in my briefcase I carry an elephant.'

The fact that I can remember word for word what he said after more than thirty years is certainly testimony to the effect that those words had on me. But apart from being incredibly memorable, it was also the start of an insatiable desire to want to learn more about this slightly arcane world where elephant-ness was a viable topic for discussion.

Effective speakers are often slightly other. What marks them out is their ability to conjure up a world with words. What few rely on is a facility with the transition and animation functions of PowerPoint. There has been a recent phenomenon of these inspiring and informative speakers, speakers who ask you to think differently, speakers who cause the unexpected guffaw, who shock you, or simply engender a head-scratching wonder at why you haven't thought of that before. The source of this phenomenon is TED Talks.

My personal favourite is Sir Ken Robinson talking about creativity and education.[3] His compelling 20-minute lecture is a personal and yet profound tale, told with real passion and self-deprecation. He is disarmingly gentle and yet delivers his final message with a rapier thrust. The video of his talk is the most popular on TED.com having been seen more than 11.5 million times.

There are three things about this presentation which are instructive for the trainer who needs to give input during a session:

1 **Simplicity.** He delivers a relatively simple message which is the natural conclusion from the (often extremely funny) stories he tells. The end point leads seamlessly from that which precedes it.

2 **The duration of the piece.** Albeit that he is delivering one message he takes the right amount of time to deliver it with maximum impact. The speech lasts 20 minutes – of which three or four are taken up with waiting for the laughs to die down. I could have delivered the same message with one short story and one PowerPoint slide in about two and a half minutes. But it wouldn't have had anything like the same impact. In fact, it might not have had any impact at all. I think that 20 minutes is about the optimum time to listen to anything, especially in a one-way presentation as demanded by the TED Talks set up. You can't really do audience interaction with over 1,000 people in a darkened theatre.

3 **It was just him.** No PowerPoint. No fancy visual aids. As a result of Robinson's childhood polio, not even much walking around. Just a person, who exudes belief and total commitment to a message, delivering something which he has

rehearsed and rehearsed and rehearsed. Most of the really good speakers in the TED Talks series are similarly un-reliant on visual aids. When they are used, they tend to get in the way slightly.

In talking about Robinson, I referred often to his humour. In fact he reminds the viewer of a stand-up comedian. If you've ever seen a stand-up comedian perform the same show, you will have been surprised at how different one night is from another. From the banter with the audience to the funny thing that happened on the way to the theatre, an element of each night's performance is improvised. Yet these streams of humorous consciousness are interspersed with other parts which are exactly the same every time they are delivered. These rehearsed short stories are routines. Every movement, gesture and phrase is honed to ensure the best result – a theatre full of people laughing uproariously. Good trainers do the same. Their stories are honed over years of practice. They may differ slightly to match the context – communication skills, or leadership behaviours or customer service standards – but the story is essentially the same and is always used to reinforce a particular point or to deliver that most wondrous thing in a training room – the A-ha! moment.

Engagement and the A-ha! moment

The A-ha! moment comes via many different activities and experiences. Whatever route is required to get to those moments of enlightenment, when things just fall into place, one of the key requirements is that learners are engaged and stimulated. So, how does a trainer ensure that their training sessions are engaging, stimulating, thought provoking, relevant, delivering value and above all keeping training participants engaged?

The answer to this question lies more in the variety than in any one technique. Frankly, any single style or mode of delivery for a whole day will eventually seem boring, no matter how good the activities or exercises being deployed. You can think of a workshop as a continuum. At one end of the spectrum you have the discussion. A facilitator or workshop leader throwing out questions, checking understanding and exploring the implications of the information introduced in the pre-workshop activities. These discussions may be Q&A sessions where the learners are cast in the role of questioners. Rather than answering immediately, the effective trainer activates the knowledge of the group by referring the question to the others present before reinforcing their answers or extending/correcting the perceptions of the participants.

Notice the word participant. By referring to learners as delegates I think you create a mind-set which is that they are there to be informed on behalf of their teams. As participants they need something to participate in. By using this terminology, the session is instantly based on a two-way process. This should be reinforced by the room layout. In serried ranks, they are an audience, waiting to be told things. In an open U formation, circle or a boardroom-style layout, they are participating only in whole group discussions – one person can speak at once and with a group of, say, 16 people the expectation is that each individual will be actively contributing for only one-sixteenth of the time (or a little over 20 minutes of the day assuming that there are no one-way presentations at all!).

I have found the most effective layout to be the cabaret style shown in Figure 3.2:

FIGURE 3.2   Cabaret-style room layout

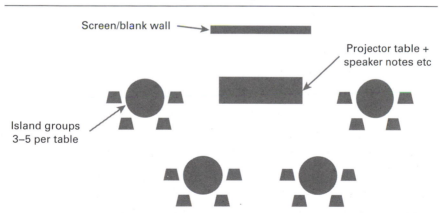

By putting participants into groups immediately, you have created a particular dynamic and established the expectation that individuals will be working with their peers throughout the workshop. What is more, from a purely logistical perspective, you've reduced the amount of seat moving where a brief discussion-style activity wouldn't normally justify physical relocation to syndicate rooms. Of course, if you have break-out rooms where groups can be isolated one from the other (useful when you may be using competition or team games as a participant engagement tool) these can be used alongside the cabaret layout. It's not an either/or solution, however. Whenever you create an exercise in which groups reassemble in a syndicate room, factor in the necessary time for someone to visit the loo, someone else to get a coffee, someone to make that urgent phone call to the office that just won't wait, a bit of time checking the blackberry for e-mails and, of course, the cigarette break. If you assume that any syndicate activity requiring relocation to a different room has a 10–15 minute hiatus while everyone gets it together to actually get on with anything, you probably won't go far wrong.

Beyond the discussion you have activities and exercises. These may be groups working together to figure out responses to questions and present back their findings, maybe undertaking research within the session and debating the issues between them in small syndicates and again in plenary sessions. Unquestionably, they will be tasks in which individuals and groups apply the skills required to achieve goals. These skills may be so called hard skills – completing a routine in a software program, creating copy for an advertisement, making something and using tools. They may also be softer skills, usually applied to those skills which require interaction between people, involving communication and emotional intelligence – working in teams, leading a group, negotiating, handling conflict, presenting a product, crafting questions to ask a buyer and so on.

The other end of the spectrum is the simulation activity. These may be case studies or replications of processes and activities which mirror those back in the workplace. The benefit is the opportunity to work collectively – apply more brains and hands to a situation – as well as the chance to take risks in a safe space or to fail in a supportive environment. Some of the simulations I have had the pleasure of working on have involved groups in designing new products, developing customer communications and planning new organizational structures. The key here is realism and giving people enough time in the session to really work through the issues. In a price war simulation for marketers developed by some colleagues of mine, the simulation took 25 people in competing groups two and a half days to work through and to see the results of their pricing and brand development decisions.

One form of much derided simulation is the role play. Of course, playing out a customer service scenario with Fiona from accounts will always be a little stilted, success determined by the amateur dramatic skills, or lack thereof, of those taking part. If realism is important, then take the opportunity to work with professional role players. With a good character brief and genuine understanding of the required behaviours, actors can transform the dreaded role play into a truly life-changing experience.

CASE STUDY

When I trained health professionals about how to explain mistakes to patients and patients' relatives, the use of exceptional actors who were sensitive to the needs of the learners in potentially very traumatic experiences but were strong enough to really put people on the spot in these interactions was incredible. This level of attention to the detail in the interaction was wholly justified when the scope and potential impact of some of these Patient Safety Incidents were taken on board. The clinicians were being trained to deal with everything from an administrative error which delayed treatment, through to incidents in which people were permanently disabled or subject to painful and long-term treatment. In the most serious and often harrowing cases, clinicians were required to explain to relatives the errors and system failings which resulted in the premature death of a loved one.

Of course, when dealing with how we behave – how we speak, interact, deal with difficult situations – the facilitator needs to ensure time to debrief properly. This is potentially pretty personal stuff and needs handling with extreme sensitivity. What is needed is time and opportunity to debrief individually where necessary. It needs a clear set of ground rules, agreed in advance. What it doesn't need is squeezing into the last half hour of the day.

As anyone who has been involved in a course knows, there is a crucial difference between a good simulation or role play and an excruciating experience filled with embarrassment. The extent to which your participants will suspend their disbelief that the experience isn't real and therefore they don't need to fully engage, depends on two factors. Factor one is the realism of the set-up. The scenario which is being created or the environment in which the task is being undertaken should replicate as far as possible the workplace in which the real implementation will follow. Too often the set-up is not as things are really experienced by those at the sharp end. The 'sunny day' experiences in which everything goes right from the off fail to engage because they are insufficiently challenging and those facing the realities of the day-to-day challenges are constantly reminded how 'life isn't really like this'.

CASE STUDY

I was observing a training session with a group of field sales people from a fast-moving consumer goods (FMCG) company. The sales teams visited small independent retailers, convenience stores and corner shops. The scenario for a role play included a long conversation – approximately 15 minutes – in which the retailer answered all the questions asked in detail and the sales person was easily able to spot opportunities for increasing the range of his or her brands on the shelves of the store. I had been out with a sales person in an inner city area visiting retail outlets just like the one apparently portrayed in the scenario. The problem with the set-up was two-fold. The first was about time. Each sales representative was tasked with achieving the goals on each call in only eight minutes – around half the time devoted to this simulated conversation. Not only that, but when these sales people visit individual stores, if the owner or decision maker is present at all, they are usually the only member of staff. They will be interrupted every 30 seconds or so by customers. The idea of having an uninterrupted 15-minute conversation simply evoked a rolled eye 'yeah, right' from the participants. The second issue was the compliance of the retailer as imagined in the brief. Small retailers are reluctant to invest in unproven brands which take up limited shelf space – they drive a hard bargain before stocking a new range. As imagined by the person who created the scenario, the retailer would be only too happy to risk his or her own money on buying in new stock so long as the sales person asked the right questions. In truth, this almost never happens without a good deal of horse trading and negotiation.

Factor two in enabling our participants to suspend disbelief is the level and detail of the feedback given on the 'performance'. Sir Dave Brailsford CBE, the Performance Director for the British cycling team which was so successful during the 2012 Olympics, talks about 'marginal gains'. These are the small things which may seem unimportant but when aggregated make a huge difference to the overall performance of an individual. Those who have seen him at work with his team members are amazed at what he sees – a slight change in body weight here, the angle of an elbow there. He is attuned to spotting anything which might gain the 100th of a second which could be the difference between success and failure. Of course, in a training session, some of the errors may be blindingly obvious and relatively easy to point out and rectify, but for feedback to aid performance of everyone, that attention to the minute detail is what's required, giving each individual one or two things to work on, building that confidence.

The ability of the trainer to spot the imperfections may have come from having done the task to an expert level, but this is not necessary. Sir Brailsford was a professional cyclist, but gave it up when he was only 23 to return to studying. Certainly, compared with the athletes he coaches and works with, he was never anywhere near as successful in the saddle. The same can be said of virtually all top sports coaches. Who coaches Tiger Woods – someone who could beat him on the course? Hardly likely. The superstars of the National Basketball Association are trained by short guys who may never have played the game past college and are probably physically incapable of the technical skills they demand of the players. Their skill is in understanding what makes a great performance and being able to analyse the small changes which will move someone from good to better. The marginal improvements are not just for the peak sports performers but for everyone aiming to improve and do things differently.

The other route for engaging learners in group activities is to divorce the action completely from the day-to-day experience. This would seem to be directly contrary to the idea of realism in the training activities, but sometimes the A-ha! moments we are pursuing come from looking at things from a completely different angle and adopting a whole new mind-set.

This is where games, competitions and other activities come into the mix. One way of achieving this is to involve the participants in simulations of enterprise-wide activities. For example, involving production workers in a simulation which includes market research and product design – creating the specification for a new product which precedes the point at which they would normally engage with the work flow. Ordinarily, we would assume that individuals may only be involved in a small part of these processes.

CASE STUDY

When SABMiller PLC, the world's second largest brewing group, create advertisements and promotional campaigns for their world-wide brands, they want to do so in a way which is responsible. Chief amongst these considerations is ensuring that their commercial communications do not appeal to those below the legal drinking age in the country in which the campaign will run and that promotional activities are not seen to promote or condone over-consumption of alcohol. To support the brand and sales teams in ensuring responsible marketing, each country has a compliance committee which oversees proposed advertising and promotional campaigns. In helping marketers to understand the codes which apply across the group, the training programme includes a board game – based loosely on the globally understood game of Risk. Participants are divided into teams of three or four and given a brand and a fictional country to start working in. At each juncture they have to consider a proposed campaign from the viewpoint of the Sales and Marketing Compliance Committee (SMCC). If they properly apply the code in their decisions, they are rewarded with additional market share and are able to move into adjoining territories. Of course, in those adjoining territories the issues may be different and a decision which is OK in one country isn't OK in another where, for example, the legal drinking age may be different.

The participants for whom the training is designed are unlikely ever to be members of the SMCC. The point of the exercise is not to train them to take on these roles, but to ensure the widest possible understanding of the code and how it should be applied. A successful outcome is that those campaigns which might be rejected by the SMCC are not pursued, with a resulting reduction in time and resources devoted to ad campaigns which will never run.

Other games might be completely divorced from the work environment. Examining the skills and behaviours required for effective team working, collective decision making, prioritization and communications can be enhanced through activities completely removed from the day to day. This is the basis for outdoor activities such as orienteering, abseiling and kayaking. Indoor-bound training can fulfil a similar purpose, including using games which cast the participants as survivors of a capsized ship or the crew of a rapidly descending hot air balloon. The trick to ensuring these activities work relies on the feedback and analysis stage of the activity. While it may be wholly appropriate to engage participants in somewhat wackier training games and team exercises, the point of the activity is to develop the A-ha! moment. This is when the group recognizes and realizes some universal truth or individuals analyse their own performance from a different viewpoint and understand when and how to use different approaches and new skills back in the real world.

Without this focused debrief of the activities, the exercises are worse than pointless because the participants may feel that time has been wasted. By being unusual, these activities are all the more memorable. The challenge is to ensure that the right thing is remembered. If the participants return to work and rave about how good the outdoor treasure hunt was without being able to explain why a whole day of work time was devoted to it, the remainder of the team may be wholly entitled to ask questions about the priority given to future attendance.

Planning, planning and planning again

So, we've created a series of experiences which have taken people from one level of understanding to an advanced level of understanding and have helped them to think differently about what they read, watched and listened to in the pre-workshop activity. We have limited presentations to the very minimum required and – given that many people use it really badly – we have not used PowerPoint unless absolutely necessary. Rather than have one-way presentations we have built dialogue into the talking sessions – asking questions and requesting examples and stories from participants to create discussion and maintain engagement. This may mean that some sessions run over and anyone who has ever stood up in front of a group will remember at least one participant who commented in a disappointed tone about the lack of adherence to the published timetable. I try never to give a timetable, but I recognize that in some organizations that would be impossible, if only because the canteen needs to know when you'll be there for tea, coffee and lunch! If a particular session lasts slightly longer than you had thought, you can employ a simple traffic light system with your course outline.

Those parts of the workshop to which you apply a 'red light' are the absolute essentials which cannot just be skipped over or squeezed in to the end of the day. The activities and exchanges that have the most value should not be shelved. Value, of course, is determined by the audience and the objective. What do they need to do in their current job or what skills are required for them to advance to the next role? How important is this section in enabling them to do this?

'Amber' sections are those components of your session which you could reference within the session but may not require much detail. Think about alternative ways of accessing this content outside of the workshop which will help participants discover more information, such as guiding participants to articles or even reference books or websites to refer to during the break or over lunch (this may also divert them away from their workplace messages and keep them focused on the matter in hand). We're not talking about missing these components out entirely, simply having other routes to achieving a similar outcome outside the workshop because the most urgent and important content and learning activities must be done by the end of the session. The focus of these sessions should be to enrich the learning, extending it to areas which go beyond the minimum requirement for the outcomes of the session and enable those who are more advanced to progress beyond their expectations and that of the organization.

Finally, you have 'green light' components which cover those sections of your material which are nice to do but can be sacrificed if time is short. I would always advocate preparing more material than you need – more exercises, games and discussion sessions – because until you have worked with a group you have little knowledge about how well things are going to go. The one thing worse than having too much material and trying to jam experiences in one after the other is to have too little and end up losing momentum and focus as you feel obliged to pad out the session to fill the allotted time. Once you have achieved the objective with the participants you have, end the session! This is not school and most of the time we don't need to wait for the crossing patrol and the school bus to turn up before dismissing the class.

The process of unlearning

> In order to start doing something new you have to stop doing something old.
>
> Peter Drucker

No one enters a training room without at least some knowledge of the subject to be covered during the session. Whether the information they have is reliable is another matter. What's more, when dealing with new techniques and approaches, recent research or developments may have made redundant things which were once considered 'received wisdom'. Before participants can take on new information, it is not uncommon for them to have to 'unlearn' old ways of doing things. This questioning of their previous learning and the attitudes and beliefs they hold is almost always painful and trainers should expect some resistance to having sacred cows of knowledge slaughtered.

Within the active components of a workshop, it is appropriate to achieve some knowledge objectives in support of the competence development which is the main thrust of the event. This is the so-called underpinning knowledge and is of particular importance when you need the group to activate what they know or think they know as part of the session. According to Wikipedia, learning is 'acquiring new or modifying existing knowledge, behaviours, skills, values, or preferences'. The process of unlearning concerns itself with the modification of existing knowledge and skills. It is not uncommon for such a modification to be required as a result of changing circumstances – different customer needs, new competitor products, legislative or regulatory changes or new technology. Regardless of how the game has been changed, those wishing to achieve the same results as before will need to do things differently.

Most people working in a particular discipline will be aware of recent changes even if they haven't quite considered what the implications may be. I was recently working with a group of trainers, helping them to think beyond the presentation. One of the sessions concerned communicating with customers in the 21st century and using novel technologies to engage them. The first two or three slides (and around 20 minutes of presentation) concerned themselves with charting the changes in mobile telephone capability, access to broadband and the growth of tablet computers. Really? The audience were for the most part twenty-somethings, working in the field of digital media. Sure, some of them may have patchy knowledge of some of the more niche communications technologies, but the images of mobile phones through the ages and some detailed statistics on the number of homes with wireless broadband added nothing.

My advice was to engage the group in describing the direction of travel in digital communications – consumer behaviour as well as new bits of kit – and describe the new environment in a sentence or two. As a process of framing the change to which the group needed to individually and collectively respond, it engaged them in a debate and a discussion in a way which simply listing the features of the available handsets could never do – whether this was undertaken using a PowerPoint presentation or a question thrown out to the group which didn't encompass the implications for consumer communications. The objective was to set the context for what was to follow.

This process is a significant element in guided discovery-based learning in a workshop. The basic premise of guided discovery is to set challenges upfront and then try to provide answers to these challenges during the course (see Figure 3.3). Not all the answers will be provided by the trainer. As well as the opportunity to learn from one another, there is also the process of finding things out, through trial and error, through discussion and debate or through the feedback provided as part of exercise and activity debrief. Even though the trainer will be in control of this feedback process, he or she does not need to be the only one commenting on performance and identifying areas for improvement. In fact, the most effective route to providing feedback involves the learner assessing their own performance first of all, followed by other participants who have observed (and learned through that observation) and finally by the trainer summarizing, reinforcing and, where required, adding comment. The key here is not to overload the individual with possible action points – especially if these may be competing. The summarizing job of the trainer is to identify the two or three things which could make all the difference – the marginal gains with highest priority.

FIGURE 3.3   The guided discovery circle

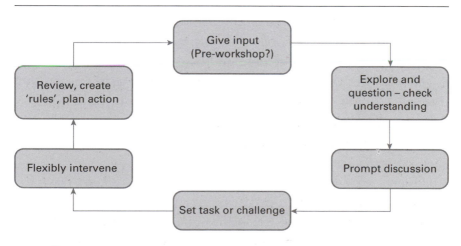

Within a guided discovery approach there are a series of actions which are the responsibility of the trainer. The first is to make sure that the participants have enough understanding of what the desired result should be, and why it is necessary to perform effectively in any activity. This input should, of course, be provided ahead of the workshop if possible. To confirm this underpinning knowledge, the trainer will explore and question the participants and also prompt discussion between participants and between participants and trainer to identify any areas of 'unlearning' which may need to happen for the practical application of the knowledge to be useful.

In setting a challenge or task always state upfront how the exercise will be of benefit to them and how feedback will be delivered. Having set the task or challenge, the trainer may need to flexibly intervene, to keep people on track to help out where participants are completely stuck and to address concerns about any risks which the session may require participants to take. Be aware though, that unnecessary support can be highly demotivating, with groups becoming quickly disengaged if they feel that the trainer is 'taking over'. Finally, the trainer manages the process of reviewing and providing feedback.

One of the important components of this debrief stage is to discuss 'rules' – the universal conclusions to be drawn from each experience. In a team activity where one individual is selected as the leader, what are the rules of team leadership which can be derived from the experience and which the subsequent leaders of activities should also apply? Where individuals are learning about how to use the features of a spreadsheet program, what are the rules which apply to other functions which will be explored and used later? Involving learners in articulating these rules – perhaps making their own top ten lists through negotiation with peers and with the trainer – ensures a deeper understanding and greater retention of the information and processes which they will need in future. In other words, they will have learned something through their experiences.

Having delivered learning and having assured themselves that participants have reached the desired goal of at least a basic level of conscious competence, the trainer has one more role to fulfil. They need to signpost the opportunities for implementation of these new skills and applying this new knowledge in the workplace. As I said earlier, the skills which are the subject of the workshop need to be skills those attending actually need and will be able to practise in the near future. If not, then 'learning fade' sets in. To put it another way, if you don't use your new knowledge and skills within a relatively short space of time, then it may have been better never to have had the tantalizing prospect of change for the better placed in front of you. The process of ensuring effective follow-up in the workplace to support the formal inputs both pre-workshop and during workshop is a trickier challenge for the training professional.

Life cycle tips

The new recruit

Unless you are recruiting a whole number of staff at the same time – for example on a graduate training scheme – the chances are that any workshop which is part of your induction programme will be an ad hoc affair. Generally, the programme is organized three or four times a year and, once recruited, the new joiner simply turns up at the next convenient induction session. That raises a question about whether the programme is of particular value. If I've been working for an organization for several months before someone tells me what the values and mission of the organization are, then it either wasn't that important in the first place or I've found out via other means.

If you are committed to running a face-to-face workshop for those new to the enterprise, think about how it could be a two-way street. Assuming you are drawing staff from across different functions, those from each function can prepare a presentation about their area of responsibility and support those from different functions in gaining an understanding of the wider organization.

Another idea might be to ask small groups of participants to critically assess and make recommendations for improvement to the induction they have had so far. This of course assumes at least a level of conscious incompetence – they will need to have an understanding of the things they don't know or have had to find out the hard way before they can actively contribute to this exercise. In fact, if you are revamping your induction, start here. There's not a lot of value in going to the directors of different functions and asking them what they think a new starter needs to know and be able to do. Ask those who are new starters first – say those who have been there for three months – and then go to the different functions with a shopping list of the knowledge and skills your inductees have said would be useful. Unfortunately, each function believes that the induction should be about them – preferably about them alone. If you go to the finance department with a blank sheet of paper, you'll find that they can design you a three-day programme about understanding management accounts very easily. Is it necessary? Well that rather depends, but probably not.

I think that there are alternatives to the induction workshop which may be more effective. Your CEO or equivalent could host a lunch with new starters every month; each new joiner could spend a day in each of the other departments. There are lots of ways of organizing this beyond a workshop and, with an effective line manager, properly debriefing the individual after each experience and checking that they have asked the questions they needed to ask and recognized how each department fits together, this can be a much more worthwhile learning experience than sitting in a training room for six and a half hours being told things that they already know.

There is one area where workshops may be important – initial training. For staff in (for example) contact centres, there is usually an initial training period of anything up to eight weeks, understanding customer service, handling complaints, dealing with people who are upset or uncommunicative, product knowledge and legislation, where appropriate. It also makes sense to do lots and lots and lots of role play, to get people used to all the different types of calls they'll make and receive. One forward-thinking organization I worked with had voice coaches from the local theatre company coming in to do vocal training exercises because they had found that lots of contact centre workers had to take time off in the first few months after their voices packed in.

The point with any of these initial training workshops – whether frontline customer service training or working with specialist equipment or achieving initial compliance before being able to be deployed – is to ensure that practice sessions replicate the real world as closely as possible and that feedback is staged, actionable and focused on one or two changes at a time.

The new manager

The skills required for first line management are – like any other skills – capable of being improved with practice and appropriate feedback. Having ensured that those seeking promotion to supervisory positions have undertaken the pre-requisite pre-workshop activities – which suggests you need a Learning Management System or similar which can track completion – your workshop should be completely focused on the skills needed to manage the team.

As well as role play for handling those tricky interactions around under-performance, conflicts in the team and performance appraisal, etc, initial scenario-based activities build learner confidence about appropriate approaches to take, enable participants to learn from each other and scaffold the learning effectively.

Try to create a continuum between the pre-workshop activities and the workshop exercises. For example, if your aspiring supervisors have used an e-learning programme in advance of the workshop, they will benefit from some online scenario activities. Let's say that you have created a scenario in which one of their team is regularly absent on Fridays and given them some options for how they might address that issue. During the workshop you can extend the same activity – during the discussion, they discover that the local bar has an extended happy hour every Thursday evening and the reason the team member is absent is because he is hung over every Friday morning. A discussion between participants to determine the options available will support learning from each other and taking on board alternative ways of thinking about the right solution to the issue.

Finally, follow this discussion activity with a role play exercise where the team member with a mid-week drink problem is actually in front of the participant and they have to practise the skills of broaching the subject and having the conversation which determines an appropriate way forward.

This approach scaffolds the learning though three stages. Stage 1 – the e-learning – will enable the learner to choose between alternatives and select the optimum choice to address the unwanted behaviour. Stage 2 will bring in a range of alternatives because there is rarely a single way of addressing such challenges, and Stage 3 will build the skills necessary to actually deal with such performance and attendance issues. The programme will have moved the learner from a programmed learning response dealing with the required knowledge (choosing one of a series of options and receiving feedback on their decision); deepened and extended that knowledge through discussion; and built skills through role play.

The specialist and leader

There's one sure way of involving these two groups in the Complete Training model. It involves them in training others. But **under no circumstances ask them to do a presentation!**

Everyone who has ever created a PowerPoint presentation thinks they are a presenter. Everyone described as a leader, or a specialist or an old hand thinks they can present. Even if they are the best presenter that ever trod shoe leather, try asking them to work with a group of learners without relying on 30 PowerPoint slides and a laser pointer.

Instead, provide the content which would have been provided through the presentation slides to the learners in advance. The day before is fine. Give the participants a 20-minute time-slot to work together in groups to formulate at least one question per table and stage the event as a Q&A session.

Don't make it a one-way Q&A either. It's really good to get senior people to answer questions but it also helps if they ask questions too. Think about it from the perspective of the learner. Not wanting to increase the pressure unnecessarily, but it does certainly sharpen the attention to the information in the pre-workshop handout if the participant knows that they need to look intelligent in front of a senior person in the business the next morning and if they are likely to be put on the spot to answer questions about the implications of the contents during the same session. I don't think this should be a general knowledge quiz. If you have a specialist in brand development attending the session, I don't think it is appropriate for the branding specialist to throw out questions about how many units brand A sells per year or how profitable brand B is. These are examples of the kinds of fact that are accorded importance because they are easy to measure. But, for example, a brand specialist asking participants to discuss and identify the issues for brand development if consumers have the opportunity to post comments about the brand's products and performance on a website (such as Amazon) – well, that's a much more useful discussion during which both the specialist and the participants may achieve a greater understanding.

That really is the holy grail of senior staff and specialist involvement in providing input to training programmes. They should learn too. The old Russian proverb has it: 'To teach is to learn twice.' How you manage their input to ensure that this is achieved will greatly increase the willingness of these individuals to engage in the debate and come along to future programmes. Nothing is worse than the big boss turning up to the first workshop and then sending along an underling to workshops thereafter. Especially if they start their Q&A session with: 'I only found out I was doing this yesterday, so I'm not quite up to speed, but I have prepared a few PowerPoint slides which I can just quickly take you through...'.

As well as supporting the learning of others, the specialists and leaders should also learn alongside their more junior or less experienced colleagues. If this is happening, it's important to agree ground rules in advance. If you are running a session for all staff – including senior people – I think it is sensible and entirely justified to arrange a conversation in advance with those senior people. If you can't do this one to one then when the strategic decision is taken that all staff – including senior people – are to be involved in the programme, agree the ground rules then. I would always give the leaders a role in the early part of the session and I would want them to explain to the other participants that they are there to learn too. It's important that they abide by all the same rules you choose to apply. If mobile phones are banned – they all are. If the session runs all day – they are in the session all day. If that's inconvenient then think again about their involvement in a mass programme.

That's not to say that they don't get the training or access the required learning opportunities, but the added benefit of networking with peers may mean that designing a programme especially for the specialists and leaders makes sense. It may provide them with opportunities to develop the required skills appropriate to their responsibilities while creating space for discussion and interaction which is not about the day to day and – at the same time – removes the potentially disruptive influence of them apologetically nipping out of the room for half an hour to take that urgent call.

Neither involving them alongside everyone else nor creating special programmes for particular groups of staff is right or wrong. Both can and do work. But these two approaches are mutually exclusive. Do one or the other.

The retiree

It is a fact that those approaching retirement are rarely offered the chance to attend workshops. This is a shame and somewhat short-sighted. A recent survey by Cranfield School of Management and Nottingham Business School[4] found that over a third of a million workers in the UK alone were now over 65 years of age. For learners in the 45–50 age bracket – those seldom invited to participate in training – it is not unreasonable to expect that they may have a working life of up to 25 years ahead of them. Unlike their more junior counterparts, they're also less likely to move on in two or three years. As I have already said, it can be challenging but also stimulating to have more experienced members of staff within the training environment – especially when they are more experienced than the trainer leading the session.

One route to enabling a positive contribution from this group is to position them tactically around the room. Using the cabaret-style layout provides a really interesting opportunity. I suggest placing one of the older more experienced team members in each table group and asking them to play a specific role, sharing their experience with more junior members of staff during exercises and activities. Even when dealing with something brand new to everyone in the group – say a legislative change or technological innovation – it is common for an older member of staff to have useful background insights which provide context for the changes. The key to organizing any training for the whole organization is to focus on skills, aspirations and potential – regardless of age.

If you are providing training specifically for a more experienced group – or perhaps organizing a workshop specifically for pre-retirement training – similar skill-building approaches to those used with others are useful activities in the training room. Helping these long-serving employees develop the skills to share their knowledge and hand over their responsibilities ensures that the organization retains its collective memory and builds confidence amongst this group that they continue to have a vital role to play in the enterprise. Developing these skills and creating an action plan for the implementation can also provide the context for amending working patterns in the run-up to final retirement.

Complete Training tools: follow-up activities and on-the-job/ informal learning

04

> *The best learning happens in real life with real problems and real people and not in classrooms.*
>
> **PROFESSOR CHARLES HANDY CBE,**
> **FORMERLY OF LONDON BUSINESS SCHOOL B. 1932**

Everyone who has attended a course knows deep down that the learning doesn't end at the classroom door. The challenge for many in the training world is that this is precisely how training is implemented. Courses are created, slotted into the required heading on the training menu and individuals book on, or are booked on by their line managers, with varying degrees of discussion around needs, aspirations and alternative development options. Thereafter, the individual is left to their own devices. They may be expected to do something different, but just to confirm that we don't have much of an expectation of them actually changing things, we get them to fill in the evaluation form before they leave class.

In Chapter 8 I'll talk more about measuring the effectiveness of training in the workplace. It is sufficient to say at this stage that you can't measure very much other than whether the participants liked you, the lunch and the people they sat with if you rely on an end-of-workshop happy sheet for your training evaluation. What happens after the formal input is much more important than anything which has happened so far. Remember, training is about ensuring people can do things differently and do different things. The next steps in the workplace matter to us as trainers and matter to the people who pay the bills for the training we design and deliver.

As part of the training continuum, we need relevant activity to take place in the workplace. This is the bit which is most difficult and most often not done to any terrific standard. The follow-up can take many forms. The work-based task is one. It is important to get participants who have worked on their skills and required behaviours during the workshop to make that transition to applying what they have learned in the workplace. This can't be underestimated. Without a chance to use the skills and behaviours required and the new knowledge uncovered and explored quickly, the learning fade will be dramatic and the chance of really delivering on the benefits identified will be slim.

The challenge is to manage the expectations. Most training workshops last between half a day and three days. While it is not entirely out of the question, in straitened financial times, it is rare for an organization to enable its staff to immerse themselves in training workshops which last longer than this. In some respects, why would they? Without the opportunity to roll up our sleeves and get on with the job, the training activities at the start of a protracted period of training are subject to learning fade as surely as if there were no opportunities to implement our new skills immediately on our return to work. In a short workshop-based programme there are scant opportunities to develop skills beyond the conscious competence stage I outlined in Chapter 3. To embed the skills and to reinforce their application requires their use in anger. What's more, the feedback model we have introduced in the workshop needs to be continued. Without someone who knows what they are looking for, observing implementation and being able to identify the opportunities for improvement, skill application becomes frozen at the initial experimentation stage. We need someone on the ground to follow up the course and support the embedding of these skills. The obvious person to manage the follow-up is the line manager.

Back to work: the line manager's role

The line manager's role starts in advance of any of their team being signed up to complete a training programme. Having outlined the knowledge and skills required and the gaps between the individual's current performance and the desired state, the line manager will explore options for closing those performance gaps. If less formal (and less expensive options) are either unavailable or inappropriate, then – and only then – will the line manager sign off the expenditure for the chosen programme.

On the eve of starting the pre-workshop activities – and at defined points as they complete the material if necessary – the line manager will sit with his or her team member and outline their expectations, remind them of the purpose for the investment and outline the follow-up activities which will take place. On return from any workshop component, this action plan will be checked for relevance in the light of the experience and the gradual application of the newly acquired skills in the context of the real world will commence. An agreement will be made between learner and line manager about monitoring progress and providing feedback. The effective trainer will support the line manager, providing tips and hints for follow-up and being clear about the standards of performance which the training programme should have produced.

A work-based task in the context of the training continuum is one in which the learning gained from doing the task is more important than the outcome of the task itself. I'm not sufficiently naïve to imagine that the workplace provides the same safe space as the workshop environment, where risks can be taken with impunity. However, this is where managing expectations comes in. After attendance at a regulation short course, it is unrealistic for either participants or their managers to believe that they will be fully competent and able to apply their new skills at optimum effectiveness.

The problem with work-based tasks is the support required. If you want or need local line managers or people within the business designated as coaches to provide this support, you may need to think about training them to undertake the process outlined above. If the manager hasn't been trained what to do, they won't feel inclined to try a new approach and they certainly won't prioritize it amongst the slew of other demands on their time.

Many will look positively pained that they will be expected to coach their team members or junior colleagues. Some will consider it an imposition – the training team pushing what should be their job onto the already over-worked senior staff. Others will simply glance skywards and ask 'when are we supposed to find the time to do this?'

It is a fact that in leaner organizations, the role of the manager as a leader of his or her people, ensuring task achievement, team and individual development has been somewhat skewed. The operational, hands-on role of many of today's team leaders and managers means that they have precious little time to spend with their people. Their overwhelming focus is to act as a senior member of the team, doing all the same things that their team does but a bit better, a bit quicker and a bit more expensively. The idea that people management is an activity which requires time devoted to it, skills to do it and a set of values and guidelines within which to undertake the tasks required, seems to be a luxury few can afford in slimmed down organizations.

Now I am a big fan of coaching but again it seems to be something which is frequently not done well. The answer is people outside the line management hierarchy who have coaching as a defined role. Even where this is not the only job they do, it might still be considered to be extremely resource intensive. However, it might also be one of the only ways of ensuring quality conversations on development issues take place.

Coaching and mentoring

Whenever I write or speak about line managers being crucially important to effective L&D I fall into the trap of describing the role I want them to take as being a coach. A few recent experiences have caused me to question this terminology. To understand my disquiet, I need to let you know what I mean by a coach. I'm not talking about someone who demonstrates what they want you to do and then supervises your first few efforts. Nothing wrong with 'sitting by Nellie' as it used to be called, but when about half the top selling training books on Amazon have the word coaching in the title, I'm guessing that all those pages are devoted to something other than simple functional coaching.

I'm also not talking about the kind of coaching that gets done by the perma-tanned external consultant in a black turtle neck. Whether they call themselves executive coaches, life coaches or personal facilitators their therapy-lite role as cheerleader and spiritual guide is not quite what I'm on about either.

The type of coaching I'm talking about is the sort that uses one of the many coaching models designed to get an individual to look at their performance and aspirations and recognize what needs to happen to the former to enable the latter to be achieved. As a 2011 survey by the Henley Business School found, this kind of internally resourced coaching is set to rise across many organizations.[1]

A couple of organizations I have worked with over many years have a so-called coaching culture. The default coach for each individual is their line manager. To have someone else involved, a team member would need to be brave enough to effectively sack their team leader as coach. Brave bordering on foolhardy!

In a classic team structure, the manager or team leader is the client of the team members. In a coaching relationship, the team member is the client of the coach. This double hatting seems to me to be inordinately tricky and likely to lead to confusion at best and avoidance at worst. If these relationship challenges are found to be too great (or thought to be too great) the conversations on which the programme relies simply won't happen.

So line managers may not make the best coaches but do they still have a role in supporting L&D? Yes they do and we should be expecting them to discuss development options with individuals. We should hold them to account for their team members taking up training programmes and using resources to develop their performance. We should expect them to follow up after training programmes – creating opportunities for the application of what has been learned.

Maybe the quality conversations which make up the effective coaching relationship should be delegated elsewhere to support an objective focus solely on the individual's aspirations.

Two examples of good practice spring to mind. In the contact centre industry, it is not uncommon for teams to have an experienced and seasoned member in the role of coach. They have scheduled time away from the telephones specifically to support individuals in improving their performance but they are not the team leader. Appraisals and staff management are not part of their brief. This seems a good approach where staff need day-to-day help to do their job.

The second example comes from education. In some universities and colleges, those staff who are currently in front-line teaching roles, but have been identified as potential faculty heads and managers in the future, have access to senior personnel on a monthly basis to discuss non-functional development. Many other organizations use a similar approach, occasionally described as mentoring rather than coaching. But the models used – discussing where the individual wants to get to, where they are now, discussing options for how they can bridge the gap and setting goals for both formal and informal development – are applied alongside an exposure to management thinking from a different department. This objective exposure to the wider enterprise seems to embody a number of advantages which may be lost if the only coaching option rests with the line manager. Similarly, the senior member of staff learns valuable lessons about life at the sharp end.

Back to work: doing something different

I am pragmatic and recognize that not every training programme or every individual could access a coach who was not their line manager as part of the training process. Line managers may have to step up to the plate and support their team members as they make the first tentative steps in using the skills they have been sent on a programme to learn. For this they will need training based on a defined competence and a standard which the organization would expect them to meet.

The best post-workshop activities are:

1 Real – participants resolving real issues and taking real opportunities as part of their daily work.

2 Agreed in advance – part of the pre-workshop activity should be the identification of the project or task for which attendance at the course will more effectively equip the participant.

3 Owned by the individual – rather than simply something in which a whole group of people are involved and our participant will have a minor role in its success or failure.

4 Beginning in a short timescale and capable of generating some results relatively quickly.

Of course, many course participants don't know what they don't know before they start the course and so completing a planning session with their line manager for a project or task to be undertaken with their new skills may be a little speculative to say the least. That's where some of your pre-workshop reading needs to come in, to more effectively set the scene and develop **at least an awareness of the knowledge to be gained, the skills to be learned** and **the capabilities to be enhanced.** To support the individual participant, think about putting together a short (one to two paragraph) brief for the line manager about how the learning could be significantly enhanced if the participant had a specific task to complete shortly after attending the workshop. You will need to give some guidance here. It is best not to assume that the line manager even knows the title of the course he or she has signed off on, never mind the detailed outcomes it is designed to achieve. Within your short briefing for the manager, you may want to include some suggested activities.

You may also want to use these work-based tasks as an ongoing part of the programme, so set up a mechanism to share what people have done. This has two benefits:

1 Others learn from the examples shared by their colleagues – colleagues whom they know and have shared experiences with during the workshop.

2 The process of reflection which learners need to engage in to produce something which can be shared. Analysing what they did, with what effect and how they would do it differently next time is a very significant learning activity.

Of course, as the project or assignment happens, the learners may need more input to make sense of their experiences. This is when a series of remote learning opportunities come to the fore. This may be follow-up e-learning – multi-media programmes targeted at learners who now have a bedrock of practice to base their new learning on – a time when fully functioning e-learning is potentially most beneficial.

Alongside the pre-prepared multi-media modules, you also have the option of using live online sessions, so-called synchronous learning. Webinars and other online group activities are now increasingly common and the software to enable it to happen becomes more and more effective. But still, these have traditionally been disappointing. Why? Because we have substituted poor presentation skills in the classroom for even worse presentation skills in cyberspace. The key to using web conferencing is to focus on the conference bit. This is a collaborative process at its best. I was recently a participant in a 75-minute webinar where the facilitator used just four information slides and presented to those involved for about six minutes of the hour and a quarter. The rest of the time, my colleague and I (who were 160 miles apart) shared ideas in a virtual break-out room and presented back to the whole group our thinking after each 10-minute activity. The discussion was facilitated by being able to vote, raise a hand, send an instant message and post questions – verbally or via the chair facility.

Because I was likely to be asked a question at any moment and be expected to respond, I didn't dare open an e-mail or review any other documents on my computer. I was transfixed and the experience was intense and worthwhile. I can genuinely tell you that I have been involved in a significant number of video conferences that have bored me rigid – including the ones I was running! I now use a piece of kit which allows me to monitor how long people spend with the webinar interface open as their main piece of software. On a webinar I was running some time ago, it was when the conference software was open on the desktop of some individuals for less than 25 per cent of the duration of the session that I realized we had a problem. The key to remote conferencing is interaction and – crucially I think – small groups to allow that interaction to be meaningful. I'll be looking at how technology can help (and occasionally hinder) in Chapter 6.

To achieve effective line manager involvement in support of your training initiatives requires three things:

1 Obtain a statement of commitment from every line manager who wants their team members to attend your programme.

2 Send them a briefing of what you expect them to do as part of that commitment.

3 Follow up and act as 'coach to the line manager' – supporting them in discussing the outcomes from the workshop and the assignment which is expected as follow-up. By modelling the behaviour you expect the team leader to exhibit, you'll start to build the required skills, prove the benefits, build your own credibility and that of your programme.

Life cycle tips

The new recruit

Defining work-based tasks for new starters from across the different functions of the organization is, and will remain, tricky. You may regard the workshop as redundant. Bringing people into a workshop simply because they haven't had the chance to attend yet is hardly a good advertisement for the services of the L&D team – especially for new starters. Regardless of whether you have a workshop or not, structured work-based learning should play a part in the induction process. You will probably want each new starter to position their new role within the context of other departments as well as to become an advocate amongst their friends and relatives for their new employer. The first activity would be to arrange interviews with key people in different functions. Ideally, each interview will have a specific brief to understand how each team in the business works towards a collective aim. It is important not to be too prescriptive about the 'how' this is conducted, but focus solely on the 'what'.

For example, asking how the organization makes money sounds like a really simple question, but in actual fact is pretty important and rarely as straightforward as it seems. This is equally valid for non-profit-making organizations and the public sector. Understanding who the paymasters are and what impact this has on what the organization does, for whom and to what object is a pretty good way of getting under the skin of an enterprise. It should provide the context for their future role. Guidance for the new line manager in undertaking a review of the organization and supporting the arrangement of interviews, etc engages them in this journey of discovery.

A further follow-up may involve submitting a report to the L&D team about suggestions for future inductions – that is, highlighting the information found out by the new starter which was of particular benefit and proposing ways in which this information could be made available to all. Rather than a dry, formal report which will undoubtedly gather dust on someone's shelf or take up space in an e-mail inbox, ask the new starter to make an introductory video for potential inclusion within the careers pages of the organization's website. The availability of video recorders on smartphones makes this a much more viable option than once it was. This kind of reflective practice should never be missed out when considering the design of work-based learning.

For initial training, ask each new starter's line manager to identify a 'buddy' from within the team – a more experienced team member who can support increased familiarity with tools, procedures and processes and act as a person to whom the new starter may turn for advice. Again, exceptional businesses in the contact centre industry are particularly effective in this regard. The facility to record telephone conversations with clients 'for training purposes' provides a real opportunity to assess performance, identify areas for improvement and make incremental action plans to increase effectiveness and confidence in what can be a challenging role. A similar approach is not beyond consideration in, for example, manufacturing, computer programming or retailing. It simply requires a process of monitoring to have been agreed between new starter and their buddy. In the case of retailing, this may require an observation role. In those jobs in which a physical or digital product is the output, there is an artefact which can be checked, a process which can be reviewed and discussed and advice offered.

The new manager

Without doubt the new manager, or aspiring manager, is one person who will benefit from having someone who can guide them through the period in which they get to grips with their new role. This guide may proactively perform the role of the coach but in most coaching models the coach drives the discussion, albeit that their role is to focus the attention of the person being coached towards taking control of their learning and the actions which enable them to develop the required skills. Alternatively, the designated individual may take the role of mentor, responding to requests for advice and support rather than driving the relationship. We know, however, that both mentoring and coaching are activities which get squeezed out by other priorities. They become OBE – overtaken by events.

When looking at coaching or mentorship for new and aspiring managers the issue of time and opportunity is an issue not only for coach or mentor. Those being coached or mentored can also claim that the day job takes 100 per cent of their attention and effort. Thinking about the skill sets required for progression and succession in a packed working day can be tricky.

If one of the outputs from this on-the-job support process is an improvement of the completion of work-based tasks, then consider using some kind of accreditation system which looks at demonstrable evidence of work-based implementation of new skills or work practices. Use a form of certification for an individual's completion of work-based tasks (whether supported by an external body or developed for purely internal use). In part this should rely on manager/coach or mentor sign-off to verify and validate the work-based outputs. In turn, this process will create situations where there is a 'pull effect' – ie new managers themselves will demand time from senior people to enable them to achieve certification. This is especially true if certification delivers other benefits such as access to promotions, higher salary bands or increased (and welcome) responsibilities. The challenge, of course, is to tie the process of completing (pre)supervisor training into the talent management and succession planning process. The first time one of your learners hears that a colleague has been promoted into the role they were working towards *without* the necessary training achievement, is the last time you'll generate the required pull. It wouldn't be the first time that L&D initiatives are undermined by the desire to promote and retain key people.

The specialist

Using work-based training to develop the specialist's skills within their area of technical expertise is always difficult. Put simply, who coaches the expert? Unless you have a whole team of experts with differing levels of skills and experience, then you may need to out-source the coaching and feedback role. In fact, engaging with external experts from other industries or from academia may provide the kind of challenge and stimulation which is exactly what the specialist needs.

That said, it is frequently not their areas of expertise which require most focus from a performance development perspective. Having worked with many specialists – from IT geeks to sustainable development gurus – it is my contention that there are two areas which prevent these individuals from fulfilling their potential and delivering the kind of impact that their organizations would want.

The first is corporate awareness. Often the specialist would appear to be of the opinion that the organization exists to provide services in their area of specialism – however esoteric that specialist area might be. I have worked with IT security experts who genuinely seem to think that the reason that the organization has an IT infrastructure is to prevent malware and viruses infiltrating the network. From an HR perspective, blocks placed on websites which give access to (free) learning resources, is all too common – whether that is a blanket ban on YouTube or the cookies which support many resource banks in remembering who you are and your areas of interest. This kind of blinkered approach to the needs of the organization is not uncommon and (let's be honest) infects a number of HR teams as well.

The second area of potential development is in those core skills which enable higher impact for those who rely on the remainder of the organization to buy in to their ideas and to adopt new practices. Communications skills – from presentation to negotiation to influencing behaviours – are essential if the left-field ideas of the researchers and the boffins are to be more widely understood and acted upon.

Both of these development areas call for a mentor from outside their area of expertise – as senior as possible to provide credible feedback and a rooted appreciation of the *realpolitik* of the boardroom. A good deal of time wasted in blind alleys would be saved if only all technical experts were guided by their personal senior adviser with the authority and influence to open doors where required and concern for their own reputation not to publicly endorse ideas whose time has yet to come or which would not command widespread support.

The leader

It is axiomatic that without support from the top, the idea of manager engagement with the learning of their team members is wishful thinking at best. The senior leaders can best support the implementation of follow-up to formal training inputs by practising what they preach and being seen to do so. I have repeatedly heard senior leaders extol the virtues of training and development at the same time as making it impossible for those below them in the hierarchy to actively support team member development. If the senior team act as though workplace development is an optional extra, then it will remain an option which is not chosen.

Every leadership programme I have ever seen suggests that leading is an activity not a status and performing that activity well requires senior managers to be actively involved in the development of their people. John Adair's Action Centred Leadership, post-graduate management qualifications, the Chartered Institute of Management competences and the like have all emphasized the point that developing others is a core part of the people leader's role. And yet, we still have middle managers wondering aloud when they're expected to find the time to undertake this role and being supported by their director in pushing back on the reasonable requests made by their colleagues in L&D. Everyone in a leadership role should recognize that developing people throughout the enterprise is one of the activities which defines their competence as a leader. If 'nice to do' is being squeezed by 'need to do' then acting as a coach or mentor should become 'need to do'.

I do think that one of the reasons some senior leaders are reluctant to play this role is that they consider it to be 'micro-management' which they have been repeatedly told by business schools is a BAD THING. They are supposed to be strategic, right? Developing people means getting involved in their workload and that's operational, so nothing to do with the senior leader then. This kind of dialogue in one form or another – disguised more efficiently in some organizations than others – is repeated the length and breadth of executive office suites.

As an L&D team, you need to gather the statistics about the cost of lost talent. If your high potential middle managers are not supported to make the step to strategic senior leader, they will leave to go somewhere they can. A lack of opportunities for development and advancement is cited in just about every survey as the main reason middle managers leave for pastures new. In a difficult economic climate, no organization can afford to lose that middle to higher level of management.

If leaders find fulfilling this role difficult or uncomfortable, then a one-to-one coach – possibly from outside the organization – might be appropriate for them. Before embarking down that road, explore the possibility of peer-to-peer coaching for senior people – the marketing director coaching the finance director, the HR director meeting regularly with the chief operating officer. Without the hierarchical barriers which on occasions interfere with the quality of the conversations required, you may find genuinely useful insights generated from these interactions. To bring a degree of objectivity to this process, think also about using 360-degree feedback in which peers, direct reports, external contacts, stakeholders and clients get involved in providing initial feedback and identifying areas which could be worked on. If you do need to engage an executive coach for one of your leaders, ensure that the L&D team are involved in the initial briefing process. This should emphasize the organization's values regarding personal development and highlight those areas of the competence framework at the highest level which articulate the expectation that enterprise-level managers will be actively involved in developing others.

The retiree

Many of those nearing retirement are only infrequently involved in formal training and therefore rarely have access to an individual who could support them in work-based learning activities. However, if you take on board the idea that a) changes to pension entitlements mean that retirement will be postponed for many and retirees tend to be more loyal to their employers and less likely to switch jobs; and, b) that we should select people for training based on potential and aspiration rather than artificial choices based on age or length of service, then you'll want to rectify that.

It may not come as a huge surprise that many of the approaches outlined for the other groups work equally well with these more long-serving employees. One area I would definitely advocate working on with this group is the ability to pass on their skills and experience. This is the group from which I would want to select the buddies for your inductees and the mentors required by your new managers. Enabling them to play this role will require training and support – especially if this is a change in organizational practice. This is an area which organizations tend not to be very good at, so don't assume that they have a blueprint of how things should be because of their years of experience. It's probably best to assume that they have exactly the opposite – a series of anecdotes of how not to support on-the-job learning! These can be a really useful insight for the commencement of the programme. I was working on a programme which was nominally about knowledge management for a medium-sized company. I had persuaded them to give me a group of their longest-serving employees for a day. I asked them a simple question: 'What are the five things you know now which you wish you had known when you started here?' It was the only input I needed to make that day – a day which turned out to be one of the most fascinating in my professional career. The outcomes from that event completely revolutionized the way the L&D function worked in that business.

Can all the tools work together?

05

> *We now accept the fact that learning is a lifelong process of keeping abreast of change. And the most pressing task is to teach people how to learn.*
>
> PETER DRUCKER, WRITER,
> ACADEMIC AND MANAGEMENT CONSULTANT, 1909–2005

The tools that are available to us span the whole learning process, from defining needs to demonstrating mastery in the workplace. Often this collection of resources and courses, activities and work-based tasks is described as a *blended learning solution*.

The problem is I'm bored with blended. Combining e-learning with other forms of training intervention is certainly better than the blind faith that online modules can replace all other forms of training. This was certainly the mantra of the earliest adopters of internet- and intranet-delivered courseware.

The genesis of blended learning was a kind of re-balancing. From the hype of the early adopters of the online medium, there was always going to need to be an adjustment. But by then, the battle lines had been drawn. Those fearing that their entire role might be replaced by a computer, or more properly, those being mortally affronted that anyone would suggest that the things they did might be automated, were quick to the barricades. When those involved in e-learning started to use the phrase 'blended learning', it felt like a victory for those who had set their face against anything online.

Of course, this was a storm in a technological tea-cup. E-learning was massively over-hyped in the first few years and the press releases announcing the death of the classroom missed the mark. The e-learning companies, which became blended learning companies overnight, were quickly exposed as having no understanding of the process of learning. They needed people who knew their way around the training process. Most of these people inhabited the training rooms, so a rapprochement was reached. Reassured, even the most fervent opponents of e-learning loosened up and recognized that they too could adopt the blended approach.

> E-learning still stands alone in some areas – especially when it comes to computer skills, systems and software. We very quickly got over our concerns about a machine training us, when it was smart enough to teach us how it should be used. Many of those technologists who initially re-branded themselves as 'blended learning companies' retreated to the comfort of focusing exclusively on tech stuff. Here, the geeks are still in control of the code, but recognizing that that's all they know about, have focused on teaching geek stuff.

For people who have been involved in learning and development for some time this may be a diverting history lesson but nothing more. Blended learning has gone the way of empowerment – it is **so** last year. To discuss the 'blend' is no longer fashionable. Blended learning has moved from the hot new thing to the embarrassing uncle of learning and development in only a decade. In their *State of the Industry Report* in 2002, the American Society of Training and Development (ASTD) reported:

> Blended Learning: we urge caution when using the e-learning estimates reported above. In last year's report we observed that our methodology for collecting this data made it difficult for companies to report on training that blended e-learning with more traditional forms of training.[1]

In other words, one of the foremost organizations involved in work-place training in the most technologically advanced country in the world (certainly from the perspective of the adoption of e-learning) hadn't thought to measure blended learning until late 2001. This really is a short timescale for a concept to drop out of favour, even by the quixotic standards of most L&D commentators. But why has it become passé so rapidly?

Technology-based blended learning

The traditional blend started with a component of pre-workshop learning, usually delivered via an online module. This was tracked by a Learning Management System (LMS) and those who had successfully completed the online module would be allowed to attend the face-to-face workshop. At the end of this workshop, the trainer would encourage participants to plan action, perhaps writing up the action plans and sharing them with the relevant line managers by way of invitation to get involved.

Only a decade ago, this was set to become the new orthodoxy in the deployment of technology and yet blended learning is now viewed with suspicion. Why is the industry not excited by the e-learning for initial knowledge acquisition (tracked so only those who have completed can go on to the next stage), face-to-face classroom workshops for introducing skills and enabling discussion, and on-the-job projects or activities to reinforce and embed the learning in the real world?

Mostly, because it doesn't happen. Organizations are loathe to exclude those booked on workshops because they haven't completed the knowledge components delivered by e-learning – even when the use of those modules can be tracked and monitored in ways which those seeking to measure previous learning inputs could only dream of. Because those who haven't clicked the link to the pre-workshop modules are still in attendance, the trainer has to spend the first hour of the classroom session recapping the content they should have covered. In so doing, they waste the best brain time of most of the group and annoy the hell out of the people who actually did the pre-workshop e-learning. The course itself is still delivered by trainers who feel most comfortable when they're doing the talking. The 'sage on the stage' is an addictive role to play. As prima ballerina Anna

Pavlova said: 'Although one may fail to find happiness in theatrical life, one never wishes to give it up after having once tasted its fruits.' Whether performing for 6 or 6,000, there is an adrenalin rush and – if you're any good – a group of people hanging on your every word. It gets to you.

This reluctance to give way and surrender the spotlight means that what skills practice sessions have been planned get moved into the afternoon – probably late afternoon. And when the discussion runs over or the presentation takes a wee bit longer, these practice opportunities are squeezed, reduced to a quick role play, rapidly reviewed with little time for proper feedback before everyone runs for the train. Action planning for work-based implementation? A few e-mails may wing their way into participants' inboxes but they will deliver little if anything by way of results.

The concept of mixing modes of delivery and matching these to the different needs of individuals is still inherently attractive. If this can use new technology in a way which seems more natural, more rooted in everyday technology use and – let's be honest – a bit sexier than the average online module, then all to the good. In fact, if we can respond to the demands from the finance director that we spend a little bit less on traditional training methods and take people away from the job less often and for shorter periods, then it would seem we may have achieved something pretty close to nirvana.

70:20:10 – the much abused new orthodoxy

All trainers like a good buzzword. We also like something which appears scientific, concerned as we are that maybe the rest of the world thinks of us as prone to a bit of mumbo jumbo. If we can put numbers in there somewhere – hallelujah! Welcome to 70:20:10.

You might have seen the ratios 70:20:10 used elsewhere in relation to organizational training and development. I have come across it spoken about a lot in papers, presentations at conferences and in business's learning strategies. The version I last heard in a boardroom was 'most learning happens on the job – it's experience that counts'.

This focus on work-based practice and on-the-job experience resonates because it makes sense. For many – especially those outside the training department – it represents how they think they learned to do the things they do. It also neatly reinforces the prejudice that 'you can't learn to do your job out of a book or in a classroom'.

Of course, these beliefs are fundamentally true. I don't want to be flown on my next holiday by someone who has only read about how to be a pilot. My children are currently learning to drive – does passing the driving theory test make them safe on the roads? Not if the permanent impression of my finger nails in the palms of my hand means anything. The gap between theory and practice is canyonesque in proportion.

So we can all accept, I hope, that despite the apparent dismissal of the now unfashionable blended learning, we still need a mix of different learning and training opportunities to develop the skills necessary for work. What the 70:20:10 concept says is that we learn 10 per cent of our skills and knowledge through formal training inputs (workshops, e-learning, etc), 20 per cent from conversations with more experienced people (coaching, informal learning), and 70 per cent from getting our hands dirty and doing things.

I have no argument with that as a concept – but be clear, that's what it is. It isn't – as far as I can see – based on robust or wide-ranging research. Although numerous articles seem to suppose that these ratios are an immutable law created through detailed research going back over the generations, no one has actually analysed how people gained their skills and determined that the proportions of experience and input outlined in the 70:20:10 model is actually what happens. For one thing, the nice round numbers always seem suspicious to me.

The 70:20:10 learning concept was first developed by Morgan McCall, Robert W. Eichinger and Michael M. Lombardo at the Center for Creative Leadership in North Carolina.[2] What is interesting when you go to the source of the model is that the focus is not on some ad hoc process by which skills are somehow developed in an organic way through simply doing the job. Instead, 70:20:10, as imagined by its originators, requires thorough planning and management of informal and on-the-job learning if it is to work.

Failure to properly understand the concept is the big issue. From 'we have a method which will help people learn very efficiently and develop practical skills using on-the-job experience' to 'most learning happens on the job, why are we bothering with courses?' is a small leap in the minds of the bean counters tasked with finding cost savings. If the model is misrepresented as '70 per cent of learning happens on the job' – which is **not** what Eichinger and Lombardo said – then we may be inviting our sponsors and senior managers to embrace a training process in which we simply throw our people in the deep end because that's how they'll learn anyway!

Rather than a quick, cheap and exceptionally dirty response to training needs, 70:20:10 is a concept that only works with a great deal of thought and thorough planning. The holy grail of training being 70 per cent on the job (and therefore cost-free, apparently) ignores the fact that the work-based experience is much, much less effective without the 10 per cent formal training and the 20 per cent informal, coach-based learning to accompany it.

More often, the expressed benefit of 70:20:10 is time and money – simply put, the same amount of content can be delivered with less off-the-job time. The e-learning or 'pre-read' component can be undertaken when convenient. Anytime, anyplace, anywhere was the original Martini mantra of the e-learning industry. It still should be.

So, I've done a bit of pre-workshop stuff then I've been on a course and got involved in lots of activities. In Lombardo and Eichinger's 70:20:10 model, this still forms the 10 per cent – formal training. This was – for the most part – where the traditional blended learning solution ended and one of the explanations for why the terminology is falling by the wayside.

Using 70:20:10 as intended requires a mix of inputs designed in a much more robust way. It must include a plan for individual follow-up to help each learner undertake work-based activities to build their skills and knowledge. Lombardo and Eichinger defined the start point as the learner taking a long hard look at him- or herself and defining their ideal self and their real self – ie where do I want to be and where am I starting from? The idea is to undertake a gap analysis which defines the behaviours required and the learning needed to bridge the gap.

The start point of the model is for the learner to plan the 70 per cent – the experiences and work tasks, projects and assignments which will give learners the exposure to new ways of doing things and alternative thought processes which will help them build the required skills. For most of us who have designed blended learning let's be honest, we've started with the 10 per cent – planning the formal input. If any thought was given to on-the-job learning it was after the course. It certainly wasn't the start point for planning the programme.

So if we have already involved the individual learner in identifying the on-the-job experiences they would need to improve their skills or knowledge, then we can plan the remaining 30 per cent of the model. The question put to the learner is: 'What would you need to know and learn before you engaged in those experiences?' The answer to that question is the subject of the courses they attend, the e-learning they complete, the books they read and the webinars they log on to as well as the informal support they receive day to day.

This 20 per cent – conversations with subject matter experts, coaches, and peers – acts as the glue in the learning process. It supports reflection, gives feedback and adds information just in time. This could be facilitated online – especially if you have one or two subject matter experts and hundreds or thousands of people who need to ask questions.

But there are challenges. The first is in ensuring that the organization, and those whose buy-in to this process is required, understand what it is you're trying to do. If they think that this is a chance to replace formal training and development with unplanned on-the-job experiences then the process will fail.

There are good reasons for this. On-the-job experiences without support are just as likely to develop bad practice as good practice. Without requiring people to reflect on what happened and identify specific areas for improvement, then on-the-job learning – far from being an efficient method – is actually extraordinarily hit and miss.

Some rigour about the behaviours required is necessary. What happens in organizations where on-the-job learning is the only game in town is that the existing culture and current behaviours are reinforced. The learning is 'how we do things around here'. In some organizations, that well-entrenched culture is not what is needed for the future. On-the-job learning simply doesn't achieve step changes in behaviour on its own. In fact, on-the-job learning can actively undermine culture change by reinforcing the tried and tested over the new and needed. Despite these potential drawbacks, the rise of so-called informal learning is seemingly inexorable. In the ASTD *State of the Industry Survey* questionnaire for 2012 respondents were asked to quantify their spending on **formal** learning and on **work-based** learning. Work-based learning is no longer formal. It is part of the informal learning experiences which come to us out of the ether. Despite being surrounded by these informal opportunities, USA-based employers are still expected to have a budget for it and to account for it separately. If you're confused by these apparent contradictions, I suspect you are not alone. If we have to pay people to support it and create structures and systems to enable it to happen, isn't it formal? If it happens without control because of knowledge and skills sharing between workers, why does it need a budget? The reality is that within the 70:20:10 model, the 70 per cent is anything but informal. In order to be most effective it is highly structured, closely monitored and requires a reflective process – provided through the conversations which comprise the 20 per cent to ensure it achieves the raised competence and enhanced performance we would want.

This brings us neatly to our second challenge, which is to engage with those who will act as the glue in the learning process. Experts, managers, trainers and coaches are a pre-requisite for this process to work properly. They may need considerable help to adapt to this role and to have the quality conversations which make up the 20 per cent of the 70:20:10 model.

In my experience whoever provides this support – whether it is a trainer, a coach or a manager – will need significant direction to get started. As a minimum they will need some ideas for the kind of on-the-job tasks which could comprise the 70 per cent. This doesn't have to be an exhaustive or definitive list, but should give some ideas and food for thought. Without some kind of start point to open up possibilities, the conversations become focused pretty quickly on the things you can't do, rather than on the things you could or should do.

CASE STUDY

I was working with a group of product designers. Whenever they interacted with their commercial colleagues – especially those involved in marketing new products – there was rarely a meeting of minds. In fact, the product designers were often cast in the role of the people who always said 'No'. The product designers were essentially practical and pragmatic souls. When market research seems to say that consumers are willing to pay more for a product which did X or Y or Z, marketers get very excited. After all, if the market research is accurate, this could provide real competitive advantage. Since starting marketing school, brand managers have been told that the so-called first mover advantage is all important. Apple and Steve Jobs proved that. Nespresso proved that – and you can bet every brand manager in the world has looked at those case studies. The holy grail of brand development is to do it first and reap the benefit of having a monopoly of certain features and product attributes. Pity the poor product developers. They have to design something that can actually be made. Their issues are about producing it in a factory, on time and to a budget. Typically, as the finance team didn't set much store by the market research, they were also expected to produce this new wonder product for the same unit cost as the existing, less-than-wonder product. 'Why does no one understand the pressures we are under?' came the cry. 'Why do the finance team not realize we need to invest in new equipment and processes to do this? Why won't marketing accept that these things take time?'

The solution to their issue was pretty simple. They were unaware that the finance team were crying out for people to join them on short-term assignments of around six to eight weeks, to act as auditors. Finance were desperate to bring people into the mix with technical and product design experience. They had specific projects – such as new product launches and brand innovations – which needed appraising to understand why they had made money or why they had lost money and what the lessons were for future initiatives. The problem was that no one had told the product developers this.

By arranging two or three of these placements, the product developers were able to educate their finance and marketing colleagues about the stresses and pressures of commercially producing a new product. The individuals involved were also able to learn about the needs of these two functions, the stresses they were under and the restrictions and budgetary pressures they faced every day and to take those lessons back to their product developer colleagues. This was two- directional work-based learning in practice. It was highly structured and required a great deal of organization. Very little about it could be described as informal.

An experiential learning model

Alongside an understanding of the possibilities of work-based learning opportunities, those involved will need to understand how to reflect on these experiences and how to provide feedback. The reflection process is vital if those learning are to make sense of their experiences and fit them into a framework which enables recall and application after the events. The experiential learning model, put forward by American psychologist David A Kolb[3] in the 1970s (see Figure 5.1), recognizes reflection as one of the four key learning phases:

FIGURE 5.1   Kolb's learning cycle

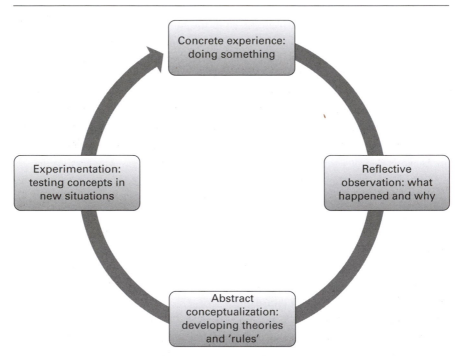

Kolb's work on the experiential learning cycle borrowed heavily on the work of Dewey[4] and Piaget[5] who looked at how children learn. Kolb applied many of these same principles to adult learning. He found that our inherent ability to learn could be considered as four separate activities, undertaken almost without us realizing that that is what we are doing. The effective learners are capable of observing what happens within an experience and reflecting on what has been experienced in order to derive concepts, theories and lessons. To consolidate that learning and to be able to apply new knowledge and skills, the learner needs to plan how those ideas could be applied in other circumstances and contexts, leading to a new experience where they experiment with those skills. In practice, each of us continuously and rapidly proceeds around this cycle and thereby continuously learns.

All well and good, except that the space for reflection is often squeezed out by the frantic pace of modern work. On occasions we experience something, cannot see how it can be applied to the immediate priorities on our to-do list and so stop short of formulating a usable theory and experimenting with its application. Further, some people are simply not that good at reflecting. The thing that happened is recalled, but why it happened, how they behaved and how things might have happened differently is still unknown to them, or reimagined to fit the pre-conceptions with which they entered into the experience. It is unfortunately the case that not everyone can learn terribly effectively by experience. This is true of some of your most successful colleagues. You will have worked with someone who has inferred from previous experience that doing something in a certain way always works. When it doesn't they are nonplussed but incapable of amending their approach to a new set of circumstances. Often, these individuals will just plug away with the same old, same old until the returns become so diminished that they are forced – kicking and screaming – to try something new.

I was once working with a business-to-business sales team. Sales had recently dropped somewhat. The sales team (of course) blamed their product and the pricing and the economic conditions. In fact, they blamed everything apart from what they were doing. On a day spent with one of the most experienced salesmen in the team, I was able to observe his 'patter'. He always established rapport with his customers by talking about sport. With the buyers who had grown up in the area and were broadly similar to him in interests and outlooks, this paid dividends. These guys bonded over a shared celebration of City's success and a joint rant about United's defensive frailties. He was smart enough to appear to be a supporter of both teams, irrespective of their intense rivalry.

When he approached other buyers, whom he knew less well and who were less similar to him in interests, age, origin and outlook he either talked about sport to a reception of blank indifference or ignored any attempt to build rapport at all! As the demographic of his customers changed and diversified, his 'local lad, salt of the earth' spiel came over as a failure to listen or appear interested in his new clients. Instead he seemed to be 'too sales-y', the kind of person who is interested in you only so long as you represent a route to earning commission.

When I reflected back to him what I had seen, I was told in no uncertain terms that I didn't know what I was talking about and that I should only come back when I had as much experience as he did. I responded uncharitably by asking if he had 20 years' experience or one year's experience which was 20 years out of date. For some reason, when the training courses were organized he was always sick or attending an important client meeting.

Ah well – win some, lose some.

The curse of learning styles

One of the reasons that individuals seem to treat reflection as an optional extra may be because they have been told this through a well-intentioned but misapplied interpretation of assessments of learning styles. There are several instruments which help people to determine their preferred learning style. David Kolb has the Learning Styles Inventory, based on the four stages of the experiential learning cycle. A well-known alternative is the Honey and Mumford Learning Styles Questionnaire;[6] 80 paired statements to be selected by an individual to help them identify their preferences and underlying attitudes to different learning processes and activities. In the UK, even school kids have completed a version of this questionnaire and plotted their responses on a kite-shaped graph enabling them to define themselves as an Activist, Pragmatist, Reflector or Theorist.

Cognitive scientists such as Professor Daniel Willingham[7] of the University of Virginia and those engaged in neuroscience such as Baronness Susan Greenfield (who famously described learning styles as 'nonsense' from a neuroscientific perspective)[8] are increasingly dismissive of the whole learning styles idea. The categorization of learners as a route to determining a range of instructional styles and learning experiences is not scientifically supported. Even David Kolb, in an essay written in 1981, specifically said that these learning style categories should not be seen as stereotypes. In tests and experiments, there has never been a correlation between a so-called learning style and an ability to learn things more effectively when information is presented in a manner which is consistent with a dominant learning preference.

However, we have a problem. Put simply, despite the absence of data, lots of learners think that the learning styles framework is a scientifically proven concept. What's more, they believe that, having drawn the kite-shaped diagram, they have identified their learning style and thereafter can only be taught in ways which are consistent with this preference. As a 'reflector' is a defined learning style in some models and some people have proved to themselves that they don't learn well by reflecting, they actively avoid the reflective process which will assist them in learning from experience.

Although the evidence that learning is more effective when matched to one's learning style is either non-existent or inconclusive, this does not mean that we don't have some experiential preferences and abilities. Often our preferences – the things we like to do – and our abilities – the things we're good at – coincide. Some people may enjoy observing what happens and others may like being thrown in at the deep end. Some may love to get into a book, with its descriptions of theories and concepts, others would prefer to look at results from an experiment and draw up their own theoretical models. The simple fact is that in order to progress around and around the experiential learning cycle, the individual needs to undertake *all* of the four different activities – from doing to observing, to conceptualizing and planning how to do something in future. If the learning styles inventory or the learning styles questionnaire or any of the similar models designed to fit learners into categories and boxes show us anything, it is that at certain stages of our learning cycle we're going to find things more difficult and less enjoyable than at other stages. This is not to dismiss the ideas of Kolb or Honey and Mumford or any of the others who worked on defining the differences amongst learners. It is simply to say that they did not invent these categories for them to be applied as cognitive ghettos where we each languish, unable to progress around the experiential learning cycle, condemned to be stuck in our groove like a damaged CD. This unbending typology is the result of a misunderstanding of how learning styles were intended to be applied. If those administering the tests had read the original literature around the concept, they would find that David Kolb also wrote:

'the learner (...) must continually choose which set of learning abilities to bring to bear upon various learning tasks.' [9]

Reflection – the lost art?

We can all learn through experience, but only if we reflect on what has happened and think about how that might change what we do in the future. Remember, the role of training is to enable people to do things differently and do different things. Reflecting on our work-based experiences – with assistance when required – is a crucial and often skipped stage in the process of learning through doing. The job of the Complete Trainer is to support this process through structuring the reflective process. This can be a simple series of questions or a pro forma template. A number of options are available for this including a simple four box diagram:

FIGURE 5.2   A four box framework for reflection

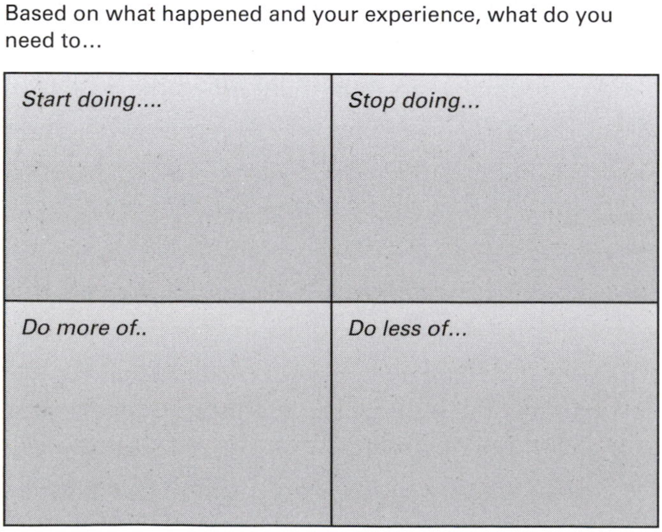

Based on what happened and your experience, what do you need to...

Start doing....	Stop doing...
Do more of..	Do less of...

In this template, the trainer is enabling and supporting the individual learners to reflect on the implications of their behaviour. This reflective process could be built into a reflective log designed to require learners to take time out to think about their experience. Typically, such a log requires learners to answer three questions, under headings like: *What?*, *So what?* and *Now what?*,[10] in which the four box diagram at Figure 5.2 represents the Now what? stage of the reflective log.

It is not a significant leap from this kind of reflective practice for the trainer to derive a mechanism for feedback and a process for checking understanding through experiential learning. The outcome of this reflection – the log or diary of experience – is also an artefact which can be shared with others to provide wider access to each individual's insights into their learning activities. However, as a learning process, reading the logs of others is no substitute for the real experience and personal reflection of the individuals involved. For some learners, though, the process of contributing to the knowledge pool of a group is an effective motivator which ensures that the reflection process is not skipped.

The log also provides a basis for the individual engaged in workplace learning to share and discuss what they have done with their coach or line manager. While we all recognize that supporting the development of individuals is a key role for managers, the reality is that it is done with very variable results. Some take to this role with alacrity and are extremely skilled, but as everyone in training knows they are usually the exception. Building individual and team capacity is not often on many managers' to-do lists and if it's there at all, it often slips down to priority number 27.

The line manager is key – again!

How do you get the involvement of line managers in the development of their team further up their to-do list? It comes back to the central tenets of training philosophy in modern organizations – what gets measured gets done. If the organization embraces a learning philosophy which puts experiential and work-based learning as somewhere close to 70 per cent of the learning journey for each individual, then they can't be taken seriously without a commitment to requiring all people managers to play an active role in helping to create opportunities for people to learn; supporting implementation by encouragement, feedback and – on occasions – instruction; and checking that the learning has happened. An active role in the reflective process should follow every training event – whether so-called formal course attendance or a work-based activity organized to enable lessons to be learned and new skills applied.

These management behaviours also need to be modelled. If the senior people aren't also developing their skills in a similar way then they are unlikely to cascade that through the hierarchy. Who coaches the coaches? As a learning and development professional capable of playing a role in the very heart of the business – you do.

Instead of merely blending different training inputs together to increase the efficiency of training spend, 70:20:10 goes to a whole new stage. Simply calling something 70:20:10 doesn't actually address the planning and support required to truly make it work and to build skills and career paths fit for a changing future.

To really work, 70:20:10 requires:

- individual training planning based on where they are now and where they want to be;
- planned work experiences and tasks with deadlines and anticipated outcomes;
- a chance to learn the essentials before starting on the job learning activities; and
- quality conversations which acknowledge achievement, support reflection and are the basis for further planning.

Part of those quality discussions should be about the next training required and the new skills gaps identified. In this way a virtuous circle is created. In changing times, for training to mean anything it needs to be a continuous cycle. Developing one skill should create a demand for others. Once into that ongoing development cycle, the importance of on-the-job experience and learning is self-evident. Those who have experienced and shared their own learning with others become hungry for new and different experiences and, through their greater exposure to the breadth of the enterprise, become skilled in making and taking the opportunities offered. The great thing about those who have been exposed to this joined-up approach to the development of their work-related competence is that they never stop learning.

Life cycle tips

The new recruit

The new starter is unlikely to be particularly pro-active in seeking new opportunities and exploring chances to learn in the workplace. Alongside initial training it makes sense to expose new starters to as many other areas of the business as possible. At first this may mean an hour interviewing someone in a different team or department, or spending a day working alongside someone with different responsibilities. These should be structured, with each new member of staff given information to discover which can be recorded in a reflective log.

A kind of assignment, to identify opportunities to do things differently or to suggest improvements to procedures and working practices, provides an insight into how they are thinking and their appreciation of the whole spectrum of activity within the organization. After a set period (100 days seems a useful milestone) the new starter should be in a position to assess what it is they now need to know to progress in their new role. This is the point at which the line manager – with the support of the L&D team – should conduct the development review, using the 70:20:10 model by starting with the new recruit identifying their real and ideal selves and articulating the gaps they would want to bridge.

The new manager

New managers are often running extremely fast just in order to stand still. No new or aspiring manager should be involved in management skills development – which, of course, should precede their appointment to a supervisory role – without access to a senior manager who can act as adviser and mentor. As well as helping them to reflect on the formal inputs, this individual should be directing them towards opportunities to learn more – leading small project teams, chairing meetings, providing support to a new starter, and so on.

Once established in role, the value of the one-to-one discussions with their team members should be reinforced and acknowledged through the simple expedient of having a member of the L&D team or wider HR community sitting in and observing the session. This practice:

- underlines the importance of one-to-one development conversations as part of the manager's role;
- provides feedback and identifies areas for improvement in the new manager's approach to these vital discussions; and
- models the kind of behaviour required of everyone within an organization committed to training and people development.

The specialist

I've outlined before that often specialists find it difficult to develop their specialist skills on the job within their area of expertise. Secondments outside the business – with a negotiated and specific brief to bring back to the organization some new way of working – may be the only route to developing specialist skills. Of course, different areas of the business may have differing levels of specialism.

When working with the global brewer SABMiller, I worked alongside their specialists working on reducing the use of fresh water and finding new and sustainable ways of using this precious ingredient in their brewing as effectively and sparingly as possible. As well as sharing expertise between those in Africa, Latin America and India – all of whom had faced different challenges and developed different solutions – group companies in particularly water-stressed areas had formed partnerships with non-governmental organizations specializing in working in arid environments. This level of information sharing and joint learning was:

- focused on specific issues of importance to each group company;

- documented for cascade across the partner organizations; and

- designed to provide opportunities for these specialists to widen their impact through working with other functions and stakeholders – within and outside the business.

This kind of active partnership, providing mutual benefit, offers an opportunity to learn through doing while tackling a pressing issue for the business and the communities it works within. It also provides a test bed for those other skills which specialists need – from communicating, negotiating, influencing and educating to delivering projects on time and achieving commercially relevant objectives.

I've seen similar initiatives in companies working with universities, colleges, community groups and voluntary sector partners. Often these initiatives are somewhat unfocused from the individual development perspective. A project may be identified and the organization's best brains lent to the team for a defined period, but rather than focus wholly on what the individual can put into the process, organizations concerned about development should focus on what the individual can also get out of it by way of new experiences, skills and knowledge.

The leader

If these approaches are new to your organization, you will have what may be described as 'legacy leaders' – those elevated to their current position before the advent of the rigorous individual developmental support now available for those making their first steps into supervision of others. Some of the mentoring, observation and feedback may be of use for them as well as for the new supervisor.

Action learning-style approaches or project-based learning approaches are also beneficial for these leaders.

CASE STUDY

When Marshalls, the Yorkshire-based manufacturers of landscaping products, wanted to develop their second tier leaders – those directly below board level – they worked with Ashridge Business School to develop a project-based leadership development model. A group of 45 second tier managers – the strategic leadership group – went through a one-week taught management and leadership development programme which led into external, case study/consultancy projects with small businesses in Sweden and Dubai, followed by internal projects tackling issues of direct relevance to Marshalls.

The strategy development process identified a number of tasks to be taken forward by the strategic leadership group as part of a revised strategic focus for the business. This included a project on people processes designed to harmonize performance management practices across all sites. It involved the strategic leadership group defining the most appropriate model and management behaviours which could be rolled out across the business on all sites and for all employees. The learning gained from their role as short-term consultants in unfamiliar business settings equipped them to look at problems differently, to analyse situations from the floor up and to present their solutions in a way which relied solely on their insights and less on the power of their position or in-company track record.

This kind of focused group work with a defined learning perspective benefits the organization, which gains additional strategic insight, the companies for whom the leaders work as consultants, and the individuals who are given a specific set of skills and behaviours to work on supported by peer-to-peer and external professional feedback.

It also has the benefit of motivating and inspiring those who otherwise might be looking for that next step up into the boardroom beyond their current employer.

The retiree

As a preparation for retirement, the 70:20:10 model has much to commend it. From thinking about the ideal self **post-employment** and then working backwards to identify the inputs and learning required, those approaching their retirement can actively develop the skills and knowledge that will serve them well in the post-nine-to-five world. This can be done while sharing their work experience with the remainder of the organization.

This two-way street seems only right. If, before they leave, we want to mine the information and insights which they have collected over the years, it seems only proper that we should support them as they wind down from full-time to part-time to retirement.

Having identified the ideal life they want post-work, the retiree should have access to someone who can help them define the experiences and learning they would need to take the opportunities newly available to them. Then, through a similar mix of formal input and experiential opportunities, each individual can prepare properly for the next stage of their life and give willingly of their experience before departing.

The benefit goes beyond this simple transaction. Think about what message such a programme would send to the remainder of the workforce. In a working world in which retention of talent is a key concern for many organizations, a strong and visible commitment to the organization's most valuable asset – both in work and beyond – seems to me to provide a real competitive advantage in the cut and thrust of human capital.

Technology: what works and what doesn't

> *For this invention will produce forgetfulness in the minds of those who learn to use it, for they will not practise their memory. You have invented an elixir, not of memory, but of reminding; and you offer your pupils the appearance of wisdom, not true wisdom.*
>
> PLATO, C428BC–C347BC

Many of the ways in which technology supports learning in the 21st-century workplace are manifestations of the communications technologies which are integral to the modern workplace. Communications – as we have seen – is different from learning and development, though it forms part of the training mix. The focus on communications, information dissemination and exchange is one of the reasons why technology does exactly the opposite and acts as a barrier to things being learned and new skills implemented. Technology, and specifically communications technology, is after all just a way of doing things more conveniently and more quickly while widening access to information. From the messenger replaced by the postal service and the telegraph, in turn supplemented by and perhaps supplanted by the telephone and then the e-mail, texts and multimedia, the last 150 years have been characterized by a rapidly changing communications landscape. But simply providing greater and greater access to more information – some of it of questionable provenance – can contribute to confusion, information overload and a failure to actually learn. Why learn things when we can always look them up?

The most common and most abused technology – PowerPoint

Whereas it would be simple to think of technology as being solely about online communications, e-learning and the like, it would be wrong to address the use of technology in training without looking back at a quarter of a century of that now ubiquitous training technology – PowerPoint. What started as a tool used by DTP experts to animate presentations which transferred from overhead transparencies has now truly democratized presentations. Anyone can use PowerPoint and everyone does. In fact, with a slide deck and a few notes, anyone can become a trainer, can't they?

Well, no – as anyone who has sat through many presentations will know, PowerPoint can be a boon to some presenters but equally can be a major barrier to communication in the hands of someone who uses it indiscriminately. If you've ever experienced a PowerPoint presentation you will have your own horror stories of how the abuse of this technology has transformed a promising meeting into an endurance event of mind-numbing futility. There are four key crimes:

1 **The bullet point.** It is a rare presenter who doesn't fall back on the templates provided by Microsoft to create slides with lists of facts to be memorized at the rate of around six or seven per slide. What's more, that dread phrase 'I'm just going to talk to a few slides' very often means precisely that – a presenter facing their own screen reading through bullet after bullet after bullet, making much of the audience wish they'd brought bullets of their own and a means of propelling them.

2 **The preparation is all in the slides.** Even where bullet points are avoided, the presenter who doesn't prepare what he or she will say, but focuses all their preparation on the creation of the slides – preferably with a few whizzy animations – soon loses their audience. It is tempting to use the PowerPoint slide deck

as the structure, notes *and* visual aid. The result is almost always too many slides, containing too much information and stories, anecdotes and discussions are mown down by the sheer weight of information.

3 **Graphs and tables**. There's nothing wrong with including graphs and tables if they have been specially created for the presentation and if they add value (although they should be illustrative of trends rather than anything more detailed). The real problem is that they are rarely produced specifically for use in a presentation. Instead the dreaded print screen button is used to extract the chart being referenced. When it spirals onto screen it is usually accompanied with, 'I know you won't be able to read this, but what it says is...'. It's supposed to be a visual aid. If you can't see what it is supposed to show, just whose vision is being aided?

4 **The use of *slideuments*.**[1] You may not have encountered the word before, but you know what it means – it is a PowerPoint slide deck produced as a handout – another built-in function of the software which should make everyone at Microsoft hang their head in shame. Used in this way we move from PowerPoint being used as it should be – a visual aid – and into something else. When used in this multi-purpose way, rather than being able to flex its technological muscles to fulfil both requirements, it fails miserably to do either. Because the document needs to serve as both a record of what has been presented and a space for participant notes, the trainer feels obliged to include lots of detail on the slide. Inevitably, we're back to bullet points and 200–300 words in small text or tables which can't be read. Because the participants may be following our presentation, we can't possibly miss anything. We are instantly less responsive to the needs of the audience and incapable (or at least extremely unwilling) to skip sections or even tear up the whole presentation and do something less boring and more useful.

You can probably identify each of your own particular *bêtes noires* about the use of PowerPoint in these four main problems with presentation software as a medium. Although less widely used there are other presentation tools, advocates of which claim they are impervious to PowerPoint's ills, but if these four horrors raise their heads, then I find the specific software choice makes little difference. A bad presenter, over-reliant on text on screen is still dull, whatever whizzy piece of software they have downloaded.

The key to resolving the issue is actually found within PowerPoint (and I'm sure other tools). It's the word 'Show'. Although called a slide deck or set, the term used by Microsoft is 'slideshow'. Thinking about the show component of the presentation might be the single most important change for many presenters to make. Having recognized that a PowerPoint slideshow is a performance, the objective is to use the PowerPoint slides as a backdrop to the messages included in the presentation. The most effective way I have found is to follow something akin to Cliff Atkinson's model outlined in *Beyond Bullet Points*.[2]

Essentially what Atkinson advocates is three things:

- a title for each slide which is a sentence giving a key message;
- clear images which reinforce the message – diagrams, pictures, models;
- extensive use of notes to ensure that what the presenter says adds value to the slide being shown rather than using the slide as a script to be read from.

I like to augment this approach by including three other useful techniques:

1 Summarize every six to eight slides with a reminder of what you've covered and a signpost to what's coming next. If necessary, use a bullet point screen (rules are there to be broken) containing the key messages taken from the preceding slide titles. My advice to the presenter when they use these summary slides is to shut up and let people read!

2 Include prompt slides asking for responses from the audience – questions and provocative comments. One-way PowerPoint lectures, without participants having the chance to participate, have served to give the software tool itself a bad name.

3 Include memory slides. These will certainly be the summary slides, but may also include important concepts, charts or graphs, created specifically for the presentation rather than simply pasted in from elsewhere. These memory slides can then be extracted from the presentation and included in a workbook for participants where there is an expectation of a handout covering the presentation. Using selected highlights in this way provides a concise record of what has been covered, enables the trainer to follow useful diversions to meet the audience's specific requirements and reduces the printing bill. A simple signpost mechanism on each slide in the workbook ensures that an audience which has become accustomed to having access to the whole slide deck can use the workbook effectively.

This reduced version of the presentation also assists the trainer in using PowerPoint as a visual aid. I was working with a leading figure in issues of sustainability and global development recently. His presentation in the first part of the session simply included a series of large numbers placed on screen. As each number came up, he asked the audience what they thought the number represented. As an example, at one point he showed a slide with the figure 16 per cent filling most of the available space. He asked what people thought it meant and after a few stabs in the dark, he clicked to reveal the answer – the proportion of the world's population aged over 65 by 2050. He then asked what the current proportion was – it was just over 8 per cent – and entered into a discussion about the implications for governments and development agencies of the ageing population over the next four decades. Could you imagine this working if everyone was reading the slides with the answers on? A bit of surprise in your visual aids can turn 'Ho-hum' moments into 'A-ha!' moments.

E-learning – does it have to be so dull?

Very often e-learning starts from the presentation which previously made up the bulk of a training session and is converted – with vary-ing degrees of effectiveness – into something which can be launched online, studied by each individual and their progress (or lack thereof) monitored by a Learning Management System (LMS). Those e-learning programmes which began their life as a set of PowerPoint slides and were converted into a so-called multimedia programme are rarely the most exciting learning activities that anyone ever engaged in.

In e-learning terms, good practice is often determined by the absence of 'bad'. So what makes 'bad' e-learning? The answer to this question is, 'It depends.' I know. Not that exciting is it, nor particularly helpful, but to a great extent context is all. One of the reasons that companies would appear to be embracing e-learning is cost. It is perceived to be cheaper to roll out a module online than to use an alternative, face-to-face programme. The Institute of Directors conducted a study on Training in the Recession[3] in 2009. They found that moving training to either on the job, online or both were methods of increasing the availability of training without a corresponding increase in costs. However, telling employees that the previously available mechanism for developing new skills (which involved nights in hotels, time away from the office and a chance to chat to colleagues from other departments) is to be replaced by a computer programme which they are expected to use in their own time, isn't a great starting point for learning.

Let's define a few terms first of all – by e-learning I mean a packaged application (or linked series of applications) launched on a computer, either locally or from the network. I'm not distinguishing the myriad of technologies used because I've seen amazing e-learning content using technologies from the late 80s which blew my socks off and brilliant examples using the very latest technologies. I've also seen complete dross using terribly sophisticated software.

The other defining feature is that an individual can use it on their own – the training or instruction is embedded into the program or application and the computer 'teaches' the user. Now right from the off there is a whole host of issues in that sentence alone. A computer 'teaching' someone something? Is this a weird dystopian vision of the future where, *Matrix*-like, we are all plugged into the network to have 'knowledge' piped into our memory banks? Are we to be reduced to walking memory sticks? No, but self-management is one of the most tricky areas when it comes to what makes a good or bad e-learning programme. The willingness or ability of the intended audience to learn independently of a trainer is fundamental to whether e-learning will work or not. And that is the crux of bad or good, surely? Bad e-learning doesn't get used. Often that is nothing to do with the design of the programme but the culture of the organization where a desire to learn and an understanding that the individual needs to manage their own learning has not been established. If your learners only ever want to be taught by an 'expert' with PowerPoint slides and handouts and a shortbread biscuit at 11 o'clock, then you're probably onto a loser from the start.

There are no universally applicable, or accurate, figures about e-learning completion rates in the corporate world. However, if we look elsewhere, a mature student entering university is undertaking a good deal of self-managed learning. In the UK, the benchmark figures for mature students leaving their chosen course within one year is 17 per cent (ie universities have to explain themselves if their figures vary from this benchmark). Now I know that factors that are nothing to do with learning – money, work, changing family circumstances – greatly impact on university completion statistics. However, these students are volunteers who have expressed a strong interest in undertaking additional study. Many will be paying the costs themselves. Most corporate learners do not fit into this category. We can assume their level of completion will be significantly lower (in one pilot study in a UK government department, it was below 5 per cent – fewer than one in 20 people actually completed all modules).

It seems to me that, even if corporate e-learning is as successfully completed as the university benchmark, saying that around one in five of the people targeted by a training initiative do not complete the programmes isn't sustainable. Designing a great course and sticking some or all of it on the intranet as an alternative form of learning or knowledge management isn't going to work on its own.

So, what can organizations – and learners – do to ensure that the guilty secret of self-managed learning isn't 'no one's doing it!'? There are three key actions which organizations can take:

1 Acknowledge it's an issue and provide support – the leading organization in the world for distance and self-managed education is the Open University. It provides pages and pages of

study skills and 'managing your learning'-type information on its website. They recognize it's a big deal to start learning on your own.

Providing support might mean creating guides giving hints and tips, or communicating with managers and influencing the organization and its senior management to insist on the achievement of team learning targets in managers' annual objectives. After all, what gets measured gets done and you should measure. Be clear and tell people what you expect and if completing an e-learning course or a pre-read booklet before a workshop is important, don't let them on the course till they've done it. Being supportive isn't always about being nice.

2 Design learning in chunks that people can complete in short sequences of time and support people finding what they want quickly and easily. That sounds like a really simple message, but if you've looked at the average Learning Management System interface you'll know it can be about as inviting as a hungry crocodile in a swimming pool. A long and boring list of a series of impenetrable course titles with associated course numbers and codes is really not going to make anyone's eyes light up.

If you want to know what simple is, think about the last time you bought something online – a book, a DVD, a music download, an airline ticket, a reservation at a hotel. How simple was it? Did you persevere through a rubbish interface which took ages to load and then asked for irrelevant information? Did you have to take the vendor's claims as gospel or could you read what other people just like you had said? Did you give up and go somewhere which made your purchasing experience easier and more enjoyable?

If like me you actively reject complicated transaction sites, then you get the drift. Never forget, your people have a job to do and may well not want to do your course in any case. Let's wise up on how people find and use information in a connected, Web 2.0 world.

3 Talk to learners and get them to give you feedback on what works for them in their busy day. Use this information to decide

what is really necessary. Do all of your courses and all the e-learning modules have to be designated as mandatory? Really? For everyone? No, I didn't think so.

Once you've consulted, go out and talk to more learners about what you've found out and why self-management is required and how it's been designed. Don't rely on reluctant managers and the Chinese whispers of your cascade system to get that message across. You need to manage the communication – consistently and repeatedly.

Let's assume that you have sorted the cultural and practical issues and people are prepared to complete some e-learning. The easiest way to do this is to make the e-learning part of a blend of different interventions. Not because e-learning is intrinsically flawed, but because it is very good at some things and very poor at others. As are face-to-face courses.

I'm often invited to observe face-to-face courses on technical subjects. Very often what I witness is a pretty average presenter, displaying slide after slide with 12 point Arial text in bullet points animating onto screen one at a time before being read out to the assembled group – many of whom have been able to read independently since they were about five, some without moving their lips at the same time.

Bad e-learning simply replicates this without adding the myriad costs of taking people out for the day. If you count the cost of participants not working, I reckon that the real unit cost of a one-day course is around £2,000–£2,500. Run the course 10 times – £20,000+. If all you're going to do with this 20 grand is talk at people, then not only will e-learning reduce the cost of the exercise, but it will be quicker and more effective. Even rubbish e-learning is better – ie more of the information will be retained by the audience – than poor presentations.

But as we know, PowerPoint is often used really badly and copying a sub-standard PowerPoint presentation is not going to make good e-learning. One of the indicators of poor e-learning is the extent to which it is a passive medium where learners are expected to interact only with the next button while they read through text on screen. Even worse is the e-learning that requires the learner to go through it in a pre-prescribed path, using every screen in sequence, each unit in order. The ubiquitous 'screen 2 of 24' at the foot of the screen becomes less of a guide to where you are and more of a threat.

One-directional online presentations do have their place. The British Army discovered some years ago that insurgents in Iraq were positioning dead camels across the road and booby trapping them. When moved to allow vehicles past they exploded, killing or maiming the people moving them. By creating a simple presentation, launched through an LMS which tracked completion, the Army were able to get this information to the troops on the ground and monitor how many of them in each location had seen it. This presentation was 'fit for purpose'. Creating any other form of interaction would have lengthened the experience and created a barrier to its use.

This military example from Iraq was a communications piece. Comms is not learning. Where e-learning is reduced to simply telling you stuff, it gets a bad reputation and falls into disuse. Most organizations don't have to communicate urgent lifesaving information like the Army, but still are over-reliant on approaches fit only for short, urgent messages.

The techies who build this stuff know it's boring. They come up with ways of trying to make it more interesting. My personal favourite is the talking owl – because as we all know, owls are wise! The use of cartoon characters used to be very fashionable. It was a mainstay of award-winning programmes. People were intensely proud of their ability to create a virtual manager who chatted away to you. The problem is, it's patronizing. There's a fine line between child-like – learning as a child does, the natural way we learn most stuff – and being childish. Most e-learning which adopts these techniques crosses that line.

Recent developments in the e-learning space have focused on replicating some of the experience of online games. This is called 'gamification' of learning – an inelegant word but one we seem to have been saddled with. Most games include a facsimile of action – ie you have to do something within the online environment, usually stealing cars or blowing up the enemy. This has been translated by the advocates of gamification into the development of skills. This is of course true. I will develop the skills to play the game using the computer keyboard or games console. One games maker actually recruited real racing drivers through an online competition using its software. So skills can be developed but only over many hundreds and hundreds of hours using tools which replicate the real thing – ie a steering wheel and realistic car controls on the console. This is the basis of flight simulators, which are to all intents and purposes just a very sophisticated and expensive console video game. If you are not engaged in using the right tools, you learn about the game but not how to convert the game's facsimile of action into real life. Take a simple golf simulation game. I may be able to beat Tiger Woods or John Daly at the 12th hole at Augusta through my magnificent choice of club and angle of approach, but that's in the world of the PlayStation. If I tried to do the same thing with a real club on a real golf course I wouldn't win. I might pick up some knowledge of the game and the clubs to use in different circumstances through the in-efficient trial and error of playing the game, but it wouldn't translate into a set of skills.

Whatever the environment created, clicking a four-option multiple-choice response to a question asked by an avatar of a customer on a screen is very different to the real thing. The use of games in customer service training, sales or similar interpersonal disciplines has been tried and I've rarely seen a smart enough algorithm or good enough design to pull it off. The main spending has been allocated to the graphics which, despite the sums invested, still have a whiff of old-fashioned amateurism.

The expense of creating credible and useful serious games is significant. The graphics used in computer games cost a lot of money. In fact, video games now regularly cost more to make than feature films. Your training budget isn't going to match that and the imperfect or old-fashioned graphics on the training games that I've seen simply turn people off. Rather than attract learners through the sophistication of the graphical interface and the depth of learning experience, the exact opposite occurs. What's more, these tend to be targeted at subject areas that young people need to learn. The idea that anyone under 25 can't learn unless they're playing a computer game is, frankly, patronizing.

Being patronizing is always a cardinal sin. The most regular transgression is the use of the pre-determined path. If you require a learner to follow a prescribed, mandatory route you are not only saying to your audience, 'You are all the same and you know nothing'; you are also using web technology, the most amazing communications aid since the invention of the printing press, in a counter-intuitive way. The web is about surfing. It's about being in control. Good e-learning allows users to choose and gives them control of what, when and in what order they use online resources.

This is the antithesis of one variety of e-learning which is incredibly common. I refer to the wonders of the compliance programme. Learning Management System purveyors have made a significant case for the ability of their software to track learner completion and register pass marks and the like. Such has been their focus on this, that it is entirely natural that those who are more interested in ticking boxes than providing learning have been quick to recognize the benefits that tracked e-learning provides in the area of covering the corporate back against claims that training was not provided.

A friend of mine is a tech wizard. In fact so sought after are his skills that he is called upon by major corporations to resolve network issues which have taxed those with enormous brains and the sallow complexions of those whose dedication to computers means they rarely experience daylight. In a recent assignment for a major telecoms company, he was required to complete a piece of health and safety e-learning and pass the end-of-programme assessment before being allowed on site. He let me glimpse the wonders of the programme which he had been required to complete.

Here was a technologically advanced organization where everyone uses computers and the latest technology is an intrinsic part of their day jobs. And yet the e-learning which my friend had to sit through was an example of the very worst use of computer-based learning I could ever imagine. I honestly thought that click-through pages, heavy text on screen with barely relevant images pasted on to each page were things of the past – the ancient past when learning programmes were distributed on 3½ inch floppy disks. Interaction was limited to hovering over a so-called hot spot which launched determinedly lukewarm pop-ups. The assessment – which plumbed the depths of the question writer's art – was of course locked until every page had been viewed. Once arrived at, the usual sins had been committed. The longest option was always right and every repetitive four-option multiple-choice included an answer which was so clearly wrong that the phone-in quiz setter for daytime TV would have been embarrassed to take the premium rate phone charges off those who called in.

Heinous though these e-learning crimes were, the best (or worst) was yet to come. One size fits all apparently. Yes, in order to come onto site to resolve a computer issue, an operation which he assures me provides no greater danger than dropping the end of a dunked digestive down his shirt, my friend had to complete the section on working at heights. My desk-bound, technologically brilliant mate needs to prove to someone (who?) that he can work safely on scaffolding before being allowed through the security gates!

This is the triumph of box-ticking over common sense and unfortunately is not that uncommon where regulatory compliance e-learning programmes are concerned. Attracted by the audit trail provided by the LMS, those charged with ensuring compliance are enthusiastic adopters. Across the whole of the learning and development spectrum measurement of outcomes provides us with this dilemma. Importance has been given to that which is measurable rather than an effort made to measure that which is important. Two things disturb me about this.

Firstly, if the health and safety of visiting contractors is important – and we do have an absolute duty here – surely they deserve something better than this? How about a programme from which they might actually learn something? How about a process which truly ensured that they were safe in those areas of activity in which they were likely to be involved? This catch all, tick-in-the-box programme achieves no objectives apart from giving a false sense of security to the Health, Safety and Environment manager that he or she isn't going to find themselves in court in the unfortunate event of an incident in which someone is injured or worse. (On that point, however, I wouldn't want to be the barrister representing anyone who used this programme as the central plank of their defence!)

Secondly, very many organizations start their journey into e-learning with compliance programmes. Everyone needs them and the LMS allows for automation of the updating of each individual's training record. Whether or not to use e-learning seems a no-brainer. But if this is the standard of learning programme which employees and contractors are being expected to use, is there any wonder that e-learning is often seen as a poor substitute for traditional alternatives?

My final gripe about e-learning is the stuff which is hopelessly optimistic about users' desire and time to learn. I see programmes that use good techniques – meaningful interaction, appropriate audio, a range of different inputs including video and good graphics which enhance rather than depress learning, etc. The problem is they go on forever. About 20 minutes is the longest duration which actually delivers the benefit of greater recall. That's not to say the course need only be 20 minutes long, but that it should be broken into 20-minute sections.

Web 2.0: the hope and the hype

In a networked world we should be expecting our people to use the web to learn. We should be helping them by providing proper learning tools – not just pointing them at information. We should remember that they are adults – with different learning needs and different learning preferences. One size does not fit all. Your audience needs to know their needs have informed the development of the resources which are designed to support them. 'If we build it will they come?' was the big e-learning question about a decade ago.

We built it. They didn't. With any area of dissatisfaction there's a natural human desire for the one-stop cure – the silver bullet. Take the slimming pill. Now, intellectually and rationally we all know that losing weight is tricky but there's only one sure way of achieving success – eat less, do more. It's not a secret which is kept from us by the medical profession. Despite this rational knowledge, emotionally we want the quick fix, the magic cure which will banish bingo wings and give us a six pack your granny could do her washing on.

My experience with this is limited to my mother many years ago enjoying life enormously when she was prescribed some magic pills to help her lose weight back in the days when GPs did that sort of thing. It was only when we noticed she was dusting like a whirling dervish at two in the morning that we realized she had been prescribed some kind of amphetamine to help her burn those calories. Certainly, my brother and I had a few months of having our Y-fronts ironed at high speed (and I use the word advisedly) but weight loss was only achieved later through a balanced diet and trips to the local swimming pool.

With e-learning everyone wants it because they recognize that the cost of people attending face-to-face courses is simply unsustainable in more straitened times, but there's a dissatisfaction. The concern is that feedback says people miss the human interaction, the chance to chat to colleagues, to share our work problems and discontent with Albert from accounts over a chocolate HobNob and a hotel buffet. The loss of a mutual and shared experience of squeezing a stress ball in a hotel near Reading weighs heavy on our training delegates.

And now the slimming pill for e-learning is upon us. Social media. By signing up to Facebook or similar and building a Twitter community we will be able to replicate that human interaction – and what's more do so in a way which is all zeitgeist-y and 'down with da yoof' and more suited to our multi-tasking times. The universal panacea for lonely e-learners is upon us – praise be.

Except it's not. Again, rationally and intellectually we know that many of the attempts to harness the power of social media become a damp squib pretty quickly. The posts dry up, the trainers lose interest after spending their time talking to themselves and even social media evangelists explain that it's only by posting a blog (rather than by reading the often ill-informed or self-promoting posts of others) that we actually learn anything through reflecting on our experience enough to articulate it and package it for general consumption.

What's more, using Facebook is a particular issue. How does Facebook make money? It gathers personal information, parcels it up and makes it available to those who would wish to commercially exploit it. It is simply an advertising channel and – given the travails of their share price since flotation – not one that the markets are entirely convinced by. Imagine you enlist the support of Facebook to create an on-the-cheap learning community. Assuming anyone uses it, perhaps their presence indicates a willingness to learn, a desire to invest time in their own development. Perhaps they will add the occasional frustration about their current employer and the lack of opportunity to progress. Now that's not useful to anyone who might want to target advertising at your learners is it? Oh, hang on, what if you were a savvy recruitment consultant looking for dissatisfied Gen Y-ers with a hunger for self-improvement? Perhaps the Facebook model works after all – just not for you and your ability to retain those in whose development you have invested. In Bridging the Gap,[4] the 2012 benchmark study from Towards Maturity published in November of that year, the researchers found that increasing numbers of organizations were facilitating employee access to external social media tools as part of their learning and development activities. This contrasted with a decreasing number who were building their own collaborative learning applications. I think there is a problem here with using free, external social media sites. The business model of these free platforms is based on marketing a product. That product is you and me – and, by extension, your trainees. But worry not because, as a learning tool, existing routes to social media such as Facebook or Pinterest provide a pretty poor model.

However, online collaboration does have a part to play in the modern learning environment. But cut through the hype. Your learners – be they graduate trainees or middle managers or customer service teams – have no real desire, or sufficient time in their working day, to initiate a series of online discussions in the hope of using the reflective process to develop their own skills and understanding. Now I should point out that I've always been a little sceptical about online communities. I've seen very many launched and read the posts about 'how cool this new forum is' and then a few weeks later I've logged back on to see those same posts created in the first flush of enthusiasm and nothing since. One of my clients very proudly showed me an online community for trainers located across the globe. There were 26 separate discussion threads – and 27 posts. The first 25 discussions had been started by the person showing me the fantastic site. Despite provocative questions, requests for information or links to new materials, not one had been answered or commented on by the community of around 80 people. One post had been created by someone else. This had got a response – from the person who created the first 25 posts. It said:

'Thanks for your great contribution!' and included the obligatory smiley face. This would have been funny if it wasn't for the fact that this global group had been created to advance the use of technology for learning across the organization.

What the people in our organizations do want to do is look things up. They want to look things up which explain things which they can't find in the bland corporate communications of modern organizations. That creates an interesting analogy for me. When I'm visiting a place and have to stay over, I'll often consult online reviews of hotels – making my purchasing decision on the comments I find there. These are things that aren't in the brochure – the fact that the rooms are subterranean and local cats have headaches as guests attempt to prove the old maxim that there really isn't room to swing one; the fact that the rooms overlook a busy road or are next to a nightclub which kindly organizes Friday night fights so that the police don't feel under-employed; the fact that the rooms are OK but that the food is dreadful or expensive or (too often) both. For some reason I trust these reviews so much more than the artful photographs which depict a dream bedroom.

But while I will visit TripAdvisor or any of the other sites with guest reviews, I don't necessarily contribute to these sites or feel compelled to do so. I may – if invited – award some stars for bedroom cleanliness, value for money or customer service or whatever I'm being asked, but I am primarily a **passive recipient** of the views of others. And that's how 90 per cent of people who log on to these sites interact with them. As part of the transaction which they are involved in they will utilize the network of previously untold stories – often cataloguing the egregious problems with the place and occasionally extolling the virtue of a hotel's location, value for money, kind, informed staff and spaciousness.

When I do feel moved to enter a star rating (and assuming it's not too much trouble and I'm not too busy that day) I become an **active recipient** in this transactional network. Very rarely – maybe on two visits to one of these sites out of 100 – I'll add a comment, usually sharing my knowledge that the hotel is OK but rather than fork out £20 for some undercooked elderly bacon, future guests would be better off at the greasy spoon 100 metres away which does a cracking,

The use of social media as an aid to learning – or in some respects as the one true route to learning and development – is very much the flavour of training conferences and the Twitter-sphere. This is the so-called heady world of 'social learning'. Now this is a phrase which I have some issues with. Many organizations ban access to Facebook and the like via their internal networks because the 'social' domain of shared pictures, updates about nights out and hangover-inspired bleak Friday mornings have no perceived value in the world of work. They have recognized that the social of 'social' networking is why people use these sites and work is, by definition, not primarily part of the social sphere. But, as I outlined at the start of this book, there is a more significant issue which I have with the phrase 'social learning'. Social learning is a term which is already taken. If you consult any psychology book – especially about child development – you will find the name of Albert Bandura, the most often cited living psychologist. He came up with his 'social learning theory' in the 1960s by looking at how children imitated what their peers and important role models did through observation.[6] This is not what is happening online in social networks. Whether employees have access to a publicly available social network such as LinkedIn, Facebook or Twitter or whether there is a purpose-built tool on the corporate intranet, the process is not imitative, it is information sharing. What's more, the information may be of variable quality, but alarmingly taken as gospel truth by thosewho read it. Sharing and collaboration is good, and communities of practice, facilitated by online tools, may have a role to play primarily for specialists and those with a high level of expertise in a particular area.

A new set of skills for new opportunities

The nature of user-generated content on the web is that it is predominantly comment and opinion and not always informed or true. Conspiracy theories abound on the web and spread with alarming speed and are accorded a status which far outweighs their validity. Using the user-generated web as an information source needs some caution and some pretty acute skills.

First among these is being a skilled information seeker. I first used this phrase around 10 years ago. The internet was still relatively new and we were just coming to terms with the impact that these new sources of information were having on work. An organization called Echelon published a report based on a survey of HR directors and training managers. In a nutshell it said that work roles were now so complicated and required such a depth and breadth of knowledge that an individual couldn't realistically be expected to know (in terms of having memorized) everything they would need to do their job. In short, knowing how to look things up was going to be essential for the future.

If only we'd known quite how far things would go! I spoke to a group of teenagers recently, none of whom knew their home telephone number. It was speed dial 2. As the wealth of digital information and disinformation has grown, being a skilled information seeker has become not only a foundation stone, an essential capability for the 21st century – it has also evolved as a skill set. No longer is it enough to know how to search and navigate various information sources. Now it is necessary to have a degree of media literacy previously undreamt of. The differentiator of the successful information seeker is not simply an ability to find information, but to critically analyse it, to sift the definitive from the deceptive, to know the difference between the proven and the porky pie. Many don't.

Those reviewing dissertations and theses from students now have to explain very, very slowly to their charges that Wikipedia is not necessarily a reliable reference source. The co-founder of Wikipedia, Jerry Sanger, was a philosophy professor at Ohio State University. He would deduct five marks from any student who cited Wikipedia as a source. When asked about this, Jimmy Wales, the other brain behind the 7th most visited website in the world, agreed with his former colleague's practice. To quote Wales in an interview with the *Independent* newspaper in the UK in 2010: 'Whatever 26-year-old tech geek males are interested in we do a very good job on. [But] things that are in other fields we could do with some more users participating.'

Those who will lead our organizations in two or three decades' time will have proven themselves to be skilled information seekers with the ability to differentiate reliable from unreliable information. What's more, they will not only be able to sift the important from the dross, they will be able to remember crucial information by replaying it to others or using it in their work. If the knowledge thus acquired is not used – and used quickly – to consolidate and re-inforce, it will just be something looked up that will need to be looked up again next time – except it won't because we think we've learned it already. The half-remembered nugget is insufficient for us to act, so when that doesn't work we revert to the way we always did it in the past.

Think about the last time you went to a furniture store and they gave you the equivalent of a tree, an allen key, some bolts and a diagram. Did you learn how to put the furniture together? Would you know how to do it next time? No, you looked up some information and followed instructions. Useful for one-off activities like assembling a regency TV cabinet, but not for things you want to do repeatedly – like most of the things you do at work. Information seeking is important, but it's not the same as learning.

The real value of online connectivity as part of the learning process is not necessarily in the raft of information thus made available. It is in the process of constructing these artefacts of our work experience that real value will be – and already is being – generated. Working on a project recently in which groups of learners from different locations were brought together for short periods, the value of the ongoing remote community was discussed. We all agreed that membership would be reserved not for those who turn up for the workshops, but limited to those who contribute to the ongoing debates through posts, blogs and online experience sharing. Contributing is not an option; it is a requirement.

One of the increasingly prevalent areas of collaboration and contribution across the web is so-called synchronous learning – where online discussions are facilitated by everything from Skype to specialist online meeting software. In Chapter 4, I outlined the benefits of this technology but once again the message is clear. If we take the worst practices from the training room they don't improve just because we beam them around the world and deliver them from our desks.

Life cycle tips

The new recruit

I've already outlined ideas for new starters to undertake pre-joining learning online before starting with their new employee. Once in post, if you require them to blog about their new experiences, this provides that vital reflective process, checks what they have learned and introduces them to their new colleagues across the business. It also handily provides the raw material to use on the careers pages of your website as part of the continuing drive to attract new talent to your business.

The new manager

New managers benefit hugely from the opportunity to learn online in and amongst other interventions designed to support their transition to a supervisory role. Alongside traditional e-learning, designed to help them understand the principles of managing a team and the specific application and policies within your organization, online collaboration should complement the online modules.

Access to a mentor, which I recommended in Chapter 5, will most probably be conducted – in part – via an exchange of e-mails. It seems a shame to me that these discussions are always private. While I appreciate that some things should be kept between the two of them, much of the discussion could take place on a public forum and be available for others – both to learn from and to add their own comments. The creation of a 'new manager community' won't be easy, however. This will need to be properly resourced and managed if it is not to fall pretty rapidly by the wayside as a nice idea which is overlooked amongst the myriad of other things to do. To assist, ask each new manager to post a short blog post or even a status update each week as part of their 'apprenticeship' as a team leader. Recruit mentors who have a track record of creatively engaging with online tools and ask them to comment and post regularly. If people use these resources they can gain some traction. Sure, not everything posted will be of significance and some of it will just become part of the overall background noise on the company intranet. But occasional nuggets and a shared sense of undertaking a journey together means that benefits will accrue.

The specialist

Specialists should be blogging on a regular basis and sharing their knowledge and experience. As the individuals in the business who keep a weather eye on developments in their field, they have an absolute duty to share insights from the field with their colleagues. In fact, why not require them to complete at least one blog post per month and incorporate this into their performance targets for the year? As learners, the requirement to update a regular blog will be an added incentive – should any be required – for them to keep themselves updated.

As well as blogging, one would hope that specialists will be working alongside the L&D team on creating e-learning programmes. The role of the subject matter expert (SME – not to be confused with small and medium-sized enterprise) is an important one within the creation of digital content. However, this is not all plain sailing. Being cast as an expert is alluring and would add to anyone's sense of self-esteem, but unfortunately it rarely comes with an allowance of time to actually contribute. In other words, they do have an unfortunate habit of saying 'yes' when actually the time and energy required isn't matched by the availability of these precious resources.

Another problem is the single-minded focus, described as 'the curse of knowledge' by Chip and Dan Heath.[7] Effectively, the curse of knowledge renders specialists and experts unable to imagine what it could possibly be like not to know this stuff – and yet the first stage of being a learning designer is to understand and empathize with the novice who will use your materials. The curse of knowledge also strikes when our specialists cannot possibly understand why everyone is less captivated by their area of specialism than they are.

A few pointers if your SME is similarly cursed:

1 **Their job is content.** Setting the learning objectives is something you would ask their advice on, but do not give them

the power of veto over the module outcomes. Determining the way in which the content will be delivered is also your job. Understanding the interactions, exercises and opportunities to explore the subject online is a learning design strategy, not a content strategy.

2 **Educate yourself.** You're much more likely to have a good relationship with the SME (and inspire their trust and faith in you to do your bits well) if you can hold an informed conversation about the subject. You're not going to know everything, otherwise you wouldn't need the SME, but at least you should have a grasp of the vocabulary and jargon.

3 **Be clear about what you need doing and when and stick to the timetable.** Usually in an e-learning project, the SME needs to sign off scripts and storyboards for factual accuracy. It's an important role. One of the challenges of e-learning projects is that the script gets sent to an SME and then disappears into an e-mail shaped black hole. Ensure you have your SME signed up to a timetable and that the project sponsor endorses this and can follow up on your behalf if things get stuck at this juncture. Remember, they are signing off on factual accuracy and matters of internal policy. What the message is is their job. How the message is delivered is yours. Build your own credibility as an expert in learning design of comparable standing to your SME and stick to the protocols agreed at the start.

The leader

Technology provides two options for leaders to get involved in learning themselves and helping others to learn. *Alien* had the slogan 'In space no one can hear you scream'. E-learning should have a slightly more prosaic version: 'In cyberspace, no one can see you put your hand up.'

One of the problems with leaders is that they feel they may lose face if they engage in training programmes alongside their subordinates. This is in no way universal – I have come across leaders who make a big thing of continually learning and are proud to ask the 'stupid' question that others might be afraid to voice. However, these leaders-as-learners might not be that common and questions of status may limit the leader's ability to admit what they do not know.

Self-managed learning, either on- or offline, removes this possible embarrassment and can be a positive boon. In fact, you can trick the leader. I remember working with a senior member of staff who seemed to struggle with the financial side of his job – figures were not his strong point. I asked him to be involved in an e-learning project and gave him access to a module we created earlier so he could see what he was going to be engaged in. That module was about the basics of accounts management. He not only used it, but had the good grace to say he found it extremely useful. 'Good to be reminded of some of those things when you get to my age,' he said. Whatever.

The other focus is for leaders to engage in content development. The blogging CEO sometimes has a poor reputation, but this is usually because the blogs are written by the internal communications department (or even worse, an external PR team). These come over as corporate speak propaganda rather than the views and comments of someone engaged in the same endeavour.

CASE STUDY

Sue Clark was the Global Corporate Affairs Director at global brewing company, SABMiller when she started blogging under the headline 'Sue's Views'. These fortnightly posts were only available inside the organization and were written by her from wherever in the world her role had taken her that week. They celebrated successes, gave candid opinions of trends in the industry and commented on government pronouncements about the myriad issues which surround alcohol consumption. They also gave an insight into what the challenges were in other parts of the world. If you were reading the blog in Bogota, you might be given an insight into what issues were being faced in Botswana. If you were based in Cape Town, learning about developments in Colorado could spark an idea.

As well as continually reinforcing the organization's values and the corporate affairs function's role in the business, it had two other important benefits from an aspirational perspective. Sue Clark was, at the time she started the blog, the only female member of the Global Excom – the executive committee which led the strategy of the world-wide operation. She was also open about the global nature of the work she was engaged in and – by implication – everyone else was engaged in as well. From addressing issues of HIV/Aids in Africa to water shortages in Latin America and irresponsible drinking in Europe, these were big issues. Messages about being involved in a global organization, which takes its role as a corporate citizen seriously and, potentially, provides really exciting opportunities across the world, are a boon to the HR team. From a senior, powerful and articulate woman in the boardroom? What's not to like.

The leader's blogs and online presence do not make learning. It is information, context and culture. All of these things are important in the learning process and the role of the L&D team is to harness these components and align the learning and training opportunities we create to these important anchors.

The retiree

Very often the last people who are considered for access to online learning are the learners who are more senior. There is a real prejudice issue here which suggests that their computer literacy might not be up to it. This is trotted out alongside the often rehearsed arguments about not training the experienced that may be close to leaving in any event. All bunkum as anyone with any sense knows, but nevertheless, older learners are not often thought of as the recipients of online learning.

I undertook a survey of learners for HM Prisons Service in the UK. What we found about attitudes to e-learning was very interesting. The main target for online learning efforts up to that point had been new joiners in the 20–30 age range. In fact those learners under the age of 25 actively disapproved of e-learning. They were far and away the least enthusiastic age group in our survey. Paradoxically, the over 45-year-olds were the most enthusiastic and also were the ones who were most likely to have undertaken e-learning at home related to a non-work issue. Time didn't allow us to explore the reasons for these unexpected responses any further, but anecdotally some younger trainees explained that they had used e-learning at school or college and didn't like it. For those who were avowedly non-academic (as many of these learners were) the association with school and also the poorly resourced and often not very well designed educational e-learning had clearly left its mark.

The older workers had less exacting demands of online learning – save that it should be pretty well designed from a navigation perspective, easy to use and clear about what you had to do next. However, even if the programmes were not terribly well designed or navigationally intuitive, our older learners found a way. Another branch of the UK Home Office launched a pilot e-learning scheme for workers in the border agency. They found that not many people completed the modules and gained some important learning even though the pilot appeared to have been a bit of a flop. One thing they learned was initially overlooked. The people who completed the learning were all aged over 45. They were also all women and they grouped together in their lunch hour to study together, helping each other out and discussing the things they were learning about a particular software tool. This approach mirrored an existing collaborative culture of mutual assistance which pre-dated the idea of user-generated content and online modules. Although now somewhat out of fashion, learning resource centres and areas where people get away from their desk to learn using online resources might provide the secret for the older members of our organizations who need to access learning and development provided on a self-managed basis.

Knowledge management and performance management: mutually exclusive?

> *Failure is the key to success; each mistake teaches us something.*
> **MORIHEI UESHIBA, FOUNDER OF THE MARTIAL ART OF AIKIDO, 1883–1969**

The process of knowledge management is at the heart of ensuring that your organization has a memory. Capturing knowledge and capabilities across the whole workforce ensures that lessons learned – often the hard way – are incorporated into daily routines. So why does it seem that many organizations spend a good deal of their time 'reinventing the wheel'?

This feeling of reinvention is compounded by a partial knowledge that things are being done somewhere in the organization which are portrayed as new or innovative but which often sound like something we've done before. This is especially the case where large organizations have a performance management approach which is based on the celebration of success. In some organizations prizes are given at the end of the year for teams which have had particular success and individuals who have led the way. It is not uncommon for the Christmas trimmings to be accompanied by the hearty slapping of backs and awards ceremonies which are an uncomfortable hybrid between school prize day and the Oscar ceremony. Gaining an internal award for the most improved customer service or the best marketing campaign or the biggest percentage cost reduction is perceived to be of particular value when the individual seeks a move up the greasy pole. Winning is career enhancing.

Even where no such awards for doing your job exist, the annual performance appraisal discussion can feel a little like a league table reckoning rather than a sober reflection on objectives achieved and plans for the next period. In many cases the monetary benefits of being given a top rating in the performance appraisal system are so significant that the whole process is skewed in favour of promoting successes. Inevitably, failures are less visible as a result. One of my clients has a four-stage performance appraisal outcome. Based on an assessment of the individual's work over the year in relation to their performance objectives, an individual may be awarded an 'inadequate' rating, a 'nearly there' rating, 'succeeds' or 'exceeds'.

An 'inadequate' rating leads to significant pressure on the individual with a short-term performance improvement target which may – over several further reviews – result in the disciplinary process being used and the individual moving to pastures new. 'Nearly there' provides for a less draconian monitoring process, but nonetheless, the individual concerned is given pretty stark warnings to push on or push off. Neither of these ratings qualifies the individual for an end-of-year performance bonus. The presence of pay in the mix and the potential threat of dismissal, means that very few 'inadequate' ratings are given but a 'nearly there' has become subject to a reverse grade inflation. It is so rare to withhold bonus which, for many, is already calculated in annual salary, that individuals with a 'nearly there' rating on their records are generally heading for the door pretty quickly. These additional factors of pay and potentially career-ending appraisal skews the system to such an extent that rather than its intention – to deliver high-performing teams – it undermines this objective by delivering safety-first objective setting and encouraging the burying of mistakes.

The top two ratings – exceed and succeed – attract annual bonus and for an 'exceed' rating that bonus is equivalent to 120 per cent of annual base salary, paid in cash and shares or share options to keep those high performers in the business. The manager who conducts the appraisal is in part measured on his or her team's achievement of their objectives, so there is an unholy conspiracy to ensure high performance is recorded and noisily celebrated. This may be an extreme example, but I'm convinced that most performance management systems which impact future promotion prospects, annual pay or individual and team bonuses, are equally likely to alter that which is being measured. In other words, it is impossible to measure performance accurately and objectively when:

a there is room for some subjectivity or extenuating factors;

b there is a shared interest between appraiser and appraisee in obtaining a successful outcome; and

c there is much riding on the result.

Far be it from me to draw your attention to any similarities between these types of activity and the performance of some of the world's best known banks in the last few years. That would just be a cheap jibe and we're above that. Aren't we?

When pushed, the bankers' bosses talk about the need to recruit and retain key people. They outline how they are 'rewarding success' and 'following market conditions' in the setting of remuneration and reward. Governance committees are mentioned and contractual terms. Above all, the finance top brass explain their employment contracts by channelling the spirit of the 'High Performance Team'.

High performance teams

High performance teams (HPTs) have been around since the work of the Tavistock Institute[1] in the 1950s. As a management and organizational development theory, the HPTs really took off in the late 1980s and as is usual in management theorizing, briefly went out of favour in the 1990s before becoming popular once more on the back of the work of McKinsey and Company, specifically partners Jon R Katzenbach and Douglas K Smith[2] and Phil Harkins[3], formerly of Raytheon and now CEO of Linkage Inc. One specification of high impact leaders, visionary companies and high performance teams as defined by these writers is that they do not tolerate under-performance. This has often been interpreted by leaders and – particularly by HR directors – as a routine commitment to performance appraisal systems which have as their basis a commitment to celebrate success while rooting out those who do not contribute to the end goal or company vision.

Now both these features – celebrating success and not tolerating under-performance – are part of the HPTs' message, but not in the way they are often implemented. Rather than focus on the whole picture of the high performance organization, which involves leaders in articulating a clear vision of the organization some time into the future; active listening and open communication with everyone in the team; and establishing clear and measurable targets – it has been easier just to go down the goal setting route. The focus has been resolutely on the things which can be measured, with all the attendant complications you may expect having got this far through the book.

Without the communication, discussion and learning which supports the high performance team approach, the targets are simply boxes to be ticked and numbers to be achieved. There is a very good reason why these moves should bother us if we are concerned with training and development. If organizational development is focused on hitting short-term targets, the employees are tacitly – and occasionally actively – encouraged to present a rosy picture of performance. This is regardless of whether the picture presented is actually a true representation of what has been achieved. In short, it's sometimes easier to fiddle the figures than achieve the long-term goals.

Achieve at all costs?

Why should this bother us? Well, think about our quest for knowledge management. If we cover up mistakes for fear of losing bonus or not being 'tolerated' by our manager and our team mates, then how are we to learn from them? As the Oscar-winning screenwriter of the 1958 thriller *The Defiant Ones*, Harold Jacob Smith, said: 'Most people would learn from their mistakes, if they weren't busy denying them'.

FIGURE 7.1 The alternate spirals of knowledge management and performance management

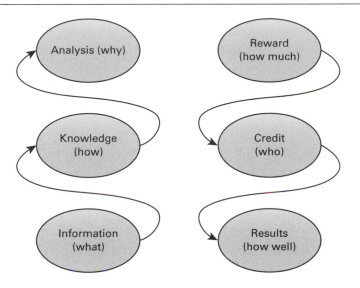

In Figure 7.1 the direction of travel is significant. Where a flawed performance management approach is elevated above knowledge management – looking good and appearing successful as opposed to learning from what happened and why – the start point and the key driver is the reward. What is to be gained (or lost) is so significant that it outweighs all other considerations. This is why the impact of badly implemented performance management systems is to spiral down. Rather than performance driving reward – which is the desired direction of effect – the reward drives the performance – or at least what gets recognized as the performance. Massaging results, focusing on the positives and overstating one's achievements is only natural when the alternatives are so unattractive.

This is equally true of organizations – whether striving for market analyst approval to boost share price or gaining contract continuation from a funding body or client – the appearance of goals met, targets achieved or exceeded and credit appropriately obtained – outweighs other considerations. In arm's length organizations – prominent in the interface between the public sector and the private or not-for-profit sector – the service level agreements (SLAs) specify escalating payments for results achieved, not dissimilar from individual bonuses. Without these additional payments, the organization simply may not be viable. In this environment, the appearance of high performance and achievement can be a chimera. Even when unravelled, the resentments caused by the inevitable attribution of blame means that the questions about what went wrong are rarely asked, let alone answered.

I was working with an organization, supporting their efforts to establish a global community of practice. One of the resources everyone wanted was case studies. We discussed what these case studies might include and what could be learned from them. This was followed by a comparison between the features of a good case study, as defined in the wish list, with the actual case studies available on the corporate intranet. Bingo. We had identified one of our issues.

The requirement which the community had of a case study was a warts and all exposé of what happened, what went wrong and the pitfalls to avoid. It was a classic case of wanting to learn from the mistakes of others rather than replicating the earlier corporate cock-up. No cupboard should be opened without the skeletons inside examined with the enthusiasm of a forensic scientist let loose in a pathology lab for the first time. But when we looked at the available case studies of projects past and approaches of yesteryear, what we saw was not an honest analysis of the routes taken, dead ends followed and errors made which could have been avoided. What was available was part of the celebration. Mountains had been moved and overwhelming odds battled. Thanks were given and everyone basked – ever so slightly smugly – in the reflected glory of the team's achievement.

And the reasons why these case studies were overwhelmingly positive? The performance management system in this organization had everyone running around in the final few weeks of the financial year, desperate to ensure achievement of year end goals before the managerial judgement of success or failure is made. Reports will be filed, evidence presented, targets checked off in time to ensure bonus payments and the chance for advancement. By default, the very information regarded as an essential spark of the community of practice was extinguished by the performance management process.

Is there a way for the performance management system to be focused on generating learning and knowledge sharing rather than celebrating success (and covering up the mistakes)? By establishing a case study framework which addresses the needs of the community of practice, can we set targets for project leaders and implementation teams to complete these frameworks as part of each of their deliverables? Can we create a new vision for success which puts reflection and learning as a central part of what 'good' looks like?

I think we can, but it might mean a significant culture shift. Changing organizational opinion about what constitutes success and what is involved in project reviews will need all kinds of reassurance to those individuals who – for the first few times – may feel somewhat exposed when disclosing their mistakes so publicly.

Building organizational memory

Wheel reinvention has another root within the corporate drive for performance. In recent years, innovation and creativity has been valued above all else in organizations. The schlock of the new is often the basis for the failure to revisit what happened in the past, what can be learned and what can be built upon. Asked to innovate, the average corporate creature seeks to invent from the ground up. 'Obviously,' they will say, 'if there were ways of doing things in the past which were good or could be learned from, the organization wouldn't be so demanding of my creativity now. I must invent new ways of doing things badly. The old cock-ups simply won't do!'

It doesn't need to be like this. One of the lessons to be gained from project management approaches is the Post-Implementation Review (PIR). I am sufficiently cynical and experienced to know that these are rarely done well. It is uncommon for the PIR to be properly re-sourced. As a result, the in-depth analysis of what happened, how and why is undertaken in a rush. Usually, in larger organizations, the project team has been disbanded and moved on to pastures new in any event. The opportunity for reflection is another box-ticking exercise to say we've done it and abided by our PRINCE 2 project management principles.

CASE STUDY

There are models of good practice in the PIRs which I have seen carried out properly. At Shell in the late 80s and early 90s specialist knowledge managers would conduct these reviews, carrying out group interviews via new-fangled virtual meetings. The role of the knowledge manager was to contextualize the data which he or she found and catalogue the various experiences – which may have been markedly different depending on the stages of the project or locations of the project team – in order to draw some lessons for the future. The next stage was to detail the conclusions drawn and disseminate this information.

By the first years of the 21st century this process of contextualization, conclusion drawing and dissemination had been transferred to wikis. These in-company encyclopaedias were capable of being created by project teams, used for real-time record keeping and information sharing – everything from plans to meeting agendas – and finally for the capturing of learning from the project experience. The challenges of ensuring people in the project teams used the wikis and consulted the information there were addressed by a powerful advocacy of the wikis across the business. Not in a big bang, but through personal discussions by the knowledge managers. By the time the wikis were actually launched in the business, they already had 6,000 users and many high-profile entries from senior staff who were well known and respected across the organization.

As well as the quality of the material available, knowledge managers created useful tools such as 'How to Create Your First Wiki' and 'Basic Wiki Skills' – using more traditional e-learning modules to bridge the gap between interest and practice. Prizes are awarded in categories such as 'most links', 'most page impressions' etc. In other words, the public celebration of success is refocused on reflection, sharing and collaborative learning. This process enables the wikis to grow and grow – by the end of 2007 the Shell version of Wikipedia was receiving over 5,000 views per day from 17,500 active users.[4]

Creating the platform and enabling people to use it is only the first stage of the process. In the Shell experience, the number of articles and different wiki pages soon grew to a potentially unmanageable size. The role of the knowledge management and learning teams (which are practically one and the same thing) is to support use of the available information. This includes glossaries for specialist terminology and tagging of entries to ensure rapid and effective search. Effectively, the knowledge managers have taken on the role of librarian – helping the uninitiated or the novice find their way around the relatively high-level technical information.

It is not uncommon amongst users of Web 2.0 tools for the person who tries to organize the material generated to be referred to as a curator. This is another example of using a more attractive but misleading title for a role. Curator sounds sexier and more creative than librarian, doesn't it? The fact is that the job of a curator is to make choices, to exercise their judgement to display some things rather than others and to do so in a way which provides depth and aids interpretation. This would suggest an editorial role in the world of user-generated content. However, this editorial role would seem to fly in the face of the basic tenets of those who applaud the use of social media and other Web 2.0 tools in learning and development. All contributions are valid, all comments valuable. But if that's the case, the person making it easier to navigate and find information is not a curator. He or she is a librarian. A perfectly good word to describe the activities involved and an honourable profession on which to model the skills required. But not that sexy. Language matters.

The combination of project logs and technical information found in the Shell wikis is not of interest to all. To contextualize the number of active users (over 17,500) we should recognize that the system is available to all employees as well as some external suppliers/partners. Shell worldwide employs over 90,000 people. In other words, only around one-sixth of the total workforce regularly uses the wiki. Now, I think this is a remarkable number, highly demonstrative of the value of such a platform and the desire of individuals to share their knowledge and keep themselves updated. But let's not run away with the idea that the wiki and user-generated content is the answer for everyone who needs to keep themselves up to speed with progress, innovations and practices across the business.

Situated learning and the corporate intranet

This is a form of what Lave and Wenger called 'situated learning' in their publication of 1991 – *Situated Learning: Legitimate Peripheral*

Participation.[5] Simply, situated learning takes place in the same context as that in which it is applied. This is most often 'learning on the job' but in distributed teams of specialists – like those found working for Shell at the forefront of oil and gas exploration – the context for the learning may be computer-supported collaboration over time and distance. Networks and intranets and continuous connections have become an essential part of the day-to-day world of the knowledge worker. The context in which they apply their skills and knowledge is online. The wiki and the blog and collaboration room in cyberspace is not an adjunct to their workplace, it is their workplace. For them situated learning takes place online and becomes a continuous process of referencing and updating.

For others and for those who are new to this world, yet more stuff on the corporate intranet only works if you're really interested in the subject and have more than a layperson's level of understanding in the first place. We can choose to be both fluffy and zeitgeist-y and misapply the term 'social learning' or we can recognize that this is simply a relocation online of an established face-to-face process, such as situated learning. Whatever nomenclature we use, most online information sharing is actually a remote yet public conversation between the knowledgeable, occasionally interrupted from the sidelines by those with something to sell.

Where it works, it will work for those with a relatively high standard of prior knowledge and learning and will work best when those looking up information are also actively contributing their own insights, experiences and ideas. It will be most enduring when it is organized by someone who recognizes the potential learning benefit of the resources which are being created. As a source of information for those undertaking training using more traditional methods, such information sharing will be a useful support, providing up-to-date information, building confidence and encouraging reflection.

Although this is technology and apparently similar to the online social interaction so common amongst the younger members of staff, this is not a job to be given to the 22-year-old intern. Without significant experience of the organization's work, the challenges faced and the barriers to effectiveness and efficiency, establishing the platform and organizing the information and analysis which lives there is going to be impossible. The crucial difference between the knowledge management platforms which are used and those which are ignored is only occasionally the content. I can make this assertion because the records of use are available and what becomes clear as soon as even the most cursory of investigation is undertaken is that people are not rejecting the content – because they are never even looking at it! Often what they are rejecting in these collaboration platforms is the difficulty of getting on to the system – unnecessary passwords and the like – and their inability to find what they want when they get there within the limited time they have available in already stretched workplaces.

Once again, think about the online resources which you use – where you get your online news, which shopping sites you use, and your search engine of choice. The chances are there will be three key features which enable you to use them quickly and efficiently:

a it is easy to get on the site – security is fit for purpose and you don't need to enter your password 23 times;

b navigation is intuitive and finding your way around the site is simple; and

c the front page regularly changes with news updates which can be personalized to match your own interests.

There is one other factor which influences our use of particular websites – necessity. The website I use for internet banking is not the simplest to use. The security required – now with added card reader gizmos – takes time. However, if I want to use my bank account online – which is significantly more convenient than posting cheques or visiting the branch – then I am prepared to tolerate the elements of this site which are decidedly not user friendly. These same rules rarely apply to your wiki or knowledge management site. For those workers who will benefit from an online repository of resources gained from experience across the organization, it should be simple to get onto – the Shell wiki is not password protected once you are on the Shell intranet; it should be obvious how you get to information which should be launched from your regularly updated and personalized home page. If there are sources of information or activities which can only be performed from within the system, ie it is essential to use the site, then so much the better.

There is yet another challenge in the usefulness of the information provided. As I outlined in Chapter 2, experienced performers – ie the ones we would want to contribute to our resource bank – are often not very good at describing why what they do works. The analytical ability is often rare and occasionally clouded by the need to celebrate success as we have seen. This is another role for our knowledge manager and one which may justify the use of the title 'curator'. It is not enough simply to manage the information which has been created – which will most often have been created for one purpose and isn't always fit for its intended secondary application as a tool for learning and knowledge sharing. If left to some specialists, materials created only for knowledge sharing will represent an opportunity for them to teach everyone everything – regardless of the level of learning actually required or capable of being undertaken.

This requires a new role in many L&D teams. This role may be called knowledge manager, curator or moderator. Whatever name chosen, this person needs to do three things:

a acquire content from those with subject matter knowledge, project experience or involvement in innovative ways of working;

b assess the content and apply a level of analysis with the content supplier. This is an iterative process in conjunction with the individuals involved, not an editorial process; and

c make the content available and easily found – tagged appropriately so it appears on search engines, properly indexed and in an appropriate format.

This final activity also involves the knowledge manager in widening awareness about what is available and using internal communications and marketing activities to raise awareness and encourage access. Some of this can be done, like the Shell wiki, by simply ensuring that certain role-critical information – such as meeting times and agendas – are only available from the wiki or resource repository. Other techniques include direct mail shots, subscriber e-mails and information to be included as signposts in other training. The most effective way of advocating the use of this material is as part of the pre-workshop activity and post-workshop follow-up outlined in previous chapters. It's important that this information is built into training programmes and that participants are first of all enabled to use it and subsequently required to do so. Of course, it's a given that when our learners have made the effort to consult this information, the resulting case studies are based on the warts and all exposés which people want and need if they are to learn through the experience – and mistakes – of others.

The provision of resources online won't suit all workers. Those on the shop floor without daily or at least all day access to a connected computer terminal will not be able to use these systems as a route to learning from past experience. But learning from experience, replicating successes and avoiding past errors, is a vital component in the learning process. It is especially powerful if the people who were involved in the earlier experience are available to share what they have learned.

Quality circles and role models

In the latter part of the 20th century, quality circles were a significant part of the drive for Total Quality Management and Kaizen. These concepts, borrowed from the super successful Japanese manufacturing systems of the 1970s were in part an attempt to play catch-up by manufacturers in the rest of the world, but also a recognition that while things were done right, they weren't done right often enough in many organizations.

The quality circle was a combination of situated learning – ie learning done in the context in which it would be applied, for the most part the shop floor – and action learning, specific projects which are undertaken within a work place for the purpose of learning and training. Groups of co-workers would be presented with a problem – or would ask for time to resolve a problem – and be given regular space and time away from day-to-day production schedules – to work out possible solutions, create prototypes and design a replicable resolution to the situation faced.

The 'replicability' of the solution was important. Those involved in the quality circle were also tasked with sharing the answers they had arrived at with other teams undertaking similar work. This included face-to-face meetings and demonstrations. The background to the issue was outlined, the options explored and the rationale for the final choice explained as well as a step-by-step guide to the new process or practice.

Quality circles – along with TQM – seem to have dropped off the agenda in recent years. I haven't seen them mentioned seriously for a decade or more but I think they present an interesting model for workplace learning and knowledge sharing. Have you ever walked past a high street store and seen that they are closed for staff training until 9.30 am on Tuesday? Ever wondered what goes on? I suspect it is simply a communications exercise rather than anything more significant, but imagine how you could use one hour a week to share knowledge and ways of doing things between colleagues. How good would it be if the people delivering those sessions were people just like your team but from a different site, a different team or from a different part of the factory? Would that count as knowledge management? Certainly it would be situated learning and all the more powerful for it. Sometimes we need to get away from the platforms, the networks and the design of the interface and look at what we really want to happen to enable people to share what they know and what they have discovered.

In the quality circle model, those who led the quality circles – who were rarely the official team leaders – became role models for others. The essential profile of a role model is somewhat different from those presented to us in organizations. It's not necessarily the individual with the best figures. The chances are the performance management and reward system will have skewed the collection and presentation of simple target achievement in any case.

While working with a relatively small company, I was introduced to their top performer. He had smashed his targets by at least 100 per cent for each of the past three years. The company clearly thought a lot of him – almost as much as he thought of himself. I asked how he had managed to be so successful. There was no analysis. It was apparently a God-given capability which no one else could possibly replicate. He was just so much better than his colleagues. I pointed out that if he couldn't outline how he'd managed to achieve his phenomenal success either he'd just got lucky, the targets had been set too low, or a combination of both. The silence was deafening.

The role model we want to encourage is not only aware of how they do what they do, but why it works. They need to be able to explain the interplay between the knowledge acquired over a period, the skills developed and their ability to manage their workload. This last seems an odd inclusion in the requirements but there are a couple of good reasons why it is there. Whenever you listen to sports commentary, you will hear top players described as having 'so much time'. This skill seems not to be confined to those on the football field, cricket pitch or basketball court. The top performers we wish to encourage do seem to have more hours in the day – including time to achieve, time to reflect and time to share their knowledge. As they are good at managing their workload – or perhaps because they see their role in knowledge management as intrinsically one of their responsibilities – they make the space and time to work with others.

Some role models, of course, don't need to do anything to be role models. They simply do what they are doing and people are able to observe the steps they take and the behaviours they exhibit. However, the most effective are also able to talk intelligently and analytically about what they are doing. They can break each task down for a relative novice. Walking the walk is one thing, but it is so much more powerful if you can talk it as well.

Not all the experienced people in our organizations can act as role models. Some of them seem to stop learning at key points in their career. For some, the knowledge, skills and behaviours which served them well in their ascent in the organization may now be out of date.

The Knower's Arc

When we start out on our journey in an organization we learn ferociously. We are embroiled in daily discovery of new ideas, concepts and practices. We hunger for new experiences and projects which allow us to implement these half-understood approaches to our work and refine our own ideas in that cauldron of creativity.

Over time, we become the learned – acknowledged experts in our domain and in our field. We become the person to whom others turn when stuck or nonplussed. After a while our expertise is recognized in the corporate world and we move up the hierarchy – from doer we become manager, from executionally engaged to executive.

That can be when we stop learning. From being a learner we become a knower. We can represent this trajectory in knowledge and skill acquisition through what I call the Knower's Arc. (See what I did there?)

FIGURE 7.2   The Knower's Arc

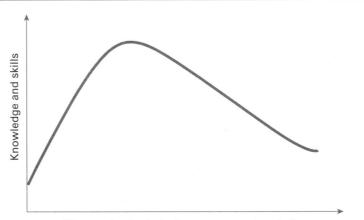

As the potential specialist begins their career, they already have some understanding and knowledge of the field – an indication that they might be quite good at something. The link between being accomplished and being interested is, I think, pretty universal. Are you good at something you like or do you like something you're good at? The answer to that question is almost immaterial. The link between ability and enjoyment is what's important. Through self-motivated exploration, the specialist will already have developed some talent and built their understanding before committing themselves to learning as much as possible.

Then there is sharp ascent of the knowledge and skills ladder (see Figure 7.2). During this time they become extremely skilled, keeping up to date with the latest techniques and through a synthesis of what they have learned with their own take on the subject, creating new and unique approaches all of their own.

Eventually they are promoted into a new role – perhaps managing a team. For the early stages of this role they will continue to be hands on but inevitably their new responsibilities compromise their ability to keep up to date. New technologies are available and others will have built on their own advances.

Once our specialist has become a fully-fledged knower they may stop learning quite as much or quite as quickly. Their executive responsibilities may have reduced their time for learning and their time for maintaining their skills. At this point they actually start going backwards – their skill set is no longer up to date. In some industries – such as software design – this process may be really quite rapid as young industries tend to promote people more quickly and the development of technology advances at a mind-blowing pace.

There is, however, a major disconnect. Our specialist is expected to know everything – that's why they're in that position. But they simply don't have time to keep up. The process of bridging this gap is problematic. As an expert and potential role model for others, how do I admit my own lack of understanding, running the risk of undermining my status within the organization? How does my organization resource and support me to keep constantly up to speed? How do I maintain my skills, honed over many hours of trial and error and working with the tools of my trade?

Imagine if we were talking about an athlete. Imagine I am the best bobsleigh driver in the world. I am so good that others flock to my training camp to learn alongside me. In providing the benefit of my experience around the world's tracks I have less and less time for my own training. First, I reduce my involvement with the manufacturers of state-of-the-art bobsleigh equipment. I don't have the time to work with them on reducing drag and increasing the efficiency of the steering and braking mechanisms. Then I reduce the time I spend in the gym; my fitness starts to decline a little. Eventually, I am so busy organizing the training of others I only get on to the ice a couple of times a week, then once a month, then whole weeks go by and I haven't sat in a bobsleigh. To be honest, with the weight I've put on I might not even fit in it anymore. The Winter Olympics come round again. How well do I perform?

In sports, this would be ridiculous. The top performers continue to hone their skills and train hard. World-famous South African golfer Gary Player was once described as 'lucky'. His oft quoted response, 'The more I practise, the luckier I get',[6] seems to sum up the idea of maintaining peak performance through hard work and continuous focus on the fundamentals.

In business, this is common place. I am indebted to insights provided by Dr Matthew Lieberman,[7] Professor of Psychology, Psychiatry and Biobehavioral Sciences at the University of California, Los Angeles. He is Director of the UCLA Social Cognitive Neuroscience laboratory and he recounts this illustrative story in a blog on the *Psychology Today* website:

> Consider Amber, an animator at Pixar. She came right out of college, having studied computer programming and graphic arts back in the 1990s. She spent the first two years at Pixar apprenticing under one of the top animators. Then she got her sea legs and started to really excel in her work. She's rapidly acquired new techniques and integrated them in innovative ways that others hadn't seen before. Within a decade she was managing her own division and is now herself one of the top dogs. As manager, Amber has implemented a program for the top experts to teach the new animation techniques to the crew in monthly training sessions.
>
> Amber has risen to a level of prominence where she is responsible for the team's overall vision, but she doesn't actually do animation day-to-day anymore. In the last few years, there have been rapid advances in animation methods and Amber hasn't had the time to learn about them. So the big question is whether Amber goes to these training sessions and asks questions, in front of her employees, that will reveal that she no longer is up on the latest techniques. The stronger her identity is as an expert, the harder it will be to put that identity aside to become a learner again.

The first step in combating the Knower's Arc is to acknowledge its existence. Thereafter, smart L&D teams check in with the experts around the organization and work with them to plan their updating. A process of Continuing Professional Development (CPD), similar to that used by licensed professionals such as doctors, lawyers and teachers, might be required – requiring our organization's human knowledge resources to spend a minimum amount of time on learning and developing. This might need to be done privately in order to retain face and the mystery required by many organizational experts. (Let's be honest, having a conversation with a junior member of staff which finishes with them saying, 'How on earth do you know all this stuff?' is a fantastic ego-boost.) That said, the organization which appropriately encourages openness amongst its whole team about their learning needs, is often led by people who themselves admit to not knowing and publicly embrace learning opportunities. Role modelling is more than functional expertise – it is essential that senior people model a hunger to learn if we are to engender a learning culture throughout the organization.

CASE STUDY

When Tom Farmer set up tyre and exhaust business Kwik Fit, he insisted that everyone in head office – from executives to administrative assistants – spent two weeks every year working in a service centre, changing tyres and brake pads alongside their front-line colleagues. Not only was this a great insight into the real world of the customer-facing teams, it also ensured that those who had progressed from shop floor to executive floor kept their skills up. I can imagine that those same individuals spent a couple of hours a night in their home garage before their two-week assignment changing the odd tyre and tinkering with the car – so as not to be embarrassed. Avoiding embarrassment can be a great spur to learning and the Complete Trainer isn't too precious about using such low cunning.

Towards wisdom management

However you choose to ensure that role models are available and visible, if informal learning is to aspire to be more than an ad hoc and barely organized exchange of ideas amongst those in the know, then some formal management of these so-called informal processes is required. The idea of knowledge management in organizations is usually a conversation between the converted – big dogs sniffing each other in ever decreasing circles. What's actually needed is a process of engaging with people and jointly working out how something can be achieved based on our past experience. It needs to go beyond the celebration of success. It needs to progress even beyond the raw data of what really happened (warts and all) and move towards an analysis of how the lessons can be applied. In Chapter 1, I advocated that we should drop the term knowledge management and replace it with wisdom management. This requires an understanding that people need knowledge to lesser or greater depths depending on circumstances and planned application. Do I need to be aware of something or do I need a greater level of detail to enable me to make decisions or approve the decisions of others? Can I navigate my way around the corporate memory banks, even if I don't know what I don't know?

Ideally, wisdom management will be self-perpetuating. Not only will it deliver to individuals the information and guidance at the appropriate level of detail, it will do so in a timely way and in a format which is suited to the purpose. By creating simple opportunities for users to contribute, it should enable the enthused and encouraged to learn more. This process catalogues the organization's collected wisdom, ideally in a way that creates additional interest and supports the newly intrigued in finding those things they didn't know they didn't know.

Life cycle tips

The new recruit

From a knowledge management perspective you should expect inductees to be net users of the information which the current employees have amassed. However, there is an interesting opportunity here. A kind of video diary of the inductee's first weeks and months in the organization can – in the hands of a skilled knowledge manager – generate a number of short insights which may be of use to future inductees, or even those yet to be recruited. It is also an alternative to the reflective log I advocated in Chapter 5 which may seem less arduous than writing a report, however brief.

Pairing inductees with positive role models (as buddies or mentors) is a useful tactic in the first few weeks. But make sure these role models are modelling appropriate behaviour across the whole range of your competency framework – including the skills to learn, keep updated and share their knowledge outlined here. Breeding positive behaviours takes time but is well worth the effort.

The new manager

The same techniques outlined for the new starter, above, are equally applicable to our new managers. One extra reflective process which helps with the knowledge management piece is for their new team members to be engaged also in reflecting on what worked and what needs extra attention. Care needs to be taken that this doesn't become an opportunity for the over-looked to have a good whinge, but in my experience, when given the opportunity to express a view about the performance of a new manager, team members are often extremely supportive and constructive in their comments.

When collected together, the insights from team members become a knowledge management resource in those areas where there are specific trends identified. For example, team members from across the organization may comment favourably about new team leaders who implement regular team meetings – that's a useful area for further investigation and new managers whose team meetings are particularly highly rated by their direct reports should be interviewed and asked what they do (information); how they do it (knowledge); and why it works (analysis).

A similar approach can be used for those regularly cited examples of less effective new manager behaviour, but obviously this needs to be handled from a knowledge management perspective with care. Interviewing someone about why they are rubbish at something always needs tact and discretion. Despite the inherent difficulty and for fear of seeming impolite, this should still be done and understood. In most organizations the errors which appear as trends are rarely individual mistakes but system failings or issues with the underlying culture.

The specialist

The specialist often has the most interaction with our knowledge management processes and systems; after all they have the knowledge to start with. It is vitally important to do two things:

1 Ask for their input to a specific brief. In the move towards wisdom management, we need to discourage the subject matter expert from simply downloading their enormous brain for the rest of the business. Over-supply of information on a subject is as bad as, if not worse than, too little. Be specific about the particular chunks of information required by each audience and involve the specialist in the modularization process – breaking their knowledge down into appropriate chunks to be understandable and usable by the uninitiated.

2 Ensure that your specialist interacts with the users of their expertise. Part of the process of choosing the right tone of voice and style, the right medium and the appropriate volume of information provided is to understand in as much detail as possible who the recipients of the information are and their needs.

Specialists can fall foul of the belief that they are doing everyone a favour by providing their information. In fact, the more useful attitude is that everyone else is doing the specialist the favour by accessing the information and developing their behaviour based on the principles communicated. It is an enormous privilege for a specialist to increase their impact and influence in the organization through effective dissemination of their experience and learning. Make that clear during your interactions with them.

From a learning perspective, the specialist should be in contact with other specialists in the field. Through such communities of practice the future organization may be shaped as issues are addressed, innovations adopted and opportunities identified. Ensure that each such community of practice is open only to those who are most able to contribute – it should be an honour to be invited to participate. Identify a different role for those who style themselves as experts but actually just want to cherry-pick the ideas of others. Give each community a facilitator. This individual should ensure that the discussions are properly documented and contributions happen in a timely and appropriate fashion. They should also be on the lookout for outputs from these closed and specialist communities which should be shared more widely. At least once a year, each community of practice established within the business should – rather like a project team – produce a report of progress, identifying the issues covered over the year and those under consideration in the next period. This stops the community of practice becoming a directionless talking shop.

The leader

As we saw from the Shell case study, the presence of well-known and influential figures using and contributing to knowledge management tools boosts user numbers. It is also appropriate to have leaders contributing to wikis which allow other, less exalted users to update the information which they have written (rather than a blog which simply allows those other users to add a comment). This is a bold step for many organizations but a leader inviting others to edit and amend information that they enter sends a resounding message across the organization.

Rather like our specialists, a leadership community of practice is also a good idea. Where leadership councils or executive committees only meet monthly or less frequently a community of practice may shape thinking as they address day-to-day strategic challenges within their area of responsibility. This process should also utilize the skills of a facilitator – keeping one eye on the debate and prompting the flow of information, but also keeping their other eye on the needs of the remainder of the organization and enabling wider access to certain wiki entries where this would be beneficial.

Peripheral members of this community of practice, perhaps those at the level one below the senior leadership team, can observe the wiki and use that as part of their learning. Whatever structure is introduced, if the wiki exists only for the benefit of others or as some kind of high-profile commitment to information sharing, it will soon stop being used. The wiki needs to have a benefit to those who use it as part of business as usual. Using it as a tool for sharing management information along with evolving strategy papers, meeting minutes and agendas, will both keep the information on the wiki current and ensure its use. The artefacts thus produced become a model of transparency – for example, one CEO I worked with published his 360-degree feedback results on the senior management wiki as well as his own development action plan. They also represent a unique source of information for those working with individual leaders on their development, whether executive coaches or internal mentors.

The retiree

If you have senior people with many years' experience around the business, the opportunity to use their learning in knowledge management activities is a no brainer. Videos, interviews and war stories generated from these individuals can be an unsurpassable source of information to feed into the organization's memory. However, it is as commentators on the initiatives of others that these individuals can have most impact.

If you have a knowledge management system in your organization – especially some kind of wiki site – the chances are that only the young or the technologically confident are using it. This misses out a whole dimension of the business. Where project reviews are posted onto a site for enterprise-wide consumption, make sure that you specifically invite additional commentary from those older heads in the business. It is difficult for anyone to work from a blank sheet; even one entitled 'everything I learned while working here'. Where to start? However, the stimulus of recent activities, such as project closure reports, unlocks stories and lessons learned from the past. The connections between current issues and past challenges are often a rich seam of learning.

Where individuals are being prepared for retirement or leaving the business, the creation of a community of practice around the issues faced as one reaches the end of work can also be highly supportive. It also potentially creates a highly motivated group of recent ex-employees who will act as powerful advocates on behalf of the organization.

What gets measured gets done

> *He uses statistics as a drunken man uses lamp posts – for support rather than illumination.*
>
> **ANDREW LANG, SCOTTISH POET, CRITIC, ANTHROPOLOGIST AND HISTORIAN, 1844–1912**

How do you calculate the benefits of training? In modern organizations there is tremendous pressure to ensure everything can be monitored and expressed in financial terms. It is an understandable pressure. A 2009 study by UK recruitment consultancy, Robert Half, found that 51 per cent of CEOs of top companies now had an accountancy qualification and background. We all work in finance these days. The trouble is that international accounting principles – used to ensure one business's results are comparable to another – treats training spend as a cost rather than an investment. Making the case for training *investment* is rather tricky when in the minds of those holding the purse strings we are actually asking for additional *cost* to be incurred.

Whether you choose to put forward a return on investment calculation (ROI) or a cost–benefit analysis, the fact is that the resources required for training need to be secured over the long term if effective training is to take place. Within the training industry, we may have been our own worst enemies in this regard. Wherever you turn – whether to vendors or to case studies of award-winning training programmes – benefits are rarely quantified and in the absence of figures linking training interventions to quantified performance improvements, the arguments put forward are centred on cost savings.

Return on investment: quality vs cost saving

I am well aware that training needs to be conducted in ways which are cost effective and I am also well aware that there is always more than one way to do something. However, as soon as the only financial argument which can be made relates to cost savings, we are in danger of killing attempts at innovation and improving quality. Instead of doing new things or doing things better we have become an industry content to do the same things cheaper.

A classic example of this was in the early days of e-learning adoption. A case study put forward to a congressional committee of the US government made the case for an increased investment in infrastructure which could support e-learning (this was before universal broadband was available). The argument showed how a company was rolling out a series of new contact centres. Under the traditional route of face-to-face systems training along with compliance training to ensure adherence to financial services regulations, it had taken a year to ensure that new centres were running at full capacity with qualified and competent employees. Under the new system, which made significant use of e-learning, the timescale had been reduced to three months. Nine-twelfths of the annual profit from one of these centres was in the region of $2 million, and yet the bill for the e-learning programme was only $250,000. The ROI was proudly shown as 800 per cent and conferences were regaled with tales of how one company had 'gotten a return of $1.75 million from one e-learning programme'. Can you see the problem?

What was the initial training programme like? Why did it take a year to achieve the required level of competence? What else could have been done to improve the more traditional approach? What about the performance of the individuals – is that not also significant? Did the teams in the centres using a traditional approach perform better than those trained online? The question that wasn't asked is the one we might not want to consider. What happens if you don't do any training at all? Could you, conceivably, receive an ROI of the full $2 million?

Some studies do look at results and quality. In his book *Designing World Class e-Learning*,[1] Roger Schank tells the story of a US financial services company that introduced a new Customer Relationship Management system. As chance would have it one group of new hires were recruited in time for the e-learning to be used while the group recruited before the e-learning was available for use could only learn the new system by attending a classroom course and 'sitting by Nellie' – learning from experienced operators and system super-users who talked them through all of the enhanced functionality. The results showed a 40 per cent improvement in performance in terms of reduced re-works and referrals to sales advisers for those trained using the e-learning method. Similarly, experienced staff who had been trained how to carry out their existing responsibilities using the new technology in a training environment were 25 per cent more likely to make mistakes and 25 per cent less likely to refer clients to the sales team. This measure of added value is worth infinitely more than the spurious measurements showing time reduced and hotel bills saved used by many e-learning vendors to justify their bills. This is based on whether anyone changed their behaviour and improved their performance. Isn't this what we are all about?

CASE STUDY

A few years ago I was asked to revise a new sales person training programme for the UK retailers of Peugeot. The original programme was a two-week residential event available to all new dealership staff for free. The franchise companies, who sent their new recruits along, simply had to meet accommodation and travel costs. The programme I was involved in designing started with a detailed research process which looked at the modern car buying cycle in the age of the internet. We found the existing programme some distance away from being fit for purpose and so we weren't simply changing the delivery mechanisms used, but revolutionizing much of the content.

The revised programme included two residential training sessions of three days and two days. In between these two sessions, participants were required to complete a series of online modules, each of which was completed by work-based tasks supervised by the sales manager or a more experienced member of the sales team. Access to the second residential programme was contingent on having completed the e-learning and the work-based tasks – a process which took around four weeks. During the two days of this second classroom workshop, learners tried out their new-found selling skills with customers played by professional actors. These interactions were staged in a mocked-up sales area and each was filmed to support subsequent feedback. Because of the reduction in training time and accommodation costs, the overall programme was certainly cheaper to deliver than the one it replaced and because of the reduced classroom time, the costs of the redesign and redevelopment were realized within 12 months.

But the brief to me, and the team with whom I worked on the project, was not simply to reduce costs. We were asked to improve the outcomes from the training. The fact that we decided a chunk of this work should happen on the job was not driven by cost reduction but by improved effectiveness. One year after the roll out of the programme, we took the performance statistics for those trained in October to December using the old training programme and those trained from January to March using the new materials. The revised programme was implemented from 1st January and the numbers of participants roughly equivalent. Within the intervening period, the models of car were the same, promotional campaigns the same, market conditions were the same and the marketing in the press and advertising on TV were the same. Any change in average performance between the two distinct groups of new sales people can be confidently explained by the differences between the two initial training programmes. One year later, average performance against the key indicators was between 20 per cent and 40 per cent better for those on the revised programme. The indicators chosen were the metrics already used to monitor sales person effectiveness and used to calculate commissions and bonuses for those who delivered the best performances. Unit sales, conversion rates and unit profits were the measures that mattered to Peugeot, to the dealer principals and to the individual sales people. Those were the metrics we looked at.

Measuring impact – control groups

If we are converting a programme from one intervention to another and we want to prove the effectiveness of that change, only a control group and some kind of comparison of results between those trained in one way and those trained differently, will do. By using the metrics which already matter to the organization – customer service scores, mystery shopper feedback, sales, and the wide range of results that organizations use to check if they are on track compared to previous years' performances – the training team can at least check that one training route has had an impact on organizational performance when compared to an alternative delivery mechanism.

Unless we focus on the metrics which the organization considers important, justifying training spend can be highly subjective. Basing success on participant feedback or even success rates in test scores is not usually of significance to anyone outside the training team. In truth most organizations don't bother even with this level of cost justification. For them, the challenge of calculating all the myriad costs of different training approaches is simply not worth it. Besides, who is interested in the real costs? The training department are only really concerned with their own outlay; the costs of venues, trainers, e-learning programmes, perhaps the costs of maintaining servers to host them, and the overheads of their team. The participant costs – from expenses and wages to opportunity costs and lost production – are mostly met by the different functions in the business. What's more, many training departments actually cross-charge their services to those functions – thereby placing all the costs on the employing departments and on occasions even making a paper profit. When reworking an existing training programme, very often what appears as cost saving is merely a cost reallocation.

Thinking in silos is not the preserve of the training team. I was once working with a group of project managers and we started to talk about the cost reductions of using technology. I was telling them about an instance in which I had produced an online training programme which paid for itself inside six months simply through reducing the print budget for the workbooks which it replaced. I was interrupted. 'We did something like that,' said one of the project managers. 'We saved £20,000 per year by issuing our quarterly newsletter to all staff via a pdf attached to an e-mail rather than printing it out and distributing it via a desk drop.' We all nodded our approval. Our point was proven. 'The trouble is,' he continued, 'we hadn't factored in the £100,000 increased spending on colour printer cartridges across the organization. This was mostly explained by everyone printing out the four-page, full-colour newsletter!'

We reeled for a moment as we took in this information. 'So, I suppose you are sending it out as hard copy again now,' someone said. 'Oh, no,' came the reply. 'My departmental budget pays for the external print costs, but we don't pay for the printer cartridges. I'm still saving twenty grand a year!'

When starting a new programme to meet a recently discovered competence gap, the comparative costs of 'the way we did it before' are not available. Similarly, prior to the investment, there are no results which can be measured, even if it were possible for control groups to be set up and outcomes compared. What exists, for the most part, is a series of input costs from previous programmes. This is a really slippery slope. The tendency is to focus on repeating the past, but for less money, rather than doing something new. What's more, the way the L&D team talked about last year's activities seemed like a great success. If the L&D team are hoist by the petard of claims made in the past, the enthusiasm of the FD for additional spending on innovation may be dampened. If it was OK last year, why do we need to significantly increase spending this year?

But not to worry. The spend on training is at least perceived as a necessary evil by those in control of budgets. To underline and attempt to quantify the nebulous benefits of training being 'a good thing' some commentators have attempted to link training spend to organization value. In a number of studies – most significantly one by the American Society for Training and Development in 2000 – the share prices, shareholder yields and other financial indicators of success from a range of private businesses were compared with the available details of their training spends.[2] Those firms which spent most on training were in the upper quartile for most business success measures – from profitability, earnings per share, share price and revenue growth. What do we learn from this? Those companies with more disposable income use more of it on training and development. Hallelujah! The direct link between organizational performance on the basis of published and significant business metrics and the quality of the training provided for the increased investment is hardly demonstrated by such numbers. Of course there may be a cause and effect between these two disparate statistical sets. But it is equally likely that there isn't. What about marketing spend? R&D spend? Production efficiency? Unsurprisingly, other departments would also want to claim some of the corporate credit for these upturns in fiscal fortunes.

Credit where it's due – but where's that?

This is often an issue with training programmes which claim business benefit. Bluntly, the other departments will be competing for the plaudits and consider the linkages drawn between the presence of training programmes and organizational success to be attempts to steal their limelight. If we want to prove the benefits of what we do, another way is required.

Donald Kirkpatrick, Professor Emeritus at the University of Wisconsin, articulated the most widely used evaluative model for workplace training in 1959,[3] although his seminal work on evaluation wasn't published or widely adopted until the mid-1990s. He defined four levels of evaluation which were added to by Dr Jack Phillips of the ROI Institute in 2005.[4]

FIGURE 8.1   Five levels of evaluation: after Kirkpatrick and Phillips

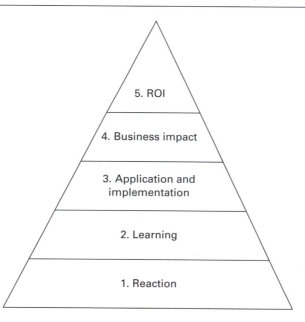

The five levels of evaluation start from assessing the reaction level from those directly affected by the training programme. This may be from learners and, occasionally from their managers. Subject matter experts may also have a role to play here in commenting on the

programme's design. Commonly this is as far as evaluation goes – the much used and abused 'happy sheets'. As workshop participants are running for the train or trying to beat the rush hour traffic, we thrust a form in front of them and ask them to tick a series of scales asking for their opinion about the trainer, the course and the catering. In some cases they can circle happy or sad faces on the form – doesn't do to get all formal and use numbers after all. Unless they've had an absolutely miserable time, such feedback is barely worth the environmental impact of cutting down the required trees. If the programme is roundly condemned, then it may indicate that something needs to change, although rarely what. Most of the time when poor feedback has been received the problem falls into one of two areas (or possibly both).

1 the trainer was ineffective. Either they didn't know the subject or struggled to explain it and relied on a series of pretty dull presentations which added confusion rather than clarity; and/or

2 the wrong people were on the course. Either the audience doesn't see the need for the programme or participants' prior knowledge and understanding has not been factored into the design. This generally results in the trainer assuming that they know nothing or know more than they actually do and there is an inevitable mismatch of expectations.

At the end of totalling up the number of smiling faces your programme has been awarded, you may choose to include that data in your cost justification arguments, but in reality it won't play very well. Certainly, the enjoyment of the experience is not linked in any significant way with whether your programme participants can and will do things differently or do different things. In many organizations, this is where programme evaluation ends.

The second level of the evaluation model concerns itself with learning. Through any number of assessment mechanisms we can understand whether the participants know and understand something and can use these skills to a required standard. From end-of-course tests for checking out knowledge to observed role plays and on-the-job assessments, there should always be some measure – for both trainer and trainee – of progress made. Ideally, these checks will mirror a testing regime which precedes the training – so that not only can capability be monitored, but there is an individual benchmark which demonstrates added value – *additional* competence rather than simply competence.

If this competence improvement can be monitored in the workplace, then you may well have been able to move to level 3 and the measurement of implementation and application of the learning. Here, unquestionably, you will require the support of line managers – both to create opportunities for the learning to be applied, and to support the measurement and ongoing feedback which will build on-the-job competence. Without this embedding and reinforcement, the transition to level 4 is all but impossible. Observed and confirmed line manager involvement is a useful performance indicator. Performance indicators are misunderstood, I think. The clue is in the vocabulary. They are *indicators* of performance, *not* performance. A good way to think about performance indicators is to consider what happens in their absence. So, in this case, if a manager is not scheduling activities in a way which creates opportunities for the newly trained to apply what they have learned, then we can be safe in our assumption that nothing will change and the investment will come to nought. But even if we observe that managers are supporting the learning process, we can't be sure that what is happening in the workplace is any good.

For this assurance we need to advance to level 4 – the impact of each trained individual on the performance results of his or her team. As I have mentioned before, usually the only measures which matter in an organization are:

- quality – things being done better; fewer re-works and better scores on other quality measures routinely used in the business;

- quantity – more from less; greater efficiency meaning that more things are achieved without an increase in inputs;

- cost – (usually) reduced costs, which may be a combination of quantity (above); and...

- time – the speed with which things are done, usually considered a measure of efficiency.

With all the measures used to check business impact, the numbers of performance indicators used should be already operational in the business. This precaution avoids the situation where we provide training opportunities which are focused on the wrong things. You can very efficiently train people to do things, but that doesn't mean that you've trained people to do the right things. Using business metrics supports your assessment after a programme that you have positively impacted business performance.

Finally, Jack Phillips added the fifth level by advocating a calculation of ROI. This is undertaken by a simple equation, such as this one, which shows the payback from the programme:

$$\frac{\text{Total Programme Benefit} - \text{Total Programme Costs}}{\text{Total Programme Costs}} \times 100\%$$

Imagine you have undertaken a technical operations training programme introducing a mechanism for waste reduction. You have observed the learners in Plant A use the activities which were introduced and practised during the workshop and implemented back on the job with line manager support. The waste reduction in the financial year has reduced materials costs by £100,000 and has also reduced the charges for waste disposal by £50,000. If the total programme (including participant costs, production downtime and all the costs of development and delivery) cost £30,000, you would have an outcome of:

$$\frac{£150,000 - £30,000}{£30,000} \times 100\% = 400\%$$

Simple isn't it? Except that the specialist team of external consultants who designed the waste reduction methodology will also be claiming the credit. The operations director will also be explaining to the board that the increased efficiency and reduced waste was all his or her idea. You may be able to generate the numbers, but that doesn't mean anyone will agree with your interpretation of the training's effectiveness.

However, measuring the ROI of a training programme is technically possible. We can use such a mechanism for calculation and – so long as we have a control group who can act as a benchmark for the measurement of performance improvement – we can use existing business metrics to evaluate the benefit of training to the bottom line. Are you going to do this? Probably not; and if so, you won't be alone. Hardly anyone actually bothers to do this stuff because however well designed the data collection process, the results come from the interplay of departmental strategy, adoption of new work practices and last of all, and usually considered least of all, training.

Supporting the strategy

The competing claims for results mean that taking each project as a separate entity is fraught with measurement challenges. We may need a different approach to justify our existence. I think we need to hook our trailer to the strategy wagon.

Strategy changes or the adjustment of the organization's focus are usually the subject of start of year mass communications. Using a combination of cheerleading and dire warnings, the strategic team communicate the vision, the challenges and the new opportunities to the managers one level down. There's a healthy dose of 'don't screw up' and a fair bit of eye rolling from the audience as last year's targets are increased while budgets freeze.

As each function commits to the board to deliver new programmes and activities, the 'from... to...' PowerPoint slides fly through the ether to teams who must take their share of the heavy lifting to realize the organizational plan. Ideally, these objectives, plans and strategies would be parlayed into the warp and weft of the organization. Team targets would lead to capability maps and capability maps would transform themselves into individual training plans, building the team's capacity to deliver. This should be a chance to work smarter; to link learning to business objectives which in turn deliver value to shareholders, service users or funding bodies.

Theoretically that all makes sense, but in practice? In practice the middle managers don't quite get the strategic vision, and if they do, don't have the time, resources or capability to explain what this all means in operational terms to the poor bloody infantry.

How do you get the managers and team leaders who weren't involved in the inner sanctum of the business planning process to fully understand what's needed and, having done so, to explain the needs to their team members? In many of the organizations that I work with, that's the bit where it all goes somewhat awry. The barriers seem to be three fold:

1 Achieving more from less, or doing different things in a changing environment is tricky. Without real clarity of purpose, real explanation and (be careful, here comes a dirty word) education ... the fact is that many of the people to whom the grand plan has been delegated simply don't get it. Yes, they can parrot the words, they may even be able to describe the key strategic thrusts and priorities, but does that mean they know what everyone should be doing on Tuesday? No, it doesn't.

   Our first challenge is how do we train and educate these important links in the corporate chain? I know one thing for sure: there's anything but clarity in many organizational strategic pronouncements. Read the average outline of future strategy and your eyes will be awash with a torrent of corporate clichés and a tsunami of impenetrable jargon. The stand-up routines of the directors speaking to the massed ranks of employees are littered with meaningless phrases. My particular favourite is 'going forward'. I thought that the future tense expressed the concept of 'it's going to happen in the future' not the need for an extra phrase. Going forward is a meaningless verbal tic. Except it isn't. What it actually denotes and transmits is a person desperately wanting to be seen as thrusting and dynamic but actually not having any clear idea about how or if something's going to work. By its very fatuousness it communicates more than they could ever know.

   In a world of naked emperors, the middle manager pretends not to notice and commits to taking the key messages – whatever they are – back to the front line. As route planning goes, this is a real case of 'if you want to get there, I wouldn't start from here'. Nonetheless, some team leaders and divisional heads do try their utmost to make sense of the corporate demands and break it down so that the people who have to actually do the job might understand the general direction of travel. Trouble is, what this means for the day-to-day work has probably not been worked out, so our teams are building a house without a blueprint. This is our second barrier.

2 In most organizations, there's a disconnect between the front line and the strategists in head office. Some try to understand the reality of what it means to do the job – or did the job themselves a few years ago – but even with real-life experience things change. Things change because the strategy changes and the day-to-day job that Tony the strategy director used to do 15 years ago is a very different one from the role Antonia fulfils today. What's more, one of the reasons it has changed is because Tony changed it. But still, field experience from yesteryear seems to command incredible authority in planning circles.

   The truth is, our modern-day manager of the front line has a series of targets and financial goals to achieve, but no one who set the strategy has explained how it can be achieved, nor indeed if it can be achieved. One of the reasons no one seems to know if it's possible, is the third barrier.

3 The plan which is now being communicated isn't the strategic plan dreamed up over the last few months. In fact, the plans for the current financial year will be at least a year old. In fact, just as last year's plans were being rolled out the strategy for this year moved from being a gleam in some strategist's eye to being a much loved and fussed-over baby. In other words, the plan was created at a time when the conditions on which it was based were speculative. Because of the long, drawn-out planning process, most large organization strategies assume the projections from the previous year's business plan are fact. Any change in those projections – whether negative or positive – are rarely factored into the strategy now being rolled out.

   Well that's how strategic planning has to happen, isn't it? Yes, probably, but if we only have projections for where we'll be when the plan starts, perhaps the world the plan has been drawn up to shape no longer exists?

So what's needed? Well maybe it's an all-new approach to the development of business plans and the strategic planning cycle – and it starts with training and education. The learning and development team should be involved early enough in the planning process (ie before the plan is communicated to everyone else) and should be able to influence the plan by reflecting on the real people capability which the organization possesses. The L&D input should also act as a brake on the more business-speak components of the communications activity. If you've given some good people the job of actually having to help people understand how their role changes to meet the new demands of the organization (and you've given them time to push back where it makes no sense) then you could be onto a winner. The organization will have built a feedback loop with people who really do have an incentive to get it right. Remember, these guys don't do 45 minutes with a 'from... to...' PowerPoint slide. They do six hours locked in a room with the great unconvinced. Everyone who has ever run a training course knows that it's no fun trying to train people to do something which you think can't possibly be achieved while those same people are telling you it can't possibly be achieved! Despite our fervent pleas, messengers are regularly the ones who get shot.

Learning and development teams will also have established a deep understanding of the capacity and capability in the organization. Most internal trainers can outline exactly what understanding and skills the people they work with have and, as a consideration on which to build strategy, that's probably more use than a blind faith that 'in 12 months' time we will have hit all the targets we've only just set'.

This approach requires a bit more planning and a few more people in the loop. You may need to think about bringing some people in who can help you to dissect the skills that your new plans demand and build some tools to help your people gain them. It is of paramount importance that the Learning and Development function in your organization is central to the strategic thrust of the business. Not to include L&D teams in the strategy planning process is to make a clear statement: 'Our strategy is not based on the capability of our people.' Include that in the glossy annual report and see what the market analysts make of it!

One of the reasons L&D teams seem to be excluded from this strategy process is because they usually report through the HR director. Now I am prepared to be surprised, but I've never met an HR director who thought he or she had the same clout on the board as the FD or the chief operating officer. It is most often a senior role in name only, with the real power lying in marketing, sales, production/operations or finance, depending on the business that you're in.

I could call for HR to be taken more seriously but I am a realist. In most companies, if the HR director is on the board, they tend to be a pretty junior member. The power still rests with sales, finance and operations. I don't think we can afford to wait for the HR director to be given equal status. Besides it might never happen. I think we should turn to other models to find our solution.

The performance director

In the sports world, the athletes, swimmers and team members may gain the plaudits, the profile and the pay cheques, but the power, influence and strategic direction is located elsewhere. In each of the different national sporting bodies or successful teams one person oversees the process of spotting and nurturing talent. They do this by painstakingly looking at each individual or team and identifying opportunities to make marginal gains – those small, incremental changes in performance which make the difference between winning and losing. This elite sports training is focused, structured and formal. The required disciplines are available from medical to mental, technical to technological. All this phalanx of support is overseen, in each discipline, by a performance director.

Think about that. What if the head of L&D in your organization was called a performance director? What if a proportion of the available training resources were focused on identifying the next crop of peak performers? What if the elite performers – perhaps the people in our business we might say were strategically important – were in receipt of focused, structured and well-resourced training, where their performance was constantly analysed to spot those opportunities to make marginal gains? What if the training looked at the competition and focused outwards as well as inwards? What if there was competition for these training places and the performance director was the power behind everything which happened?

I think every board which says that their people are their biggest asset – and most of them do – should have a performance director amongst their number. That performance director should be at the heart of the business: this is not a separate role or something farmed out to a different function. Instead the performance director should head up the most strategic function. If your business is built on brand marketing – the marketing director should fulfil the role. If you are world-class manufacturers, the production director should do it; if your organization is research led, the director of R&D. You get the picture.

Making requests of the L&D team to be more involved in the strategic processes followed by most businesses is to ask the powerless to rise up and grab control. It is a request for a revolution and one which most likely will be put down at the earliest opportunity. Instead, those in power need to understand learning and development and how to build the capability of the people who will ensure future success. Once that becomes the role of the most powerful people in the business, proving the benefit of training will be as unnecessary as it is currently meaningless.

Life cycle tips

The new recruit

If you work in a large organization you may have multiple sites or a graduate trainee scheme. This should enable you to set up control groups to monitor any changed process. Just as Peugeot had a natural control group – ie those trained before the introduction of the revised training programme acting as a benchmark for those who benefited from the new system – you can compare one intake of new recruits with the performance of another. Whether the control group are based at a different location or recruited over a different time frame depends on your circumstances. You may need to adjust for changed conditions – economic circumstances may be different and organizational strategy may have evolved. So long as there is sufficient similarity between expected activities to ensure performance comparisons this process should enable you to isolate the impact of changed training methods.

Using existing business metrics, over a sensible timescale for your business, enables you to check whether the latter group, trained in the new way:

1 worked at a higher level (quality);

2 achieved more with similar resources (quantity);

3 at a comparable or lower cost; and

4 reached the required competence levels, as defined by your existing competence standards, more quickly (time).

In organizations of any size, an effective measure on an individual basis will require a pre-start profiling exercise which seeks to identify a start point in relation to current skills and knowledge. Re-running the profiling exercise at, say, 100 days into the new recruit's employment, provides an opportunity to calculate the value added by the induction process. As this is roughly three months into the new starter's career, when probation periods usually end, this process of appraisal should already be built into the organization's processes and therefore does not require significant additional resources to implement.

The new manager

A similar process of initial testing followed by early, post-training appraisal works for new managers – particularly if you have a clear competence framework for your new managers to work to. However, it is business results which really matter. Although it may be a big ask, using your more established team leaders in similar disciplines as a benchmark works well. Does the team led by your new manager achieve similar results to those teams led by more experienced supervisors? If teams led by experienced people significantly outperform your new manager's team, then you may need to investigate further, but if there is no significant difference or if your new man-ager's team does better, then you can confidently consider your training to have been successful.

Of course, this doesn't address general management level perfor-mance. It may be that doing as well as everyone else is still not good enough. In these cases, isolating the team manager's contribution to general under-performance starts with reviewing the competence framework and the associated training for all team leaders. Training new managers may be easier than tackling the more experienced as there will be fewer bad habits to undo. Setting new managers up to do things right and better than the more experienced is a useful way of testing that the competences you feel are important and the working practices which you believe will deliver better results actually work. Well trained, your new managers could be the bench-mark for everyone else to work to.

The specialist

One of the important roles for specialists and subject matter experts in measuring the benefits of training is in supporting the evaluation process. Where a training programme is designed which relates to their specialism, consulting widely at each stage of the design and roll out (see Figure 8.1) can form part of the evaluation process.

At level 1, reaction, the specialist's opinions on training materials design should be canvassed. At this point, you are looking for confir-mation that the material is factually correct; the messages contained are accurate and the skills and standards for their application will be effective in improving performance.

At level 2, the specialist should be helping to define the learning – setting assessments, tests and identifying those crucial components of any assessment which would be the key indicators of future success or failure. A word of caution here: specialists tend to think every-thing is important and demand 100 per cent test score results before an individual can be said to have 'passed' this stage of the training. This is rarely necessary and usually an impossible outcome to specify. However, certain tests should act as a barrier to progression. I don't want anyone who crashes the flight simulator every time they practise landing to progress to the actual flying part of the training. Similar barriers may exist in your industry. But catastrophic competence gaps are rare and generally isolated to certain sectors, where health and safety or protecting the vulnerable are paramount. Achieving a sensible level of assessment – which is as tough as it needs to be but no tougher – is important and the advice and approval of your subject matter expert may be required. What 'good' looks like in relation to the implementation of new skills on the job (level 3) is also an area where specialist and experienced input is required, as is how this successful application of skills will result in business impact (level 4). If they're right, checking those impacts should facilitate the ROI calculations at level 5. Don't forget to cost their inputs into the overall investment figure.

Assessing the performance of specialists is very often difficult to do. The person who knows what 'good' looks like *is* the specialist. Even when looking at the skills specialists need in relation to their area of expertise – for example, presentation skills, influencing skills and project management capabilities – specialists can be so used to being the only arbiter of what they should be doing that assessment mechanisms fail to gain traction. The most effective way of resolving this potential impasse is to involve the specialist who is undertaking training in setting their own goals before the programme. It goes without saying these should be SMART, and capable of being objectively assessed after the event. The feedback process on these key indicators of achievement lies, in the first instance, with the specialist. 'You set the goals – what progress towards their achievement have you made?' is a powerful question when reviewing the benefits of training for this group.

The leader

Leaders are usually net recipients of evaluation data and the insights derived from the information collected. Where you are reporting back on a training programme, it is advisable to bear two things in mind:

1 Good leaders aren't interested in inputs. In order to justify the amount of investment required you may need to delve into the

detail of how the budget was used, but equating success with numbers of training days delivered or the equivalent is usually met with bored expressions at best.

2 They have already defined the results which indicate success. These may be outcomes defined by a customer or funder; they may be timescales or simple financial results – more profit, lower costs, higher yields for shareholders, etc.

When preparing a report for the leadership team, always think about the things which keep them awake at night. If they have specific areas of concern and indicators which give rise to those concerns, then those are the results which really matter. Your training will be judged as a success when they worry less and sleep more.

For their own training, a combination of self-determined goals and 360-degree appraisals are the highest impact assessment tools. Whether your leaders prefer to have access to an executive coach from outside, sign up to a peer mentoring scheme with their colleagues or trust one of the internal L&D team to discuss these things with is not vitally important. It is the goals they set themselves, the opinion of their peers and direct reports which will ultimately determine the success or failure of any leadership training you have put in place.

The retiree

Assuming you have a programme to prepare those about to leave employment for the world beyond, the measures of success will not be immediately obvious as the application of what has been learned will be after employment in the organization. Do you have a customer service measurement process? If you have a mechanism for researching what your customers or consumers think about what you do, it can be adapted for this group. You may want your recently retired colleagues to act as ambassadors for the business. Asking them to complete a questionnaire about their readiness to do so may be the single best indicator of the success of your programme. In a tight recruitment market, where identifying future talent is important to every employer, this may be an outcome worth pursuing.

Set targets in advance and gain the buy-in of those approving the investment and proving the benefit of your approaches becomes pretty straightforward. The other benefit of asking the questions is that those approaching retirement consider future advocacy of your organization as an employer a feasible option – perhaps for the first time.

Where you are looking at providing training for the often overlooked older members of your workforce, the same assessment and business impact considerations apply. Training older workers and investing in their continued capabilities should be just the same as for everyone else. If they are part of the human resources available to your organization, your role is to ensure that those resources are being put to the best possible use.

Growing your own talent and succession planning

> "We are told that talent creates its own opportunities. But it sometimes seems that intense desire creates not only its own opportunities but its own talents.
>
> ERIC HOFFER, ITINERANT LABOURER,
> LONGSHOREMAN AND SOCIAL PHILOSOPHER, 1902–83

Every year the Association of Graduate Recruiters[1] survey more than 200 of the UK's top firms to assess the picture for university graduates and the organizations looking to employ them. The picture is not good for those looking to join graduate training schemes. For every graduate vacancy, there are over 70 graduates in the market for that job. This pattern has been on a steady uphill trend since 2010. Even though the AGR has found that the proportion of major employers offering graduate schemes has increased, demand still outstrips supply. With an increasing 'backlog' of under-employed graduates from previous years, the competition for each place increases year on year. In retail and, amazingly, given recent reputational issues, investment banking, the number of applicants is more than double the general trend. If you're a retailer with a graduate scheme, expect to have to wade through more than 150 applications for each available place. It's a tough time to leave university.

However, there is some good news here. As well as a commitment to train from the bottom up, it also appears that training teams are increasingly – and rightly – being given a role in both selecting and building the talent of the future. Maybe one of the reasons for the increased investment being made in graduate training may be the widely held belief that universities aren't equipping graduates with the skills that employers need. Fed up with graduates who don't seem equipped for the world of work, organizations may be taking things into their own hands and are now seeking to grow their own talent by setting up intensive training and experience programmes for those who have recently left academia.

The role of higher education

However, I don't think the universities and colleges should be criticized for not developing the skills to work in current business. Academics are at their best reflecting on what has happened and through analysis and reflection drawing out the universal truths. It is a process which includes looking backwards and grounding their theories on the lessons from history – however recent. A theoretical understanding of what has gone before and why one approach worked and another was doomed to failure, is important. But the key skills gained from university should not be facts about the performance of *Fortune 500* companies in the past, but the ability to learn. Organizations desperately need people from a range of backgrounds, all of whom should be able to analyse what happened, draw conclusions and articulate the resulting rule sets clearly.

Those who complain about the skill sets of graduates are often talking about their ability to do job X or perform function Y. Although university funding bodies and the like demand that faculties and degree courses should prove their relevance for employment or justify their existence in terms of 'work-skills', it really isn't their role. When I started university the history professor who took my very first tutorial said to me: 'Welcome to the course. You are commencing a programme where you will be taught to read and write to degree level.' That pretty much is what I think universities should do. Universities are not equipped to train. They *should* be looking backwards. You and I wouldn't be that impressed by someone who drives a car forward but focuses all their attention on their rear-view mirror.

So, why would we want to employ someone with business skills learned at university? This will be a skill set which is already out of date by the time they have a chance to use it.

Louis Ross, former Vice Chair of the Ford Motor Company, famously addressed a group of engineering students with the words:

> In your career, knowledge is like milk. It has a shelf life stamped right on the carton. The shelf life of a degree in engineering is about three years. If you're not replacing everything you know by then, your career is going to turn sour fast.

This is not just about undergraduates. The applicability of the things learned in education is less direct and more tangential than is sometimes made out. When combined with experience, it can help individuals place their existing knowledge into a framework of research and contextualize what they pick up through work-based learning. Viewed in that light, all learning is applied learning – it just requires the opportunity for its application.

I am clear that in disciplines like medicine, some of the sciences, the law and similar, the drivers of new thinking are to be found within the universities. But I see little evidence of that being true in subjects such as management, marketing and business – and even if it is, the latest conjecture, hypothesis and blue sky thinking rarely make it onto the undergraduate curriculum or onto the syllabus of the cash cow courses, such as the MBA.

I was once working with a graduate recruiter. He was bemoaning the number of 23-year-olds with MBAs who he regularly interviewed at university recruitment fairs. 'It's all very well being taught how to run a FTSE 100 company, but these guys will need another 30 years of real learning before that's what they're going to do.' I often think back to that and wonder if any of them have got anywhere close in less time and whether they have recalled, remembered or applied anything they learnt on their MBA en route. We are told the only constant is change. As Eric Hoffer, whom I quoted at the start of this chapter said:

> In a time of drastic change it is the learners who inherit the future. The learned usually find themselves equipped to live in a world that no longer exists.[2]

We must look for those individuals with the universal skills which will enable them to take advantage of the uncertainties of the future.

Selecting the best

Graduate training schemes are an expensive option. As well as the cost of dealing with the huge numbers of applicants, some companies expect to invest as much as £200,000 on each graduate trainee over a two-year training period. That's a lot of money and, in order to gain maximum return on this considerable investment, it would be wise to ensure that you select the right person in the first instance. Being spoilt for choice doesn't make it any easier. Many of those surveyed by the Association of Graduate Recruiters specifically recruit from those who have existing work experience with the firm. Internships or placements during studying are now a pre-requisite to being selected. If this work experience is essentially an extended interview and selection process, then that seems OK to me.

Recently, I conducted a survey of recruitment preferences amongst HR teams with whom I worked (see Figure 9.1). The results confirmed those published by the Chartered Institute of Personnel & Development in their Learning and Talent Development Survey.[3] This had found that talent management was a significant issue which was growing in importance. The CIPD survey results showed that formal approaches to talent management were the preserve of large organizations seeking to develop senior managers and so-called 'high-potentials'. The issue is, where do these potential leaders come from?

For two-thirds of respondents to my survey, experience in undertaking a similar role elsewhere was the main factor in whether an individual was recruited or not. The second most important factor was organizational fit – whether the person under consideration had an attitude and outlook aligned with the organization's values and culture. Interestingly, qualifications were far and away the least important factor considered at recruitment. Half of all respondents said this was the least important consideration when making a hiring decision. In a world in which having held an internship at the firm may be your best chance of gaining access to the graduate recruitment

FIGURE 9.1   Survey of 50 UK HR professionals, October 2011

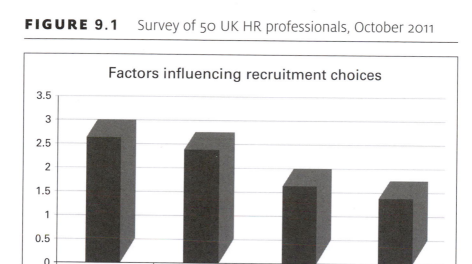

Respondents were asked to rate these four factors using a four point scale in which 4 = most important and 1 = least important. Average scores (out of 4) shown.

scheme, it is to be hoped that these internships are open to all. Being 'just like us' hardly seems a great basis for investment in someone's potential.

Grow your own

I am in favour of organizations growing their own talent and I hope that they are casting their net as wide as possible to find those whom they will nurture to be the future leaders. In fact it can be like hunting for a needle in a haystack, or more appropriately a diamond in the rough. So before seeking our gem of a graduate, we need to determine what would make someone a gem.

If you're expecting to have to train them on your graduate training scheme then what set of skills do they need? Well, the clue is in that phrase 'training scheme', isn't it? The most important skill for a new recruit from university will be the ability to learn – and not just academic study skills. They'll need a real understanding of what it takes to be motivated to pick up new skills, and not only learn **about** stuff but learn **how to do** stuff – to apply their knowledge in a constantly changing world where learners will be increasingly valuable. If, however, qualifications are among the least important factor in determining the recruits selected to enter the training scheme, what indicator of learning skills does the organization have?

If you are overrun with applications for graduate places in your organization a traditional interview isn't really going to cut the mustard. Perhaps you need an assessment centre – putting people in different situations and seeing how they get on as team players, problem solvers and – most importantly – as learners.

Let's assume that they have demonstrated how effectively they can both learn and use what they have learned in a series of group and problem-solving activities through the assessment centre. Now, you have employed someone who has proved that they are a skilled learner, you'd better deliver on the expectation you will have created.

This means creating an environment in which ongoing learning is central to the experience of working in the organization as a graduate trainee. For the most part this won't be formal training. What it may require is a culture change amongst managers – especially if they haven't always been the most supportive of development activities. If your line manager's involvement in training is limited to pulling people off courses at the last minute – and when I speak to L&D people this still seems to be a major issue – then expecting them to be coach, guide, mentor and shoulder to cry on may be asking rather a lot.

However, this too is an opportunity for organizational cultural change driven by the L&D team. Most teams should be happy to have a graduate trainee on board. In many organizations they're not considered as part of headcount figures and the costs of having them around are met by a central budget. It's a great way of increasing the team without apparently increasing costs. So, my advice to L&D teams is to use this for all it's worth. If my informal conversations with L&D teams are to be believed, some rogue team leaders are regularly unsupportive of training, slow to encourage people to use e-learning programmes, usually behind in agreeing personal development plans and likely to be the first phone call pulling someone off the course on the morning they are supposed to be attending.

If you've got someone like that would you want them to be involved in developing the next generation of leader? No? I didn't think so. Unfortunately, trainees are often placed in teams based on functional fit rather than whether the individual team leader is the right person to model the desired organizational values.

By publicly rewarding those managers who take their people development responsibilities seriously you ensure those with a good track record get to model the right behaviours to the next generation and get an additional pair of willing and highly motivated hands. If we learn as much from our role models as we do from formal interventions, expose your new graduates to those whose behaviour we would want them to emulate. By so doing, you also communicate to other team leaders the importance of continuously developing their people.

But putting the graduate trainee with a supportive line manager is only part of the story. Providing that line manager with support, creating structured work-based tasks for the graduate to complete and having learning materials available just in time for these digital natives should all be part of the mix. If you have selected your trainees on the basis of their ability to learn, utilizing that capability and drive to create a new learning culture across the teams they join will have wider benefits.

It is a fact which organizations often overlook that the graduates they recruit and invest in now will be retiring after 2060. What role will we be preparing people for? What will that future look like? Imagine someone joining an organization in the 1950s and retiring this year? Look at the change they have experienced. Data processing in the period just after the Second World War involved hand-written ledgers and countless clerks. Will this year's graduates look back at our current highly technological work environment and see something they regard as equally antiquated? They might.

One would hope with the level of investment of a graduate training scheme, organizations would be looking to keep that talent on board for as long as possible and maybe – in an uncertain world – their entire career. Recruiting people who can be developed to do the jobs we have now rather than the jobs we will have in a radically different future is at best short-sighted.

Manage the talent you already have

But talent management isn't and shouldn't be simply about the bright young things being recruited at the annual university milk round. Most organizations of any size which are looking to their future sustainability will have a plan in place for talent management and most of these will go beyond graduate schemes. The CIPD survey found that around a quarter of those with talent management systems outlined 'recruiting and attracting key staff' as one of the stated objectives of having such a scheme. People of all ages and experiences are attracted to those organizations with a strong and public commitment to developing their people and their careers.

The processes of identifying high-potentials, involving them in a succession plan and laying on career development workshops are well understood. But increasingly I see organizations where, despite the detailed planning for succession and activities designed to nurture the next generation of leaders, when senior roles become vacant they look outside their own organization. Fresh ideas are needed, new blood and someone to shake things up a bit. Perhaps, but doesn't that indicate something of a problem with the talent management process and the investment which underpins it? So what's gone wrong?

Once we have people on board we need to think about how this latent talent will be nurtured and shaped to work within the organization. We also need to think about how the potentially talented can transform the organization to ensure it is fit for the future. The focus of talent management needs to be about recognizing those crucial change agent and adaptability skills. Where talent management relies on a steady rise through the ranks, the outcome is rarely good enough. The recruitment of mid-level managers who have cut their teeth in some other organization should always be a worry for L&D teams. If we have to go outside to gain some new ideas, the work we're doing inside is simply not good enough in the rapidly changing environment of the corporate world.

Growing your own talent to work in a world we cannot accurately predict may not yet be an established practice. However, an enthusiasm for an organization and the desire to grow within it is clearly a desirable characteristic amongst those we want to recruit. Will they still display this characteristic after they have been passed over in favour of those with more experience who have been brought in from the outside to provide fresh and innovative thinking?

One way of supporting a home-grown route to talent is to recreate the career path, which was in favour a few years ago, of working in different departments. The idea, borrowed from the Japanese organizations which had embraced continuous improvement and Kaizen, was that high-potential individuals would follow a structured career path – not moving inexorably *up* the organization but moving inexorably *round* the organization. High-potential employees should be spending time in different functions and departments, learning the ropes, constantly being taken out of their comfort zone. This has the benefit of honing the individual's learning skills and provides evidence of their adaptability. It also ensures a thorough grounding in all the different functions that one day they might be called upon to lead.

As part of our talent development programme, there will be formal training input but for the most part the learning will be work-based – learning through doing, finding out, responding to new situations by developing new ways of working, new behaviours and new skills. This is not the same as some talent management programmes in larger organizations, where staff are moved round every few years, taking on new projects and new roles. The impact of these roundabout moves is rarely the deepening and shaping of strategy in response to new market conditions, but an allegedly strategic role which is subsumed beneath careerist mark-making. On occasions the talent merry-go-round is reduced to making an impact by undoing all that your predecessor has done and achieving one noteworthy thing. Then this apparently high-potential individual keeps his or her head down until the next move comes along and the process repeats itself. Trying too hard can increase the likelihood of any failure being all the more spectacular. Under the microscope of the talent review mechanism, all failures are high profile and one high profile failure may be one too many.

I spoke to some senior managers about career and development planning and performance appraisal meetings recently. Every one of them noted how the people who report to them were hungry for progression – repeatedly outlining how their potential could best be achieved by taking on a new challenge, stretching their skills in new environments. Clearly, it is easier to make a mark by sweeping out the old, than by maintaining and incrementally enhancing the familiar and 'business as usual'.

Beyond the greasy pole – the skills needed for the future

So we may need a new paradigm for the development of our future talent – a talent that will succeed or fail in a very different environment than the one we now know. That paradigm starts with identifying the crucial skills which these individuals will need in future decades.

First among these is being a skilled information seeker. As I outlined earlier, this is not an unquestioning acceptance of the information out there, but an ability to find it, verify the sources and derive what's needed. The ability to differentiate reliable from unreliable information is vital.

But looking things up is not the same as learning and the next crucial capability is to be a skilled, independent learner. In an environment where work-related learning may be fragmented – a combination of on-the-job experience, learning programmes, in part online, and developmental projects (as well as very occasional course attendances) – the multi-dimensional learner who is open to new experiences and can reflect on what they mean, will be a valuable member of any team. The connectivity I mentioned earlier will be a real focus of this reflection – not the consumption of the blogs and wikis of others, but by contributing and articulating concepts, theories, ideas and experiences in ways which resonate with peers.

My third and final skill is what I call an enquiring mind. This is not just a function of problem solving in a connected world. It is about someone who asks the awkward questions, challenges received wisdom and established conventions. When working with a group involved in innovation recently I came across 'knowledge scouts'. Their role is not to think up new ideas, but scout around for new insights about the ways innovations are being used and identify the people and organizations with the ability to contribute to the creation of commercially viable new products. They are mining the creativity which surrounds us and asking simple questions. What if we did that too? Does the fact that these consumers use X mean that if we create Y they would also use that? They are trend-spotters and observers of the zeitgeist. Not to rip off the ideas of someone else, but to re-shape novelty in their own image. They synthesize what is going on and create new opportunities from unexpected combinations of ideas and innovations. The mash-up first seen in nightclubs and music videos has become a tool for exploiting ideas by standing on the shoulders of the achingly fashionable giants who surround us.

Externships

One way of thinking about developmental projects which borrow experiences from beyond the organization is as *externships*. The simple idea is that the opportunity to build skills and demonstrate capabilities available to recent graduates in an internship can be replicated for those already employed by the organization. One of the things to look for from these development projects and programmes is how effectively the talented individuals bring their learning back to the organization. It's relatively easy to see whether the experience has led to new ideas, new effectiveness and a new appetite for their own development. The results they achieve will either improve or not. More difficult to assess – but far from impossible – is whether these individuals come back and can share their experience with others. Each externship should include a requirement for these experiences and the knowledge and skills generated through such an exposure to be cascaded to others.

In very enlightened organizations, this process of placement in different departments is accompanied by time devoted to special projects or activities outside the organization. I recently spent time with the HR director of a leading supplier of building materials. In this relatively unglamorous organization, the leaders of tomorrow were involved in project work overseas with completely different companies in different industries – looking at the management and organizational challenges outside their own experience and their relatively traditional world.

As part of their Corporate Social Responsibility programme, these same managers also worked with community organizations in developing countries. The communities in India and Africa where raw materials are quarried benefit from the management input of creative individuals to community schools and civic organizations. The sponsoring company also benefits from different experiences and learning opportunities and has the chance to assess its talent in unusual and challenging situations and – by strengthening these communities – add security and sustainability to their own supply chain. It is a virtuous circle.

This cascade of experience will be important for the individual themselves in helping them embed their experience, analyse it and reinforce the desired behaviours. For the individual, it is a crucial learning process. Constructivist learning theories[4] identify this process of making a representation of what you have learned as an essential part of truly learning something.

In a networked world, it will be more and more common for this representation of such experiences – the lessons learned and the relevance of novel undertakings to the day job – to be performed digitally. The use of wikis, blogs and other Web 2.0 tools to share and amplify this learning will not only spread the benefits. Their adoption will also create an auditable output to support further assessment of those who demonstrate their ability to apply a breadth of experience to the challenges of the future.

Curate the outcomes of this experiential development process, perhaps through a learning management system, add an enterprise-wide approach to learning and development, water well, fertilize with interesting and provocative inputs, and harvest the results. If your enterprise-wide approach to L&D involves interlinked departmental curricula and organization-wide leadership development so much the better. Through a smartly designed learning platform, the resulting well-rounded individual can have their progress tracked and their learning accredited. More importantly, this approach ensures duplication is avoided – why would you want to waste the time of these talented future leaders?

Collaboration and sharing – development which drives the organizational memory

Of course, the use of these online tools for collaboration and sharing is not yet embedded in, or taken seriously by, many organizations. It is still an immature technology for all but a few. Those who have yet to make use of the possibilities of Web 2.0 technologies often cite the lack of time to be able to contribute or utilize the potential treasure trove of knowledge which an organization's intranet can provide.

In Chapter 7, I outlined how sports commentators always describe top class athletes as 'having so much time'. Whether receiving the ball in midfield, returning serve or moving their feet to a demon fast bowler, these individuals seem to have more time to react than their less successful counterparts. Is there a lesson here for talent managers? Perhaps peak performers who have the learning skills we require for a different future and who add value, not just by learning but by sharing their insight and knowledge, also 'seem to have more time?' Why might that be?

1 First and perhaps most importantly, they do things quickly and correctly. Right first time is actually one of the best ways of generating more time to do other things.

2 These individuals prioritize the act of sharing knowledge and continually learning. They make time for these activities. In some respects, this is a selfish act. As the old Russian proverb has it, 'to teach is to learn twice', so sharing your knowledge is never purely selfless.

3 They also recognize that work is a team sport – the chain is only as strong as its weakest link, etc. Developing others, having a hymn sheet that everyone can sing from and honing ideas in the cauldron of informed debate builds a better team and delivers better performance.

Contributing to the shared knowledge of the organization – perhaps through Web 2.0 tools, such as wikis, blogs, and published online exchanges – adds a new dimension. The individual talent that is being nurtured is also contributing resources for the development of those who will work with them as they grow into the leaders that the next generation will demand. There is a record of what shaped them. When these people get to the top, knowing the route they have taken to the dizzy heights may be of immense value to those who will work alongside them.

So, as with all things, if you want something done find a busy person to do it. For talent managers everywhere, reviewing the input which these high fliers make into your corporate knowledge bank, the way they promote debate and thought in an uncertain future and the way they embrace available technology to do so, will be useful indicators of potential. Those leading our organizations into the second half of the 21st century will have mastered these ways of working and will be ready to adapt to building the skills and knowledge of their organizations to face whatever challenges may be thrown up over the course of their career.

They will also be digital natives and happily adapt their communication and knowledge sharing skills to whatever new technologies appear over the next fifty years. As a start point, organizations wanting to identify and nurture talent ought to view contributions to these systems as an essential and highly valued behaviour from those they develop.

In my survey I found that internal competence frameworks do put some emphasis on learning skills alongside other core capabilities. Almost all the respondents said that learning skills were specifically mentioned within the competence framework. A further two-thirds also include an ability to utilize disparate sources of information – though whether this includes the ability to be media literate and a skilled information seeker is a moot point. Trend spotting, change and creative problem solving were less likely to be included in the competence framework in the organizations I surveyed.

This focus on only part of the required skill set for the future is somewhat concerning. While recognizing change as a constant, it would seem that organizations still prepare strategically for a world in which business as usual continues ad infinitum.

Now look at your own organization's competence framework. In there will be a set of core behaviours and skills, common to all roles in your organization. They are intended to be the very warp and weft of your organizational culture. Do you recognize the foundation skills for growing your own talent in those common capabilities? Teaching your high-potential people the stuff which gets done in your organization is going to be hard enough. Teaching them if they don't have these essential skills in the future, will be nigh on impossible.

Life cycle tips

The new recruit

For new starters there are two important processes with regard to talent management. If your new starters are joining a formal scheme, such as a graduate training programme, the induction process needs to outline precisely what the graduate programme will include. During induction for those not recruited into a formal training programme, a similar outline of career development options and the process of career progression is equally important.

Eric Jackson, writing in *Forbes* magazine in December 2011,[5] described the top 10 reasons that large companies lose their best talent. Number 3 in his list was a poor, rushed and 'tick-box' annual performance review process and, closely related at number 4, was not having a clear career development path. This seems pretty much in touch with other surveys, except that I think the importance of a lack of career and training opportunities may well be higher amongst those who leave in the early stages of their employment. Remember, most inductees have recently been on the look-out for a new job. There is a better than evens chance that you weren't the only employer to which they applied. When a new starter gets a couple of months into their new job and that company that interviewed them just before you did finally gets it together to contact them again about a possible job, what will your new starter say and do? Will they feel that the expectations they came into the company with have been matched by their experience?

According to the Chartered Institute of Personnel and Development's annual Resourcing and Talent Planning survey, 2012,[6] two-thirds of organizations have problems with staff retention. Of those firms who are making serious efforts to address the issue 47 per cent focus on increased learning and development opportunities while 43 per cent have improved, or plan to improve, their induction process. With recruitment costs averaging around £8,000 per person for managerial and professional staff, keeping people once you have them is a significant issue.

When reviewing your induction ask yourself:

1 Does it clearly identify what the career development paths are and how an individual will be trained and assessed in order to make such a progression?

2 Does the rest of the organization share the HR team's view of career development, or are these processes over-ridden by functional managers who want to recruit from outside?

3 Are new starters clear about the need to maintain an active involvement in their own learning and development?

The new manager

The mechanism for selecting a buddy for your new manager from amongst the supervisory ranks is much the same as that for placing a graduate trainee with a team leader. The buddy should model the kind of behaviour you would want all managers to exhibit.

New managers, particularly those who have come up through an internal training route, should be great salespeople for your organization's commitment to career development. Even though they are new in role and will have many issues competing for priority status, involving them in identifying potential amongst those in their team is a real vote of confidence. It also taps into the fact that they have recent first-hand knowledge of what it takes to make a step up the career ladder. Their insights can be refreshing.

Importantly, a new team leader should have a clear expectation of what they need to do before being considered for further moves and progression. For the most part, new managers recognize that they will need to establish themselves as team leaders before any idea of further progression could be on the agenda. However, you should ensure that the timescales to which they are operating match those which the organization thinks sensible. I asked a group of recently appointed team leaders about their career aspirations during a training session recently. The longest period which they expected to be on the bottom rung of the management ladder was two years. For some, even this amount of time before their next move was considered excessive – they expected to have made their mark and moved on in a year or less.

If your organization has a talent review timescale which, for example, only considers moves through the management ranks once a person has stayed in role for three years or more, it is imperative that these managers understand this. If you don't ensure common understanding here, your considerable investment in management training may never be realized as the recently promoted move on. In the CIPD survey, one-third of firms reported difficulty in retaining those in management, professional and specialist roles. In other words, once they get a management job, they are more likely to move.

When working with newly appointed managers, ask yourself:

1 Have we prepared them adequately for the role they will play in managing the talent in their own teams?

2 Are they focused on continuous development and improvement *in this role* or do they see rapid changing of jobs as the only way to develop?

3 Are we continuing to invest in their training once they become more established in the post?

The specialist

According to the CIPD 2012 Resourcing and Talent Planning survey, specialists and technically skilled employees cause the HR team considerable headaches. They are more likely to be in demand, more likely to leave and more likely to be difficult to replace than just about any other group.

Active engagement in succession planning can buck this trend. If you have a sizable portion of your organization's knowledge and skill set in a few specialist individuals, wherever they may be positioned in the hierarchy or pay grade structure, ensure that they are both helping to identify their successor and actively working with that pool of talent to pass on their skills and knowledge.

Whether you have a formal apprenticeship scheme or not, having someone who is just learning the ropes working with your specialist talent provides two sorts of benefits. For the organization, more of the knowledge is retained if the individual specialist moves on. For the specialist, their high levels of knowledge, ability and experience are recognized. Inviting these skilled individuals to be involved in training their own replacement allows them to develop their own legacy. This is highly motivating. Very few experts worth having around would like to see the work they have done over some period of time unravel because no one was capable of taking over.

In relation to their own development, I think specialists are prime candidates for *externships* – those external experiences which bring the benefits of fresh thinking and exposure to something completely different without the talent management problems associated with external recruitment. Whether this is working with community or voluntary organizations, placements in different sectors, or work in the far-flung locations of your own organization, these kinds of experience can be the shot in the arm a long-serving specialist needs. They should rekindle some of the vigour which being in the same role and having advanced up the hierarchy inevitably brings.

The leader

The leader's role in talent management is usually to support the process rather than benefit from it. Hopefully, they have already progressed through the formal and informal career paths in your organization. Their engagement with the process is vitally important in one regard. If they do not appreciate the internal methods used for identifying and training talent, they will be minded to recruit from outside. This undermines the whole process. If the top brass look for their replacements beyond the doors of your organization, your efforts in talent management will always be severely limited.

However, if they have come through the ranks and recognize that career development in the organization worked for them then they should be powerful advocates. There is no better endorsement for a graduate training scheme than a high profile leader telling those recruited or about to be recruited, '20 years ago, I was sitting in your seat'.

The retiree

By definition talent management and career development seem at odds with preparing long-term employees for a career outside the organization. However, they have a role to play. I would always want a long-term employee to be involved in every talent review. While we are considering someone for a move through the organization, a lot can be gleaned from those who know the organization inside and out. Will high potential individual X be able to work with function Y?; will this individual have the strength of character and the integrity to address the issues in location Z? It's always a risk – which is why I think most firms employ outsiders who appear to have performed the exact same role somewhere else. An old head might provide the wisdom required and – given that they are coming to the end of their career – do so from a uniquely impartial perspective.

Using externships can also be a route for those going through some kind of career transition. In the 2012 CIPD Resourcing and Talent Survey, apparently 51 per cent of those organizations which had needed to make redundancies in the previous year had offered some kind of specific support to employees leaving the firm. This may only be limited to time off for job seeking and perhaps an interview or two with a recruitment consultant, but I think employers will increasingly be judged on how well they manage these events. Furthermore, building links with local communities is no longer considered a luxury. Perhaps a little more focus on older employees in the development mix opens up a whole host of opportunities to look good because you're doing good.

The strategy checklist

"The essence of strategy is choosing what not to do.
PROFESSOR MICHAEL PORTER, HARVARD BUSINESS SCHOOL

What does strategy mean in your organization? For many, describing something as strategic merely means important. It has been debased from its original sense and simply shortened to what the boss does or those seeking to justify their position and attendant salary. But strategy as defined by the Oxford English Dictionary is: 'a plan of action designed to achieve a long-term or overall aim'. To be described as strategic, therefore, whatever is being described must figure in that plan of action and advance the journey to the overall aim.

The main focus of strategic thinking, and of those like Porter quoted at the head of this chapter, has been looking at how organizations devise their long-term or overall aim. By and large, the focus has been on reviewing the external environment and the organization's place within it and determining how to carve out a unique position for itself – to do something which no one else can easily imitate and which customers want. The strategy needs to be implemented in such a way that is responsive – that is, if the external environment changes considerably or is thought likely to do so, then the overall aim may be redefined somewhat. It also needs to be implemented within a framework of continuous improvement. If we can do things better (quality), do more of something in more places (quantity) and make it less expensive (cost) and quicker (time), then whatever competitive advantage is conferred on us by being different from anything else available is prolonged.

Most strategies, and what is considered strategic in organizations, fit into that framework. Training and development of people within the business is strategic in these terms. It supports the implementation of strategy, continually communicates organizational purpose and supports continuous improvement. So far, so good.

The reality is, though, that training and development teams become enablers of strategy rather than strategic. There's a subtle but significant difference. An enabler is a service which could easily be outsourced to someone who can do more, better, cheaper and quicker. It sounds silly to suggest that training could be off-shored to a cheaper source of labour in a developing country, until you consider where most e-learning gets developed. Then you realize that's exactly what happened. If your organization is focused on the external environment and assuring a long-term competitive advantage, then your training and development function needs to take a similar environmental focus. Consider yourself not as a strategic part of the business, but as an external enabler of the strategy. This means you will need your own strategy to ensure competitive advantage in the face of a changing environment. This market-driven approach, which sees your organization's individual functions and teams as the customer base for the differentiated L&D services provided, is one way of thinking about the strategy for your training department.

There is a different model, though. Increasingly in the last decade or so, organizations have started to give thought to a resource-based model of strategy and planning. In a traditional SWOT analysis the opportunities and threats represent the external environment, the strengths and weaknesses the internal capability – or resources available. This balance between the external – usually how money is generated to maintain the organization and to deliver profit – and the internal – what are we good at? – is given greater or less attention as organizational strategy responds and reacts to changes in both the external and internal environment. What if your organization focuses primarily on a resource-based view of strategy? In this model, to put it simply, the overall aim of the organization is derived less from an external focus on competitors, suppliers, buyers and other things which may take the customers' money,[1] but from an internal focus on what we can do that no one else can.

This resource-based view of strategy is especially appropriate for non-profit-making organizations and the public sector. Here, competition, if it exists at all, is usually manufactured by external funders and refugees from corporate boardrooms. In resource-based strategies training and development doesn't support strategy, it shapes it. For the resource-based strategist, *the* most important resource is the people in the enterprise and the skills which they possess. If this describes your organizational strategy, then learning and development is integral to the organization strategy and you shouldn't need a separate focus from that of the organization.

However, even when an organization follows a resource-based strategy many L&D teams still find themselves marginalized in the strategic planning activities. The strategy is the responsibility of the strategy department. Functional heads are consulted but the biggest say goes to the department with the greatest impact on organizational success – usually production or sales and marketing. It also goes to those who manage the physical assets of the business. A factory manager will be considered strategically important, not because the factory employs most people, but because the equipment, buildings and other assets inside the factory feature on the balance sheet. The people don't.

Even in organizations which allegedly consider internal capability as the main focus of organizational planning, your L&D function will in all likelihood require a separate but complementary strategy of its own. I think it is always appropriate for your training team to build its own strategy to service a market comprising the different departments of the organization. Effectively you should act as if you are competing or collaborating with external training providers to ensure the best available service for your one customer.

Essentially, you'll need some way of articulating your own long-term or overall aim and the way in which you will implement the plan which gets you there. Whatever else your strategy contains, it must describe the match between your internal capabilities and your external relationships.[2] In most organizations, the external relationships for the L&D function will be supplemented with internal relationships within the organization – the customer base.

The strategy checklist has been designed to both summarize the approach I have advocated in *Complete Training* and provide you with a shopping list for your own strategy planning. Whether you are enabling competitive advantage to be achieved and sustained or creating differentiation through your capabilities, the following will give you a place to start asking the questions which need answering.

1 Where are you starting from?
Whichever approach you take, the establishment of an aim without first deciding a starting point is a little like planning a journey to get somewhere without knowing your current location.

Your initial assessment begins from understanding the capabilities of the current training organization alongside an assessment of the current state of the capabilities in the remainder of the enterprise. Of course, this assessment needs to be made against the organizational strategy – what skills does the organization need to achieve its aims? You can see that there's a possibility here of going round and round in ever decreasing circles. In truth, the capability assessment and deciding what you should do are so interlinked that they need to be undertaken together.

2 What is your overall aim?
The problem with a question like this is that it is easy to state a series of wishes in language that is imprecise. 'World-class' is, after all, just another word for good – or, perhaps, very good. It isn't a standard nor does it define a quality threshold. To be 'the partner of choice' doesn't help either. If you're the world-class partner of choice, start worrying.

The overall aim needs to inspire and to have a mission and/or vision associated with it, but it also needs to be practical and to some extent measurable. The more specific it is, the more it will help your people focus on it in everything they do. The mission of the L&D department provides the first point of focus for making the decisions about what you will do – and importantly – what you won't do.

Imagine a training team which has as its vision statement:

To become a zero-cost training operation.

Think about that. The essence of their vision would be to continually justify their activities by ensuring that no programme is initiated unless there is at least the expectation that the benefits of the programme would outweigh the costs involved. It's a bold move but if you consider the direction of travel engaged in pursuing that aim, you'll see the main benefit. By having 'zero-cost' as their overall aim, the culture and discipline created is constantly focused on ensuring the training team meets departmental needs in such a way that the benefits outweigh the costs.

3 What is your unique capability?

The mission derives from the vision and provides more detail about the What and the How. The first stage of the mission is the unique capability, for example:

> Through our unrivalled knowledge of the business and our intimate knowledge of the needs of its people...

Here, the unique capability differentiates the internal team from any potential external/alternative supplier of training services. If the team can legitimately claim it, and the customers agree that this is what they want, then the team's future should be assured. If the remainder of the business does not agree that they have that in-depth knowledge and intimate understanding, then that assurance disappears.

The unique capability also provides guidance about the process of recruiting new team members. Do they have an unrivalled knowledge of the business or can they acquire it? Do they have an intimate knowledge of the needs of its people? I think this statement makes it unlikely that the team would recruit from outside; instead, they would seek to promote to the trusted position of trainer only those people who had shone in the functions of the business it supported. However, if there is to be recruitment from within, then it is important that these trainers keep themselves updated in order to deliver on the mission's promise. Experience of working in a function in the past hardly counts as 'intimate knowledge' after a few years away from the functional day to day.

When I was a young manager, I was fortunate to be trained by the Industrial Society which was then under the leadership of the inspirational John Garnett. All the consultants who ran the society's training courses were on fixed-term contracts. After three years (or exceptionally, five years) each one was expected to return to their original discipline or profession before coming back once again to the sharp end of delivering the training courses it provided. The Industrial Society training division was bought by Capita in 2001. I hope they retained that ethos.

The use of the word 'promoted' to describe being moved into the training team is intentional. If your business is committed to transferring internal staff into trainer roles, then being a trainer in your organization should be a senior and well-respected role. Too often it isn't. One of my clients employs skills development managers in each function. The pay grade for these individuals roughly equates to a junior or first line manager. It certainly isn't a senior role. Consequently, a spell in training is seen as a short-term stepping stone on the way up. Occasionally, and much, much worse, it represents a longer-term resting place on the way down.

4 What will you do?

The next stage of the mission deals with what the team will do (and by definition, what it won't do). Our example may extend as follows:

> ... we will design and implement joined-up capability building services ...

Note that it doesn't say training or talk about the various modes of delivery. This team is focused on outputs – enhanced capability – rather than the inputs required. 'Joined-up' is consistent with the Complete Training philosophy. There are no quick fixes designed here, no sticking plasters or tick boxes. This is a team focused on changing behaviour – enabling people to do things differently and do different things. To do this requires a range of interventions from the self-managed, the actively facilitated and the work-based; from the experiential to the reflective. It is a process enabling shared knowledge and the building of an organizational memory. The L&D team will design these different and differentiated interventions and manage their implementation.

5 For whom will you do it?

You might specify those whose capability you seek to improve by grade, function or location. Any route to segmenting and defining the potential audience for your services is good. So long as it is clear. An ambiguous audience profile causes confusion and the potential for scope creep – where we suddenly find our finite resources pulled towards things which were never part of the original plan and which can only be achieved by cutting a few corners elsewhere.

Continuing the example, we might say:

> ... for team leaders and their teams, across every function and every location.

Pretty clear about who this service is aimed at, isn't it? The focus will be on the doers and the provision will be universal. Leaders are excluded from this definition of the customer base – perhaps the organization recognizes that once an individual has advanced to a leadership role their training should involve an external input and an outward orientation. How that is consistent with a 'joined-up' training approach will need further definition later in the strategy.

6 How will you do it and how will you know it works?

Finally, the how; the exact definition of the services which make up the mix provided by the team. For example:

> We will do this through defining current and future competences using a range of training methods and learning opportunities and applying appropriate business measures to gauge our effectiveness.

Here the focus is on competence definition and a mix of different inputs. The effectiveness of these inputs will be measured not by some specially concocted metrics, but by establishing how the training has supported the achievement of the important performance indicators already in use across the remainder of the business.

Our final strategy vision and mission now reads:

Vision:	'To become a zero-cost training operation.'
Mission:	'Through our unrivalled knowledge of the business and our intimate knowledge of the needs of its people, we will design and implement joined-up capability building services, for team leaders and their teams, across every function and every location. We will do this through defining current and future competences using a range of training methods and learning opportunities and applying appropriate business measures to gauge our effectiveness.'

Now I know we've ended up with quite a bit of detail, but strategies require a degree of precision which the short slogan often lacks. The vision does provide us with the key focus and you can always get it put onto a T-shirt should you wish. To be truly strategic, the mission should leave no member of the team – nor user of the service – under any misapprehension about what matters. What gets measured gets done. Those factors which contribute most readily to our success will be those which will be measured, even if such measures prove difficult.

7 How will you implement?

The implementation plan is where the whole strategic process becomes much more tactical. An effective plan to support a training strategy has three core components:

– *Defined and validated competences.* Defining what the people who will receive the training need to know and do requires both an assessment of current requirements and skills and a projection for the skills required in the medium and long term. This needs to be validated and verified with internal customers – experienced staff, team leaders, specialists and the like – and external, benchmark organizations. To avoid compromising on the organization's differentiated capabilities, ideally this will be a synthesis of the skills demanded and developed in like-minded but non-competing organizations.

- *Training approaches which are designed and piloted and refined in the light of results.* One size does not fit all, so multiple approaches will be required to develop the same competences in different individuals and teams. Using a range of techniques, in concert, ensures that everyone has the best chance of achieving the required outcomes.

- *Standards for training interventions.* These may be the standards expected for face-to-face trainers, coaches and mentors (whether part of the training team or line managers from different functions) and standards for content and media production. Having standards does not imply a standardization of approach, but merely outlines the quality we would expect from any kind of training intervention and learning experience provided. From the inputs needed through to the feedback on initial implementation, defining quality standards has a significant bearing on the resources required to implement. It goes without saying that the total amount of resources required includes the learner time needed to achieve the required competence.

Too often, there is a disconnect between the standards expected by the people whom we seek to train and the teams in which they work, and the resources available to deliver against those standards. Inevitably, this leads to shortcuts, learner dissatisfaction and a gradual diminution of the influence and importance of the L&D function.

The standards we set for training interventions correlate directly with the standards of performance we expect from those in the L&D function. Is there a fixed standard for what makes a good trainer? It would appear not. When I work with training teams I often ask them to describe the qualities, skills and behaviours of effective trainers. Apart from hygiene factors such as punctuality, if I have 10 trainers in the group I'll receive 12 different opinions. It really should be a lot more objective than this and, framed by a clear mission, it can be.

The standards you set to define your training team and the individuals within it will depend on:

- who is being trained;

- to do what;

- the organization; and

- the training methods employed.

It's important to spend some time defining what 'good' looks like and ensuring that everyone in the training team has a clear understanding of the performance level expected. It's also important to communicate these standards to the end users of the programme. I personally like internal training teams to have a version of a customer charter – defining what line managers and course participants can expect. I particularly approve of these if they form a kind of contract with the learner and their line manager.

You will know by now that I'm no fan of the end-of-workshop happy sheet. However, I recognize that for many organizations they are an inevitable component of the training process. If using a charter or a contract or something similar, then you will have at least communicated to everyone what a trainer should do. Having these contracted standards helps with the design of the end-of-event evaluation tool. Thereafter, the completion of those forms might be a little less subjective.

8 How will you use external capability?

However well resourced your training team is, there will be times when you need to enlist the support and assistance of specialist training providers or media producers. From the perspective of the strategic plan, this needs careful thought and integration into the plan's roll-out. Apart from anything else, there is likely to be a significant cost involved and so budgets will need to be accessed and financial projections made.

Many teams seem to be somewhat sketchy about how external training companies, business schools or college courses will be used. There's a kind of ad hoc approach which belies a lack of rigour in the planning process. Until you have assessed your internal capability, made a decision on the resources required to achieve the competence of the teams you will support and determined the right mix of training resources and interventions, how can you possibly determine what external help you need? Furthermore, without a set of standards about how, what and how well things will be done, how will you know who to select from the many training providers who will be anxious for your business? Of course, your training strategy may revolve around using entirely external resources as trainers and materials designers. This course booking function is a perfectly reasonable approach, though if used in relation to the vision defined earlier would be unlikely to deliver the required results.

Even when your assessment of internal capability determines that you do not have the skills or resources to staff the training required from your own people, the remaining steps in the strategy process are still required. Before selecting the partners with whom you will work, you will need to define needs; determine the measures you will utilize to measure impact and effectiveness; define the training mix required and the standards which you expect anyone involved to meet.

Usually, however, you will have a mix of internal training team and external providers. You should also have another group in the mix – the line managers and functional experts from within the business for whom training is only one part of their responsibility.

You will also need to determine where the internal training team will be located. Will you have a separate training function which reports to your performance director or will you locate trainers and developers within functions, reporting through the management lines in those business units?

However you choose to resource your implementation plan, the unifying factor will be the vision and mission contained in your strategy, underpinned by the desired capabilities you seek to build. Contracting out components of the implementation is never an easy option.

In the mission outlined above, the provision of leadership development is going to be contracted out for strategic reasons. This mix of some internally resourced training supplemented by specific skills bought in to meet training or subject expertise shortfalls, is a pretty common feature of the way most organizations undertake to build capability amongst their people. The interplay between the external training provider and the internal team is important. Take our example. If the training and development of line managers is the responsibility of the internal training team, but the development of leaders is contracted out to a business school, then there is a real danger that there will be a mismatch between management and leadership behaviours. At the point at which middle managers interact with leaders who will be acting as coach, mentor or adviser, the potential for a lack of common vocabulary, approach and shared agenda may be significant.

Many external providers of learning opportunities are rightly protective of their intellectual property. In my experience, this is especially true of business schools. Asking them to share the knowledge and capability, which is their differentiator in the market place, is likely to be fraught with difficulty. However, there is a way. I have worked with some clients where it was clear from the very start of the relationship that as well as developing a certain level of competence amongst those being trained, I was also developing the capabilities of the client's trainers working alongside me. My role was to deliver a time-limited input and effectively make myself redundant in the organization by passing on my skills, knowledge and resources to the organization employing me. This was part of the deal from the start and the contract was negotiated on that basis.

In our example, it may be appropriate to continue the external input of new ideas and approaches to the senior leadership team. The business school or equivalent which is tasked with building leadership capability would never need to render themselves redundant. But the initial contracting process should identify those approaches which will be shared with those aspiring to be future leaders and those at lower levels who need to be effective in the leadership culture thus created. A unified strategy requires unified ways of doing things.

Following these steps and answering these questions will result in a more effective approach to training and development in your organization. It will create a focused use of resources and clear direction for those designing and supporting training and those being trained. What it will also do is develop a common culture. This cannot be underestimated.

As Edgar Schein, former Professor at the Sloan School of Management at the Massachusetts Institute of Technology and one of the foremost thinkers on corporate culture said: 'We tend to think we can separate strategy from culture, but we fail to notice that in most organizations strategic thinking is deeply coloured by tacit assumptions about who they are and what their mission is.'

Schein identifies three sources of organizational culture:[3]

- artefacts and behaviours – what people do and how these actions are recorded and marked within the organization;

- espoused values – what's important to the organization, the vision, the mission, the standards of performance, codes of conduct and beliefs; and

- assumptions – the thoughts and opinions which may well be unconscious and which will exist in the gaps between the performance standards, defined behaviour and organizational competences. These basic shared assumptions define what people think should be happening, how they think they should be treated and how they expect to behave with and to their colleagues.

The key word about these cultural assumptions is shared. One of the functions of your strategy is to ensure the sharing of assumptions. The key test for a strong organizational culture is that the values and behaviours and assumptions are held in common and fiercely protected by all in the organization. Culture without commonality has another name – we call it chaos.

The vision and the mission of the training team should drive organizational culture and help to create that common sense of purpose. What people learn, regardless of how they have been trained, will be determined by the culture within which they work and learn. A clear corporate culture, with people at the heart of it, underpinned by a commitment to continuous improvement, is the unifying focus for all that the Complete Trainer is trying to achieve.

Notes and references

Introduction

1 Meltzoff, A *et al* (2000) *The Scientist in the Crib*
2 BBC Radio 4, January 2010 *A History of the World in 100 Objects*
3 Bandura, A and Walters, R (1963) *Social Learning and Personality Development*, New York
4 http://livinginlearning.com/2009/08/14/the-learning-continuum-pdr-model/

Chapter 1

1 This referred to the practice in traditional industries where shop floor workers were paid a weekly wage in cash, whereas managers and supervisors were paid a monthly salary into their bank account.
2 W Edwards Deming: US quality guru, 1900–93
3 Sarbanes–Oxley covers transparency of financial dealings for organizations which generate some or all of their income from within the USA. Failing to comply can result in imprisonment – appropriately enough, usually for the CEO!
4 CIPD, Recruitment, Retention and Turnover Survey 2009, p 31
5 Report in *People Management* of a survey conducted by the Henley Business School, April 2012

Chapter 2

1 CIPD factsheet, *Identifying Learning and Talent Development Needs*, January 2012
2 http://www.mindflash.com/blog/2012/03/infographic-how-to-train-your-employees-to-handle-social-media

3 Nordström, K and Ridderstråle, J (2001) *Funky Business: Talent Makes Capital Dance*, FT Prentice Hall

4 Dale, E (1987) *Audio Visual Methods in Teaching*, Dryden Press

5 http://www.trainingzone.co.uk/topic/leadership/tom-peters-search-leadership-heroes

Chapter 3

1 Chartered Institute of Personnel and Development, Learning and Talent Development Survey, 2011

2 O' Leonard, K, Bersin & Associates, *The Corporate Learning Factbook*, January 2012

3 http://www.ted.com/talks?lang=en&event=&duration=&sort=mostviewed&tag=

4 http://www.acas.org.uk/media/pdf/e/p/The_Employment_Relations_Challenges_of_an_Ageing_Workforce.pdf

Chapter 4

1 Corporate Learning Priorities Survey 2011, Henley Business School

Chapter 5

1 Van Buren, M and Erskine, W, *ASTD State of the Industry Report 2002* – annual review of trends in employer-provided training in the United States

2 The 70:20:10 concept is described in detail in *The Career Architect Development Planner*, 5th Edition, Michael M Lombardo and Robert W Eichinger, published 2010

3 Kolb, DA (1984) *Experiential Learning: Experience as the source of learning and development*

4 Dewey, J (1938) *Experience and Education*

5 Jean Piaget was the father of modern cognitive psychology. His constructivist theories appear in or are cited in many publications. His most famous work was *La construction du réel chez l'enfant* (1950) translated as 'The Child's Construction of Reality' and published in the UK in 1955.

6 See http://www.peterhoney.com/content/learningstylesquestionnaire.html

7 To read Prof Daniel Willingham's accessible and fascinating articles and blogs and even watch his videos, go to http://www.danielwillingham.com/index.html

8 *Times Educational Supplement*, 29th July 2007

9 In an essay, published in: *The Modern American College: Responding to the New Realities of Diverse Students and a Changing Society* ed Chickering, AW (1981)

10 These three questions are a simplified version of the Rolfe model of reflective practice as described in: *Critical Reflection in Nursing and the Helping Professions: A User's Guide*; Rolfe, G, Freshwater, D and Jasper, M (2001)

Chapter 6

1 I'm indebted to Phil Waknell, presentation blogger and director of Ideas on Stage, for introducing me to this word, which he attributes to Garr Reynolds, author of *Presentation Zen*. Read Phil's blog on http://philpresents.wordpress.com.

2 Atkinson, C (2005) *Beyond Bullet Points*, Microsoft Press

3 The survey of 1,000 IoD members covered the period January to May 2009. Read more here: http://press.iod.com/2009/06/29/employers-turn-to-training-to-fight-recession-new-research-shows/

4 http://www.towardsmaturity.org/article/2012/11/22/towards-maturitys-2012-benchmark-study-highlights-/

5 My experience suggests training-related response rates of 8% for star ratings and similar one-click responses (active recipient) and about 2% for more comments and other more detailed engagement activities (active participant). This resonates with studies of digital marketing response rates by Nellymoser Inc. and others showing a response rate of between 1% and 4.9% depending on medium used and the response rate required. For more information see http://www.nellymoser.com/news/magazine-scan-response-rates-exceed-that-for-direct-mail.

6 Bandura, A (1977) *Social Learning Theory*, General Learning Press

7 Heath, C and D (2007) *Made to Stick*

Chapter 7

1 http://www.tavinstitute.org/about/index.php

2 See The Discipline of Teams, *Harvard Business Review*, March–April 1993

3 Harkins, P (1999) *Powerful Conversations: How High Impact Leaders Communicate*

4 I'm indebted to Dr Donna Hendrix and Griet Johannsen of Shell for sharing their experience of the Shell wiki via *Inside Knowledge Magazine*, May 2008.

5 Lave, J and Wenger, E (1991) *Situated Learning: Legitimate peripheral participation*

6 This is also attributed to tennis star, Jimmy Connors but as Gary Player pre-dates Connors by about a decade, I'm going to give Player the credit.

7 Dr Lieberman's department do really interesting research into learning and cognition and this work is published in accessible language. See http://www.scn.ucla.edu/research.html for more information.

Chapter 8

1 Schank, R (2001) *Designing World-Class E-Learning: How IBM, GE, Harvard Business School and Columbia University are succeeding at e-learning*

2 Van Buren, M *et al* (2000) *Profiting from Learning: Do firms' investments in education and training pay off?* ASTD White paper

3 Kirkpatrick, D (1994) *Evaluating Training Programs*

4 Phillips, J (2005) *Investing in Your Company's Human Capital: Strategies to avoid spending too much or too little*

Chapter 9

1 The Association of Graduate Recruiters (AGR) is a membership organisation for those employers with graduate recruitment programmes. http://www.agr.org.uk

2 Hoffer, E (1973) *Reflections on the Human Condition*, section 32

3 2011 Learning and Talent Development Survey, Chartered Institute of Personnel and Development, http://www.cipd.co.uk/hr-resources/survey-reports/learning-talent-development-2011.aspx

4 See the work of Vygotsky and Piaget who separately developed constructivist learning theories. See *Fifty Modern Thinkers on Education: From Piaget to the Present Day* (Routledge Key Guides) ed Palmer, J, Bresler, L and Cooper, D (2001) which gives an overview of the work of many of the key people working in the field of learning and psychology over the last 100 years.

5 http://www.forbes.com/sites/ericjackson/2011/12/14/top-ten-reasons-why-large-companies-fail-to-keep-their-best-talent/

6 Resourcing and Talent Planning 2012, CIPD, available from www.cipd.co.uk

Chapter 10

1 Adapted from Porter's 'Five Forces'. Porter, ME (2008) The Five Competitive Forces that Shape Strategy, *Harvard Business Review*

2 Adapted from John Kay, The Structure of Strategy, *Business Strategy Review* (1993)

3 Schein, E (2004) *Organisation Culture and Leadership*, 3rd edn

INDEX

NB: page numbers in *italic* indicate figures